HUGH MACDIARMID: A CRITICAL SURVEY

HUGH MACDIARMID

A CRITICAL SURVEY

ALEXANDER SCOTT · DUNCAN GLEN
BURNS SINGER · DAVID DAICHES
JOHN C. WESTON · RODERICK WATSON
MATTHEW P. McDIARMID
IAIN CRICHTON SMITH
SYDNEY GOODSIR SMITH · DAVID CRAIG
DOUGLAS SEALY · TOM SCOTT
EDWIN MORGAN · MICHEL HABART
G. S. FRASER · W. R. AITKEN

Edited by
DUNCAN GLEN

BOOKS
10 East 53d St., New York 10022
(a division of Harper & Row Publishers, Inc.)

1972 by:
...LISHERS, INC.
...RT DIVISION

First published 1972

© 1972 Scottish Academic Press

ISBN 06 4924327

Contents

Preface

'Hugh MacDiarmid's importance is at last recognised.' So writes W. R. Aitken elsewhere in this book. He is recognised as unquestionably the greatest Scottish poet since Burns and, as John C. Weston says in his preface to the revised edition of Hugh MacDiarmid's *Collected Poems* (New York, The Macmillan Company, 1967), it is now almost a platitude to rank MacDiarmid with Burns and Dunbar as 'one of Scotland's three greatest poets'. In fact such claims were being made for MacDiarmid as long ago as the 'twenties on the basis of his first three collections of Scots poems – *Sangschaw*, 1925; *Penny Wheep*, 1926; and *A Drunk Man Looks at the Thistle*, 1926. Despite the opposition which the early work of MacDiarmid encountered, there is no doubt that Sydney Goodsir Smith is expressing an essential truth when he writes elsewhere in this book: 'In 1926, with *A Drunk Man*, he had conquered Scotland – the Young Chevalier at Holyroodhouse . . .'

But MacDiarmid moved on to his communist poetry and from being a lyricist to become, in David Daiches' phrase, a 'discursive epic encyclopaedist'. The late 'thirties, the 'forties and the 'fifties saw MacDiarmid neglected by the established publishers and there was no interest amongst publishers in critical or biographical studies of his life. The discerning minority continued to be interested in him and he continued to be a controversial figure; this meant that, as at all times since the 'twenties, much continued to be written about him. Almost all of this writing was ephemeral work, although it is of interest in showing contemporary reaction to MacDiarmid and to the battles he has fought throughout his long literary life.

The last ten years, however, have seen a remarkable change in MacDiarmid's position. Publishers now compete for the honour of publishing his books. The breakthrough occurred in 1962 with the publication of his *Collected Poems*, in New York initially and then in Edinburgh to coincide with his seventieth birthday, and since then international recognition has come to him as one of the great poets of this century. We can now confidently say: Yeats, Eliot, Pound and MacDiarmid. There has also come a steady stream of critical works. W. R. Aitken writes of these elsewhere in this book but the *Festschrift*, with its fourteen essays and Dr. Aitken's Checklist, has become almost a rarity; Iain Crichton Smith's perceptive if controversial pamphlet, *The Golden Lyric*, is also out of print, as is the special issue of *Akros*. There are other important essays, such as Burns Singer's excellent pioneering essay, which have never been collected in book form. The aim of this book is to bring together a selection of these largely out-of-print or uncollected essays covering as many aspects of MacDiarmid's work as possible.

With the exception of Roderick Watson's essay, which is based on a series of lectures given at Edinburgh University, all the essays have been previously printed. W. R. Aitken has completely revised his Hugh MacDiarmid bibliography for this book. I am grateful to the editors and publishers of the books and periodicals where the essays, or earlier versions of them, were originally printed, for permission to reprint them here. I have also to thank the authors and others who have generously given their permission.

Alexander Scott: 'Hugh MacDiarmid and the Scots Tradition' (*Agenda*, Autumn–Winter 1967–68) by permission of the author; Duncan Glen: 'Hugh MacDiarmid: Supporting Roles' (a shorter version, *Agenda*, Autumn–Winter 1967–68) by permission of the author; Burns Singer: 'Scarlet Eminence: A Study of the Poetry of Hugh MacDiarmid' (*Encounter*, March 1957) by permission of Dr. Marie Battle Singer; David Daiches: 'Hugh MacDiarmid's Early Poetry' (*Hugh MacDiarmid: a festschrift*, K. D. Duval, 1962, and *More Literary Essays*, Oliver & Boyd) by permission of Oliver & Boyd and the author; John C. Weston: 'A Critical Note on *A Drunk Man Looks at the Thistle*' (modified version from the University of Massachusetts Press edition of *A Drunk Man Looks at the Thistle*, 1971, edited by John C. Weston) by permission of The University of Massachusetts Press and the author; Roderick Watson: '*The Symbolism of A Drunk Man Looks at the Thistle*' by permission of the author; Matthew P. McDiarmid: 'Hugh MacDiarmid and the Colloquial Category' (*Agenda*, Autumn–Winter 1967–68) by permission of the author; Iain Crichton Smith: 'The Golden Lyric. An Essay on the Poetry of Hugh MacDiarmid' (*The Golden Lyric*, Akros Publications, 1967) by permission of the author; Sydney Goodsir Smith: 'MacDiarmid's Three Hymns to Lenin' (*Hugh MacDiarmid: a festschrift*, K. D. Duval, 1962) by permission of the author; David Craig: 'MacDiarmid the Marxist Poet' (*Hugh MacDiarmid: a festschrift*, K. D. Duval, 1962) by permission of the author; Douglas Sealy: 'Hugh MacDiarmid and Gaelic Literature' (an earlier version, *Hugh*

MacDiarmid: a festschrift, K. D. Duval, 1962) by permission of the author; Tom Scott: 'Lament for the Great Music' (*Agenda*, Autumn–Winter 1967–68) by permission of the author; Edwin Morgan: 'Poetry and Knowledge in MacDiarmid's Later Work' (*Hugh MacDiarmid: a festschrift*, K. D. Duval, 1962) by permission of the author; Michel Habart: 'Visionnaire du Langage' (*Critique*, December 1955) by permission of the author; G. S. Fraser: 'Hugh MacDiarmid: The Later Poetry' (*Akros*, April 1970) by permission of the author; W. R. Aitken: 'A Hugh MacDiarmid Bibliography' by permission of the author.

DUNCAN GLEN

Hugh MacDiarmid and the
Scots Tradition

ALEXANDER SCOTT

Of all the hundreds of thousands of words which have been printed on Hugh MacDiarmid's aims and achievements, some of the most perceptive are among the earliest, written by John Buchan in his preface to MacDiarmid's first volume of poems in Scots, *Sangschaw*, in 1925:

> [MacDiarmid] has set himself a task which is at once reactionary and revolutionary . . . He would treat Scots as a living language and apply it to matters which have been foreign to it since the sixteenth century. Since there is no canon of the vernacular, he makes his own, as Burns did, and borrows words and idioms from the old masters. He confines himself to no one dialect, but selects where he pleases between Aberdeen and the Cheviots. This audacity . . . is a proof that a new spirit is today abroad in the North, which . . . is both conservative and radical – a determination to keep Scotland in the main march of the world's interests, and at the same time to forego no part of her ancient heritage.

Buchan was right to stress the importance of the medieval tradition of Scots poetry for MacDiarmid's endeavour to create verse in Scots which expressed higher reaches of spiritual and intellectual concern and deeper levels of emotional and physical experience than the eighteenth-century Scottish bards had aimed at. For MacDiarmid's slogan was 'Not Burns – Dunbar', a phrase from his essay *Albyn: or Scotland and the Future* (1927), where he expressed the view that 'The history of Scottish vernacular poetry . . . since the days of the Auld Makars, is a history of the progressive relinquishment of magnificent potentialities for the creation of a literature which might well have rivalled English.'

During the early medieval period the Lowland Scots, a people of mixed racial inheritance – part-Celtic, part-Teutonic – and differing linguistic habits, came to speak a variant of the northern dialect of English, in which John Barbour (*c.* 1320–95) composed the first major work from Lowland Scotland, *The Brus*, a biographical poem on the exploits of King Robert the Bruce written in the style of the French romances of chivalry. Over the years, this variant of northern English developed into the language which is technically termed 'Middle Scots', and in the fifteenth and sixteenth centuries the Lowlanders created a literature, largely in verse, capable of expressing effectively the whole of life between (and including) heaven and hell.

Scotland produced the finest major love-poem of the fifteenth century, *The Kingis Quair*, which more often than not is attributed to King James I (1394–1437) and which certainly tells a story related to the incidents of his early life. Although James's literary method derived from the French allegories of love, he was an innovator, working towards naturalism, and if he was influenced by Chaucer, both in style and in language – he used southern English as well as Scottish forms – he looked at the world of the senses through individual eyes.

A cruder poet than James, the mysterious figure known as Blind Harry or Henry the Minstrel, who composed the heroic romance of *Wallace* around 1460, continued the Barbour tradition of military epic. In the folk-lore of the hundred and fifty years since Wallace's execution by the English, the Scottish hero would appear to have become a kind of demi-god, the victorious embodiment of his people's desire to see 'the auld enemy' south of the Border humbled in the dust, and Blind Harry's work was often violent and sometimes barbaric. But while *Wallace* may be regarded as a projection of the more brutal fantasies of the folk, in at least one passage – 'Go live in war, go live in cruel pain' – the minstrel becomes a lyric poet, achieving the true cry.

The most remarkable of the fifteenth-century makars, Robert Henryson (fl. 1480) was one of the very greatest narrative poets ever to practise his art within these islands. He was a stylist of the highest skill, with an apparently effortless ability to vary the density of his colloquialisms, and the nature of his images, in accordance with every facet of his subject-matter. Whatever his themes, and whether he wrote of them humorously or contemplatively, philosophically or tragically, the perfection of his style was such that the reader's attention is never distracted from matter to manner. Where the style of the majority of poets is at most a veil, and at least a glass, between the reader and the content, in Henryson there seems to be no veil and no glass, only a subtle manipulation of light and shade which places the content in the perspective most proper to the poet's purpose.

His beast-fables – where he was working in a well-established

European tradition, and frequently based his Scots versions on French or Latin originals – were superbly swift and racy in their use of vivid colloquialisms and proverbial phrases. In his *Testament of Cresseid* (a sequel to Chaucer's masterpiece, and equally masterly in its own manner of concision) the gravity of the language was everywhere illuminated and given urgency by images drawn directly from everyday life.

Below Henryson's narratives, and supporting them, lay a strong construction of doctrine, of social and political philosophy whose base was finally religious. In the work of his younger contemporary, William Dunbar (*c.* 1460–1520), the reader is impressed less by philosophy than by personality. Dunbar's dissatisfaction with the world was fundamental, and on this fulcrum his attitudes see-sawed violently from one emotional extreme to another – from the extravagant glee of the 'Flyting' [Scolding] poems where he escaped from his dissatisfaction with reality into a purely verbal world where nothing existed except hundreds of separate terms of abuse which he built into great mountains of insult, to the opposite mood in his moralising poems, where he turned his back on the life which had disappointed him and set his hopes on futurity.

The totality of Dunbar's work is extraordinarily varied, with tremendous range of manner, matter and metre. His control of form was consummate, whether he used the French ballade, the Latin hymns, or the old alliterative measure, and always he matched form and content, sense and sound. His allegorical poems were gorgeous tapestries of aureate language; in his satirical pieces the vigorous colloquial idiom gave the verse a sharp cutting edge; and in his poems of resignation, the quiet simplicity of the style exactly suited the passivity of the content. His scope – moving easily from the lewd to the enlightened, from the profound to the profane – was wider than that of any other Scottish poet, medieval or modern, until the advent of MacDiarmid himself; and the dark irony which ran through much of his writing still possesses compelling power.

Scarcely less remarkable was the achievement of Gawain Douglas (*c.* 1475–1522), whose Scots version of Virgil's *Aeneid* was the first great translation of classical Latin poetry into a European vernacular. The enrichment of the Scots tradition by means of translations had begun at least a century earlier, with versions of French romances on Alexander the Great, and was to be continued in every century thereafter, but Douglas's work has remained the prime source of emulation, never surpassed. Again, in some of the original prologues added to his Virgil, he emerged as the first nature poet in extra-Celtic Britain, the earliest (apart from some song-composers) to treat the natural scene not merely as a background to human action, but as being in itself interesting and significant.

An equal concern with actuality was displayed by Sir David Lyndsay (c. 1486–1555), although his was directed towards the social scene. The Bernard Shaw of his age, preoccupied with the reform of church and state, Lyndsay was a master of the art of sweetening the pill of social criticism with the sugar of comic effects, and in his still-celebrated morality play, *The Three Estates*, he cajoled his audience into agreement with his views. While he was less of an artist than Henryson and Dunbar, this was not so much because of his didacticism – there was didactic purpose behind most of Henryson's work, too – but rather because he was often so intent on what he had to say that he was comparatively careless of the form in which it got said. In this his example has been unfortunate – for MacDiarmid, on occasion, as well as for others. But if his verse was frequently pedestrian, it was just as often lively and pointed, especially in the broad comedy scenes of his dramatic masterpiece, where indecency and hilarity tumbled together so madly that criticism is still knocked head-over-heels into laughter.

The last performance of *The Three Estates* in Lyndsay's lifetime took place in 1554, when the Queen Regent, members of the aristocracy, and 'an exceeding great number of people' watched it played. Six years later the Queen Regent was dead, and members of the aristocracy who had taken up arms against her French Catholic allies had established a Protestant form of religion in Scotland. The ideological unity of the Lowland Scots was shattered, and their linguistic unity was also doomed – for the Reformed ministers used a translation of the Bible into English from which to expound the gospel, and this began the displacement of Scots by English as the language for the discussion of 'matters of moment' by educated Scotsmen.

During the next forty years, as long as the court still remained in Edinburgh, royal patronage continued to be extended to Scots poets, and Alexander Scott (c. 1530–85) composed his superbly singable love-poems, bawdy, tender and scathing by turns, while such makars as Alexander Montgomerie (c. 1545–1615) and William Fowler (d. 1612) achieved considerable success in the 'golden style' of the Renaissance. But the writing was already on the wall for all to see in the work of the religious poet, the Rev. Alexander Hume (*c.* 1557–1609), where the influence of 'the Bible in English' showed plainly in increasing Anglicisation of vocabulary and idiom, and the departure of King James VI to London in 1603 to become King James I of England led to a disregard of Scots, in favour of English, on the part of the courtier class who followed him and the poets who served them. The political and economic predominance of England, and its contemporary cultural ascendancy, helped to hasten the process of Anglicisation among lettered men. Although the large bulk of the Scottish people continued to speak Scots as they went about their everyday affairs, the literary language ceased to be used, and that part of its vocabulary which was concerned with other than merely mundane affairs dropped out of sight and out of memory.

Throughout the late medieval period, Lowland Scotland had possessed a distinct cultural identity, for the nobility, the burgesses and the peasants all spoke the same Scots tongue, the small scale of the various social organisations of the time compelled the different classes to 'live together', and aristocratic art-forms were forever interacting with popular ones. But after 1603, when the aristocratic and the educated adopted English, there was a division between the literary language of the élite and the tongue spoken by most of the population.

For more than a century, while those Scottish poets who aimed at the higher levels of achievement were following English fashions, the art-poetry of the great medieval makars was ignored, either forgotten or disregarded. However, the peasants and the townsfolk, at work and at play, went on singing the old folk-songs and ballads – and creating new ones – while some country gentlemen carried on the medieval tradition of writing light verse about the life of the 'lower orders'.

The eighteenth-century revival of verse in Scots began *circa* 1707, partly as a patriotic gesture against the Union of Parliaments, and at first the poets followed the styles of the preceding hundred years, most of which were rural. Allan Ramsay (*c.* 1684–1758) collected folk-songs and ballads, composed sequels to the anonymous medieval poem, 'Christ's Kirk on the Green', which painted a highly-coloured comic picture of village life, and wrote a pastoral play, *The Gentle Shepherd*.

But although Ramsay grew up in Dumfriesshire, he spent his adult life in Edinburgh, and while much of his verse looked back to the rural community of his earlier years, he also attempted to adapt his rustic models to depict various aspects of city life. Following the example of Robert Sempill's mock elegy on the piper Habbie Simson (c. 1640), and employing the verse form then called 'standard Habbie' but later designated 'the Burns stanza', Ramsay portrayed a series of individual Edinburgh worthies in rough, vigorous, slyly-comic verse. His work, like folk-poetry, was full of naturalistic detail, but the intellectual level was not high, and his colloquial style was incapable of the sub-lime.

Where Ramsay, in 'Christ's Kirk', had celebrated the life of a whole village community, Robert Fergusson (1750–74) used the same technique – bustling action and abundant comedy – to depict the folk-ways of Edinburgh's populace. In this, so far as the Scots tradition is concerned, he was – and remains – a pioneer, for the later success of Burns, a countryman, in the celebration of country themes, gave a new impetus to the description of rural manners.

Although Fergusson sometimes wrote on rustic themes, too, he was more often an urban poet, and always an educated one. Academic discipline lay behind the formal excellence and clarity of his verse, and easy command of his learning enabled him to incorporate classical references and Latin quotations into his Scots without any sense of strain, while he could satirise high politics as sharply as low life. When the American critic Lowell described the most effective literary style as 'the tongue of the people in the mouth of the scholar', he might have been writing of Fergusson.

Robert Burns (1759–96) brought a more penetrating irony, a more uproarious comedy, a more touching tenderness, and a more powerful passion, to verse in Scots, but he added little to its forms and themes. Greater than Fergusson's although his work was, in at least one respect it represented a retreat from a position which the earlier poet had already attained. Before the end of his all-too-brief career, Fergusson had mastered the art of intellectual discussion in Scots, treating ideas with the self-confidence of a scholar. Burns, perhaps because of an over-sensitive awareness of his educational deficiencies, tended towards a defensive jocularity in Scots or a somewhat self-conscious demon-stration of ease in English – more often the latter – whenever he became philosophical.

For the nineteenth century, however, Burns was less the philosopher than the singer – inevitably so, since twenty will sing a song where only one will read a poem, and few songs have ever been more singable, or more worth singing, than those which Burns took from 'tradition' and virtually re-created in an idiom which was at once the folk's and his own, a brilliant individual enhancement of community art. The emphasis on the lyrical aspect of Scots poetry which resulted from this achievement received further weight from the success of Walter Scott and James Hogg, during the first thirty years of the nineteenth century, in collecting ballads and in recapturing the ballad qualities of dash, drive, colour and mystery in their own verse. The highly idiosyncratic work of William Tennant (1784–1848), who developed the style of Ariosto in 'Anster Fair' and that of Lyndsay in 'Papistry Storm'd', a lively mock-epic which is the only successful extended poem in Scots between the sixteenth century and our own, was largely overlooked.

Well before 1850, Burns had come to be regarded as Scotland's patron saint of love, liberty and labour. But the evangelical revival inside and outside the Free Church caused his audience to avert their eyes from his provocative and intellectually-stimulating satires, with their radical attack on religious conservatism, and to concentrate on his domestic idylls and his love-lyrics, with his humorous character-sketches and drinking-songs as the lightest permissible comic relief. Many of the poems in the successive editions of the *Whistlebinkie* anthology (1832) reduced the range and power of Burns's genius to a lowest common denominator of amorous alcoholism, and even those verses which deftly described the surface mannerisms of the Scottish scene and the more apparent eccentricities of the Scottish character were lacking in critical penetration and emotional force. Exceptions to the rule there sometimes were – Outram, Bell Scott, George Macdonald – but the rule was deadly.

In language, too, the *Whistlebinkie* writers were more restricted in scope than Burns, who had sought the riches of Scots 'from a' the airts the wind can blaw', whereas his successors tended to confine themselves each to his own local dialect, eked out with English whenever the patois was found wanting. During the 1880's, however, Robert Louis Stevenson (1850–94) and 'Hugh Haliburton' (1846–1922) reverted to Burns's practice, weaving a literary Scots out of threads drawn from different dialects. Both poets had intelligence and wit, but some of Stevenson's Scots satires were modelled so closely on those of Burns as to be dangerously near pastiche, and Haliburton's Scots versions of Horatian odes – in a tradition as old as Ramsay – often smacked of the patronising literary exercise.

When *Hamewith* by Charles Murray (1864–1941) was published in

B

1909, Andrew Lang commented, 'Poetry more truly Scots than that of Mr. Murray is no longer written'. The Aberdeenshire dialect in which Murray wrote was one of the richest in the country, and his work was rooted in the everyday realities of the North-East community. Since he shared the humour of the characters he presented, the sly, sardonic, 'off-taking' wit, his observation of external behaviour was both exact and pointed. Yet he never penetrated the secret places of the heart or the subtler intricacies of the intellect; he became embarrassed (and embarrassing) when he attempted direct expression of personal feeling; his style, though close to the cadence and idiom of Aberdeenshire speech, was often prosaic; and he tended to look towards the past.

But the First World War compelled him into contemporaneity, and the best of all his dramatic monologues was 'Dockens Afore His Peers' (1916), a portrait of a farmer before an exemption tribunal which, as an ironically-acute study of provincial chicanery and self-interest, was an astonishing achievement in an age of civilian jingoism. Again, the most passionate of his lyrics, 'Gin I Was God', was a brilliantly forceful expression of disillusion, and his Scots version of Horace's 'Parcus Deorem' delivered a savage comic denunciation of the war and its aftermath.

The advance towards keener criticism and deeper emotional honesty represented by Murray's war-time and post-war poems was matched by others. While the work of Violet Jacob (1863–1946) belonged to the 'truly rural' tradition, her character-sketches penetrated below the social aspects of her men and women to express their more intimate joys and sorrows. Marion Angus (1866–1946) had a narrower range, most of her verse providing variations on the twin themes of sorrow for lost youth and lamentation for lost love, but within her limited scope she expressed considerable intensity of passion, and she had notable technical mastery of lyrical forms.

Tendencies towards parochialism and insularity which had dominated much of Scots verse since Burns were scarcely resisted in the original poems of Alexander Gray (1882–1968), but his translations of Heine (1920) were a return to the internationalism of the medieval tradition. No trace of the literary exercise here – Gray effected the transference of the lyrical impulse from one tongue, one culture, into another without loss of immediacy of impact or authenticity of expression. He introduced a post-romantic sensibility into a literature still dominated by earlier modes.

About this time, too, Lewis Spence (1874–1955) was attempting to create a literary Scots based on the language employed by the old makars. His verse had a chill remoteness, but its cold, langorous beauty struck a note long unheard in the bucolic good cheer characteristic of nineteenth-century Scots.

In the early 'twenties, then, there was a certain 'forward-march' atmosphere about the Scottish literary scene, due at least in part to the war which had revealed the limitations of attitudes inherited from the immediate past. Between 1920 and 1922, C. M. Grieve (b. 1892) edited three issues of an anthology of 'representative selections from certain living Scots poets', *Northern Numbers*. From 1920, the Vernacular Circle of the London Burns Club was campaigning for the revival of Scots. In August 1922 appeared the first number of a new literary review, *The Scottish Chapbook*, edited by C. M. Grieve and dedicated to the proposition, 'Not Traditions – Precedents!'

From the beginning of his career, Grieve had as one of his aims 'To bring Scottish Literature into closer touch with current European tendencies in technique and ideation', and at first he had opposed the contemporary movement towards the revival of Scots, believing it to be 'a backwater'. But Scots was his native tongue, and the current propaganda in its favour led him to investigate it and to experiment with its possibilities. In the course of this experimentation, C. M. Grieve gave birth to 'Hugh MacDiarmid', the greatest living Scots poet, in whose work both traditions and precedents were to play their parts.

Like Stevenson and Burns, MacDiarmid employed a literary Scots which, while it was based on the speech of his native place (Langholm in Dumfriesshire), incorporated words which were still alive in the mouths of the people in other parts of Scotland; and he also employed terms which he found enjoying a somewhat dubious immortality in the work of the Scots poets and prose-writers of the past. Most often, in the lyrics of *Sangschaw* and *Penny Wheep* (1926), and in his masterpiece, the extended rhapsody *A Drunk Man Looks at the Thistle* (1926), he used archaisms with fine tact, so weaving them into the texture of spoken Scots that they drew life from their context.

MacDiarmid was the first Scots poet whose original verse expressed a post-romantic sensibility; and he was the first to be acutely aware of the contemporary world. The eight short lines of 'The Bonnie Broukit Bairn' contained immensity, for the poem's concern was not confined to a single local parish, as in the eighteenth- and nineteenth-century

Scots fashion, but extended to the whole of creation, as the individual stood alone in the darkness, confronting the world and the stars above him.

> Mars is braw in crammasy,
> Venus in a green silk goun,
> The auld mune shak's her gowden feathers,
> Their starry talk's a wheen o blethers,
> Nane for thee a thochtie sparin',
> Earth, thou bonnie broukit bairn!
> *— But greet, an' in your tears ye'll droun*
> *The haill clanjamfrie!*

Again, in 'The Seamless Garment', where MacDiarmid sought to express his conception of how society should be woven into an inte-grated and harmonious whole, he used images derived from the weaving of cloth in a Border textile-mill, the images of a predominantly industrial world, not — as in nearly all earlier Scots verse — those of a community almost entirely rural.

In *Sangschaw* and *Penny Wheep*, the short lyrics possessed intensity of passion, audacity of imagery, and original and often profoundly-haunting rhythmical patterns. MacDiarmid had the power to create in a few lines an emotional force of extraordinary strength, and to evoke scenes and situations which, while they were perfectly precise and definite in themselves, nevertheless suggested a whole world of ex-perience behind and beyond them.

A Drunk Man Looks at the Thistle, the first major poem in Scots for at least a century, ranged widely over time and space, exploring the fundamental mysteries of love and death and human destiny. In form, the work was a dramatic monologue, a meditation on Scotland, the world and the universe as these appeared to an intoxicated reveller who had tumbled into a roadside ditch while plodding his weary way homeward from the pub. While his drunken imagination reeled and plunged across the cosmos, the hero delighted equally in the gorgeous and the grotesque, the obscene and the absurd, the mystical and the material, finding beauty in the terrible and terror in the trumpery. Abrupt transitions and sudden changes of mood were dictated by the association of ideas in the drunk man's mind, and the poem proceeded by means of a series of shocks of surprise, as the sublime suggested the ridiculous and the ridiculous the sublime.

Bound together by the complex character of the protagonist, who was by turns a satirical critic of Scottish life, a wondering spectator of his own situation, a lover of beauty whose senses were alive to the finger-tips, and a speculator on the mysteries of time and fate, *A Drunk Man* was at once a portrait of the author, a vision of the world, and an exploration of the nature of reality. 'A sardonic lover in the routh of contraries', MacDiarmid created new and striking harmonies from elements of comedy, satire, farce, documentary, lyricism and tragedy, the range and richness of his personality going far towards resolving the contradictions of experience.

There can be little doubt either of MacDiarmid's awareness of the Scots tradition, or of his enhancement of it. He is even more fond of battle than Barbour, and an even better hater than Blind Harry; he has written love poetry as moving as James I's, as contradictory as Alexander Scott's, as lyrical as Burns's; he has expressed as vivid a colloquial morality and as stark an idiomatic tragedy as Henryson, while surpassing him in lyrical energy; he has even more personal force and paradoxical scope than Dunbar, and greater staying-power; like Douglas, he has enriched the tradition as a superb translator; his social satire has been as stinging, and his farce as lewdly intoxicating, as Lyndsay's; he has shown himself as concerned with the contemporary European avant-garde as ever were Montgomerie and Fowler; his evocations of the Scottish landscape, as sensuous as those of Douglas and Hume, have more formal control than the first and more passion than the second; he has adapted the traditional ballad style to modern themes, and his 'Empty Vessel' is as brilliant an enhancement of folk-song as anything by Burns; his delight in individual idiosyncrasies is even keener than Ramsay's; more often than not he has all the formal excellence of Fergusson, with a more frequently-exercised ability to employ Scots for intellectual discussion; like Burns, he is equally effective in comedy, tenderness and passion, and masterly in satire of religious conservatism. Even his faults – an occasional carelessness which recalls Lyndsay's, a tendency at times to lapse into bathos which is reminiscent of Ramsay – have their traditional counterparts.

The present writer, having lived long among academics, is not partial to superlatives. Yet he is unable to resist the conclusion that Hugh MacDiarmid, who has restored Scots as a language of the highest poetical art, is the greatest of all Scots makars, and one of the great poets of the world.

Hugh MacDiarmid: Supporting Roles

DUNCAN GLEN

A recent critic was only echoing the earlier cries of not a few pre-decessors when he suggested that 'there are few things in modern verse more dismal than MacDiarmid's furious frequent flogging of the dead Scottish Pegasus'. Some bad poetry was written by MacDiarmid under the influence of his Scottish nationalism as of his other political beliefs, although I doubt if there is much of it in the *Collected Poems* and *A Lap of Honour* which were under review, but the critic has completely missed the huge importance to MacDiarmid, and indeed to Scottish poetry in general, of his vigorous flogging of the now very much alive Scottish Pegasus. He has given us the Scottish literary renaissance and has played a vital part as a poet and as a propagandist and educator, in giving Scotsmen a new cultural confidence and so giving a new vigour to the life of the nation. But even at the level of an individual poet – and at that level he has given us the greatest Scottish poetry since at least Burns if not since Henryson and Dunbar – MacDiarmid has been providing himself with intellectual poetic equipment to support his imagination.

This is, of course, a device common to many poets, although some may feel less need than MacDiarmid to turn their systems of thought into public campaigns. Much of his campaigning, no doubt, is a reflection of MacDiarmid's fighting personality (and many a younger poet has cause to be grateful for the battles fought by MacDiarmid) but the subliminal ego of the poet may have known what it was about here in that, in the fractured and isolated cultural situation which existed in Scotland when MacDiarmid began to write as a distinctively Scottish poet, this public campaign was probably as essential to the poet's survival as a poet concerned only with attempting to write major poetry as was a personal belief in his cultural theories. Nothing would have been easier for a poet in MacDiarmid's situation than to be content with a local success in a parochial Scotland. MacDiarmid was building much further back than a poet fortunate enough to be born in a time and in a culture which could give the sort of supporting environment that MacDiarmid made for himself through his nationalistic and other theories. Of course the public battles which his theories produced would have killed most poets quicker than any sense of isolation.

Some of MacDiarmid's theories strike me as a part of the 'folly' that poets have often to seem to be committing to be true to a vision which goes beyond the logic of everyday language or indeed the logic of reason. But most of MacDiarmid's theories I find very convincing and all of them stimulating and, in themselves, a fascinating monument to the most fertile mind Scotland has produced in centuries. I am not here suggesting that MacDiarmid is a great creative thinker and, indeed, I have an idea he was thinking of himself as much as Yeats when he put the following quote at the head of a poem addressed to the Irish poet: 'The philosophical content of his poetry [Yeats's] is neither consistent nor systematic. The poet was not a creative thinker, and his genius drew from many sources and influences, lacking a supreme originality. Here, in fact, is an intellectualism, which stands apart from the classic English tradition.'[1]

One of the strengths of MacDiarmid as a poet has been his ability to build up these intellectual theories in the eclectic manner ascribed to Yeats in the above sentence and, even more important perhaps, when he has outgrown them – as a poet – to disregard them as he builds up new or changed theories. He has often enough attacked others for not accepting ideas which he himself disregards in his poetic practice. These theories then, far from being a restrictive influence on his poetry, have been supporting structures for him and which he especially needed as a poet writing in isolation and in the ruins of the Scottish literary tradition. Without much doubt the most fruitful of MacDiarmid's personal theory building has been that which he built in the 'twenties and which has been important outside his poetry in that it has produced the Scottish literary revival. But for all that, his theories for a renaissance of Scottish poetry were also one of the main cultural supports for his own poetry.

These nationalistic theories for an independent Scottish poetry written predominantly in Scots or Gaelic were not, however, the first literary ideas to which MacDiarmid, or C. M. Grieve as he still was then, publicly committed himself and indeed he had a Saul-to-Paul conversion (if he will forgive the association) before he became the Scots makar.

[1] 'Poetry Like the Hawthorn', *Wales*, no. 11, Winter 1939–40. Reprinted Hemel Hempstead, Duncan Glen, 1962.

Christopher Murray Grieve ('Hugh MacDiarmid' being a pen-
name assumed in 1922 when he began to write in Scots) was born in
Langholm, Dumfriesshire, which is only six miles from the English
border and indeed Carlisle was where he was taken as a baby for
perhaps the first of the many times that he has been photographed.[1]
His father was a postman with, as his son tells us in his autobiographical
volume, *Lucky Poet*, 'his beat running up the Ewes Road to Fiddleton
Toll, and we lived in the post office buildings. The library . . . was
upstairs. I had constant access to it, and used to fill a big washing-
basket with books and bring it downstairs as often as I wanted to.'[2]

Grieve's paternal grandfather was a mill-worker in a Langholm
tweedmill and the poet claims that he resembles his grandfather
physically 'a big brow and all the features squeezed into the lower
half of my face); but when I was a lad the older folk used to tell me
I took after him in another respect – "juist like your grandfaither",
they used to say, "aye amang the lassies"'.[3] Grieve's mother's people
were agricultural workers but the poet claims that his alignment from
as early as he can remember was 'wholly on the side of the industrial
workers and not the rural folk, and it remains so today. I never had
anything but hatred and opposition for deproletarianising back-to-
the-land schemes; my faith has always been in the industrial workers
and in the growth of the third factor between Man and Nature – the
Machine'.[4] But although that may have had an important bearing on
his early allegiance to socialism and to his finally joining the British
Communist Party there is no doubt that in some of his most important
poetry MacDiarmid draws strongly on what was essentially a rural
upbringing. As he himself has said: 'even as a boy, from the steadings
and cottages of my mother's folk and their neighbours in Wauchope
and Eskdale Muir and Middlebie and Dalbeattie and Tundergarth, I
drew an assurance that I felt and understood the spirit of Scotland and
the Scottish country folk in no common measure, and that that made
it at any rate possible that I would in due course become a great
national poet of Scotland'.[5] It is not for nothing that the poet claims
in his autobiography: 'My mother's people lie in the queer old church-
yard of Crowdieknowe in the parish of Middlebie'.[6] I quote these
passages as much to show the magnificent use MacDiarmid has made,

[1] See photograph 'The MacDiarmids', *Akros*, vol. 5, no. 13, April 1970. Reprinted
The MacDiarmids, Preston, Akros, 1970.
[2] *Lucky Poet*, London, Methuen, 1943, p. 8.
[3] *Ibid.* p. 2.   [4] *Ibid.* p. 3.   [5] *Ibid.* p. 3.   [6] *Ibid.* p. 4.

in prose as in poetry, of the place and river names of Langholm and its surrounding countryside, as to give biographical information. Some people are sceptical about the existence on the map of a cemetery by the name of Crowdieknowe, and it could well be an example of the famous MacDiarmid humour as indeed is the poem 'Crowdieknowe' which shows MacDiarmid giving expression to the lively, earthy and slightly macabre humour that appears time and time again in Scottish poetry and which is very much a part of the national character:

> Oh to be at Crowdieknowe
> When the last trumpet blaws,
> An' see the deid come loupin' owre
> The auld grey wa's.
>
> Muckle men wi' tousled beards,
> I grat at as a bairn
> 'll scramble frae the croodit clay
> Wi' feck o swearin'.
>
> An' glower at God an' a' His gang
> O' angels i' the lift
> – Thae trashy bleezin' French-like folk
> Wha gar'd them shift!
>
> Fain the weemun-folk'll seek
> To mak' them haud their row
> – *Fegs, God's no blate gin he stirs up*
> *The men o' Crowdieknowe!*

'Crowdieknowe' has been given a place in the national consciousness of Scotland (whether or not it exists in the parish of Middlebie) as has the undoubtedly real Wauchope in 'By Wauchopeside':

> Thrawn water? Aye, owre thrawn to be aye thrawn!
> I ha'e my wagtails like the Wauchope tae,
> Birds fu' o' fechting' spirit, and o' fun,
> That whiles jig in the air in lichtsome play
> Like glass-ba's on a fountain, syne stand still
> Save for a quiver, shoot up an inch or twa, fa' back
> Like a swarm o' winter-gnats, or are tost aside,
> > By their inclination's kittle loup,
> > To balance efter hauf a coup.

Or in 'Water Music' with its 'multitude of rivers, each with its distinctive music':

> Wheesht, wheesht, Joyce, and let me hear
>   Nae Anna Livvy's lilt,
> But Wauchope, Esk, and Ewes again,
>   Each wi' its ain rhythms till't.

And the scenes from Langholm – The Muckle Toon – in *A Drunk
Man Looks at the Thistle*:

> Drums in the Walligate, pipes in the air,
> The wallopin' thistle is ill to bear.

> But I'll dance the nicht wi' the stars o' Heaven
> In the Mairket Place as shair's I'm livin'.

> Easy to cairry roses or herrin',
> And the lave may weel their threepenny bits earn.

> Devil the star! It's Jean I'll ha'e
> Again as she was on her weddin' day. . . .

From various autobiographical references we can see that the young
Grieve, like many of us brought up in working-class circumstances in
church-going Lowland Scotland, was brought up in a very 'respectable' atmosphere with his mother concerned, again like so many
ambitious working-class Scottish mothers, for her son to move into
the respectable profession of teaching. In some ways this respectability
continued into Christopher Grieve's adult life as for example when he
was both a Parish and a Town Councillor (1925–28) and a J.P. for
Angus (since 1926) when he was living in Montrose in the 'twenties,
but one of the inspiring facts about the life of Christopher Grieve is
that he has, as a writer and as a propagandist for a new Scotland,
firmly set his face against the cautious and safe common-sense respectable attitudes of Calvinist Scotland. As he said: 'border life was raw,
vigorous, rich, bawdy, and simply bursting with life and gusto. And
the true test of my own work – since that is what I have sought to do –
is the measure in which it has recaptured something of that unquench-
able humour, biting satire, profound wisdom cloaked in bantering
gaiety, and the wealth of mad humour, with not a trace of whimsy, in
the general leaping, light-hearted, reckless assault upon all the conven-
tions of dull respectability.'[1]

[1] *Lucky Poet*, p. 6.

Great poets can, of course, re-create their boyhood country poetically and almost anywhere can be appropriate for them but Langholm, with its contrast of mills and rich countryside, with its many rivers and with its rich border traditions, was obviously a fortunate place for the boyhood of a poet and perhaps especially so as he left it at an early age so leaving the memories youthfully pure. It is not surprising that MacDiarmid should write in the late 'twenties:

> And hoo should I forget the Langfall
> On mornings when the hines were ripe but een
> Ahint glintin' leafs were brichter still
> Than sunned dew on them, lips reider than the fruit,
> And I filled baith my basket and my hert
> Mony and mony a time?[1]

Nor is it surprising that a geographical feature near Langholm should be a central image of Hugh MacDiarmid's imagination. *To Circumjack Cencrastus* (1930), is sub-titled 'The Curly Snake' and whilst this is related to the curly snake of Celtic drawings and to the serpent image of women or of the poetic imagination, it is perhaps not without significance that there is a place near Langholm also called the Curly Snake. Indeed in his essay on F. G. Scott, the composer, written in 1955, MacDiarmid explained: 'there is a place at Langholm called the Curly Snake where a winding path coils up through a copse till it reaches the level whence, after passing through a field or two, it runs on into the splendid woods of the Langfall. It has always haunted my imagination and has probably constituted itself the ground-plan and pattern of my mind, just as the place called the Nook of the Night Paths in Gribo-Shov, the great forest north of Hillerod, haunted Kierkegaard's.'[2]

This is the 'naturally' acquired education of Christopher Grieve; his more formal education was received at the apparently excellent school – Langholm Academy. In the primary school he had F. G. Scott as a teacher and Scott was later to be an important figure in the 'history' of 'Hugh MacDiarmid'. He assisted MacDiarmid with the

---

[1] 'North of the Tweed', *To Circumjack Cencrastus*, 1930, p. 165. Reprinted *Collected Poems*, p. 200.
[2] *Francis George Scott*, Edinburgh, Macdonald, 1955, pp. 41–2. I quoted this passage in a radio programme I compiled to honour MacDiarmid on his seventy-fifth birthday, transmitted 11th August 1967 B.B.C. Scottish Home Service, and the prose parts of the programme which were all quotations from MacDiarmid's writings were reprinted in *The Listener*, August 1967, as 'My Boyhood in Langholm'.

final form of *A Drunk Man Looks at the Thistle* and had this masterpiece dedicated to him. He also set many of MacDiarmid's poems to
music, and was projected by MacDiarmid as a major figure in the
Scottish cultural renaissance. When I wrote my *Hugh MacDiarmid
and the Scottish Renaissance*[1] I took Scott as the most important supporting figure behind MacDiarmid and whilst MacDiarmid obviously
valued his advice, as his acceptance of it in his final revisions of *A
Drunk Man* shows, it now seems to me, thanks to the writings of
J. K. Annand,[2] that George Ogilvie was perhaps psychologically more
important to Grieve. He was largely kept private by Grieve whereas
F. G. Scott was a sort of public figure to Grieve as well as being a
personal friend. But it was a different kind of relationship to that
which he had with Ogilvie. Ogilvie was perhaps a father-figure to
Grieve as he himself has been such a figure to so many younger poets.
Many poets, of course, have just such *private* friends to whom they
turn for advice and criticism, and for support, even if they ignore the
practical advice or criticism given.

George Ogilvie was the Principal Teacher of English at Broughton
Junior Student Centre in Edinburgh when Grieve left his home in Langholm to attend the Centre in September 1908. He attended Broughton
until 1910, leaving not to become a teacher as was his intention in attend-
ing the Centre but to take up journalism. His first post seems to have been
on the *Edinburgh Evening Dispatch*, obtained thanks to Ogilvie,[3] but
by before the 1914–18 war he had worked as a journalist in Ebbw
Vale, Clydebank, Cupar and Forfar. Grieve joined the Royal Army
Medical Corps in July 1915 and rose to the rank of Quarter-Master-
Sergeant with service in Salonika, Dieppe and Marseilles. He was
demobilised in 1919. His first book, *Annals of the Five Senses* which
was published in 1923, was largely written in Salonika as were many
of the poems by Grieve in the anthologies *Northern Numbers* although
some of them must have been written in Montrose where he was
chief reporter of the weekly paper *Montrose Review* from soon after
his demobilisation, although he had a short spell in St. Andrews
before taking up the job in Montrose. Some of the *Northern Numbers*
poems as well as the long poem 'A Moment in Eternity', which is
dedicated to George Ogilvie and was to become the first poem

[1] Edinburgh, Chambers, 1964.
[2] See 'Introduction', *Early Lyrics by Hugh MacDiarmid*, Preston, Akros Publications, 1968.
[3] See J. K. Annand, 'Hugh MacDiarmid: Some Notes on the Poet's Early Career', *Akros*, vol. 5, no. 14, April 1970, p. 21.

included in the *Collected Poems* of 1962, were also written at what Grieve calls Gildermorie[1] but which according to the reliable authority of J. K. Annand was actually 'Kildermorie Forest Lodge, inland from Alness in Easter Ross, on the estate of C. W. Dyson-Perrins of the Worcester Sauce firm. He was employed by the Education Authority to teach the daughters of the stalkers on the estate, the nearest school being too far off for them to travel'.[2] Grieve returned to Montrose and to his old job on the *Review,* after about a year at Kildermorie, and remained there until September 1929 when he moved to London to become acting editor of Compton Mackenzie's new radio paper, *Vox.* The paper soon folded up and Grieve was out of a job and there now began a time of personal troubles for him after the safe and reasonably secure time in Montrose. He went to Liverpool for about a year as Publicity Officer of the Liverpool Organisation which was a civic publicity organisation for the Corporations of Liverpool, Birkenhead, and Wallasey. Grieve went alone to Liverpool as his wife refused to leave London and soon he was taking responsibility for the breakdown of his marriage. He was divorced early in 1932. Soon, after a spell living in a thatched cottage named 'Cootes' in Thakeham, Sussex, he was moving back to Scotland with Valda Trevlyn his second wife, first to a run-down cottage in Longniddry, East Lothian, and then, in the Spring of 1933, to the cheap but isolated life of the island of Whalsay in the Shetlands. It was a time of dire mental and physical straits for Grieve and poverty was a constant companion for the poet and his family. But it was also a period of great creative re-orientation and also of political re-alignment. The Grieves remained in Whalsay until February 1942 when he was moved to Glasgow for war work; first in a factory and later in the Merchant Service. This period of Grieve's life is a disgrace to the supposed civilisation of Scotland with a period of unemployment in Glasgow coming at the end of the war. But soon, in 1951, Grieve moved to Brownsbank Cottage where he still lives and where since the 'fifties recognition and honours have come to the poet. He received a Civil List Pension in 1950 and an honorary LL.D. from Edinburgh University in 1957. Tributes flowed in on his seventieth birthday in 1962 which year also saw the long-overdue publication of his *Collected Poems,* first in New York

---

[1] See for example the poem 'Sonnets of the Highland Hills. IV: The Wind Bags', *Northern Numbers,* second series, 1921, p. 54. The poem is dated 'Gildermorie, November 1920'.

[2] 'Hugh MacDiarmid: Some Notes on the Poet's Early Career', *Akros,* vol. 5, no. 14, April 1970, p. 23.

and then in Edinburgh and his cottage is now a place of pilgrimage for literary and/or academic people from all over the world. He is also in constant demand as a speaker and reader of his poems throughout both the Eastern and the Western World.

Hugh MacDiarmid, or C. M. Grieve as he still was then, first came to the notice of the literary world as a writer of rather mystical poems in English – the poems of the 1914–18 war period and immediately after. But it is interesting that by 1920 he already had the ability to organise supporting movements for himself – this ability is perhaps an essential of literary innovators. Grieve's first movement was known as the 'Northern Numbers' movement after the title of the series of annual anthologies he edited 1920–22. There was that sense of things happening that prevailed after that war fought to save small nations, and the young Grieve clearly intended to be at the forefront of these literary stirrings. Always he has been an avant-gardiste and the last place he would look in 1920 for advanced literary ideas was in the tiny kailyard that was Scottish literature. He was looking to Dublin and to continental Europe and to America and to London but not to the fuddy-duddy London that was represented by the London Burns Club which was then beginning to promote the idea of preserving the Scottish language. Immediately MacDiarmid attacked this as a reactionary idea and raised the English language as 'an immensely superior medium of expression'.[1] The flags of nationalism were also being raised in that he was advising Scottish writers to shed their provinciality by looking not to London but to Europe and to follow the example of the Irish and produce a comparable Scottish literary revival.

With the anglicised education that Grieve (like most of us coming even forty years after him) received, allied to the kailyard qualities prevailing in Scots writing immediately after the 1914–18 war, it was inevitable that a forward-looking, progressive writer like Grieve should react against the Vernacular revivalist movement but by 1922 there were hints that he was beginning to look differently at the potential of Scots. Reviewing a book of children's verse by Mary E. Boyle in the *Dunfermline Press* of 11th March 1922 Grieve was wondering if Miss Boyle 'writes in the vernacular at all?' and suggesting 'Failing Miss Boyle some new poet or poetess of the magic land of eternal youth may stake a claim in this delightful territory where the

[1] See 'A Scotsman Looks at His World', *Dunfermline Press*, 25th November 1922, p. 6.

soul of Scottish childhood may be revealed through the medium of that "couthie mither-tongue" – which has expressive qualities of its own not to be found in the most perfectly interpretative English'.[1]

By May 1922, in the same *Dunfermline Press*, Grieve was claiming that 'something in the nature of a Revival of Scottish Poetry, is manifesting itself today; or would be but for the adverse commercial conditions'.[2] And by August 1922 writing on the creation of a 'Scottish National Literature' he was saying: 'If there is to be a Scottish literary revival the first essential is to get rid of our provinciality of outlook and to avail ourselves of Continental experience.'[3] But as yet Grieve had no faith in Scots and continues: 'Most of it [Scottish literature] is, of course, and must continue to be, written in English. But it is not English on that account, although it is denounced on that score by the ardent minority bent upon the revival of the Doric. . . . It is no more English in spirit than the literature of the Irish Literary Revival, most of which was written in the English language, was English in spirit.'[4]

But the breakthrough into the creative use of Scots by Grieve was very near and indeed the *Scottish Chapbook* of October 1922 was about to publish the first of his great Scots lyrics and in one of an illuminating series of articles in the *Dunfermline Press* he was also introducing the first of his work in Scots. It was, of course, done pseudonymously and in the *Dunfermline Press* it was a 'friend' who had been staying with Grieve who had, as Grieve explained to his readers, buried himself for an hour or two with Sir James Wilson's *Lowland Scotch as Spoken in the Lower Strathearn District of Perthshire* which, Grieve continued, had gone unread by him and which had, I would suggest, stirred up the latent emotional and imaginative strength of Scots in Grieve who, after all, had been brought up as a speaker of Scots. But he had been attacking the revivalists and had to explain his new interest in Scots even if it was a 'friend' who had been stirred by Wilson's book.

The friend was of course 'Hugh MacDiarmid' whom Grieve was introducing in the *Scottish Chapbook* which Grieve had founded and was editing. In the *Dunfermline Press* Grieve continued: 'I have strong views in regard to the literary uses of the Vernacular which I have on more than one occasion expressed at length in this column and elsewhere in the Scottish Press. At the same time, I possess a great delight in words; and the obsolete; the distinctively local, the idiomatic, the

[1] *Ibid.* p. 6.
[2] *Ibid.* 20th May 1922, p. 7.
[3] *Ibid.* 5th August 1922, p. 6.
[4] *Ibid.* p. 6.

unused attract me strongly.' Grieve then explains that his 'friend'
passed over to him 'the two sets of verses I have pleasure in re-produc-
ing here. They serve a useful purpose, I think, in rescuing from oblivion
and restoring to literary use forgotten words that have a descriptive
potency otherwise unobtainable. Not only so but apart from that
philological interest they have, in my opinion, some genuine poetical
merit too.' Then followed the unmatchable 'The Watergaw' and the
unimportant 'The Blaward and the Skelly' and Grieve commented
'my readers will, I think, agree that a Scotsman may waste his time
in many a worse way than in giving a new lease of life to ancient words
by means of verses such as these; and I think Sir James Wilson would
be happy to know that his book has set even one of his countrymen to
such a pastime'.[1] The poet could not of course know it at that time
but in fact he was initiating the most important Scottish literary movement since Ramsay if not since Dunbar or Henryson. Innovators have
to feel their way but it did not take Grieve long to discard his previous
antagonism to a revival of Scots although he retained, and retains, his
opposition to kailyardism and backward-looking preservationists. In
the *Dunfermline Press* of 21st October 1922 he wrote: 'Possibly the
present writer was largely responsible for the extent to which currency
was given to the argument complained of, viz., "That the doric sentiment is to blame for the literary stagnation of Scotland". But if I was,
I put it in such a fashion that it was perfectly clear to every intelligent
reader that I was dealing with the doric sentiment in its present degenerate state . . .'[2]

Grieve had cleared his past and soon in his Causeries in his new
magazine, the *Scottish Chapbook* – arguably the most important
Scottish literary magazine ever – he was expounding the theories of
a Scottish literary renaissance based on the potential of the Scots language. He was busy providing a theoretical background to the movement and to his own new poetry in Scots. In doing this he fastened
on to, among many other works of course, Professor Gregory Smith's
book *Scottish Literature* which had been published in 1919. Grieve in
his February 1923 'Causerie: A Theory of Scots Letters' in the
Chapbook wrote:

Professor Gregory Smith has . . . described the great vital characteristic of Scottish literature – a distinguishing faculty, which it can

---

[1] *Dunfermline Press*, 30th September 1922, p. 7.
[2] *Ibid.* p. 6.

only shape forth poorly in English, but which is potentially expressible in the Vernacular to which it belongs. It is the predominant feature of Scots literature old and new, and yet, do not the phrases ('taking all things as granted', 'freedom in passing from one mood to another') sum up the essential tendencies of the most advanced schools of thought in every country in Europe today? We base our belief in the possibility of a great Scottish Literary Renaissance, deriving its strength from the resources that lie latent and almost unsuspected in the Vernacular, upon the fact that the genius of our Vernacular enables us to secure with comparative ease the very effects and swift transitions which other literatures are for the most part unsuccessfully endeavouring to cultivate in languages that have a very different and inferior bias. Whatever the potentialities of the Doric may be, however, there cannot be a revival in the real sense of the word – a revival of the spirit as distinct from a mere renewed vogue of the letter – unless these potentialities are in accord with the newest and truest tendencies of human thought. We confess to having been discouraged when thinking of the Vernacular Movement by the fact that the seal of its approval is so largely set upon the traditional and the conventional. The real enemy is he who cries: 'Hands off our fine old Scottish tongue.' If all that the Movement is to achieve is to preserve specimens of Braid Scots, archaic, imitative, belonging to a type of life that has passed and cannot return, in a sort of museum department of our consciousness – set apart from our vital preoccupations – it is a movement which not only cannot claim our support but compels our opposition. The rooms of thought are choc-a-bloc with far too much dingy old rubbish as it is. There are too many vital problems clamouring for attention. It is a different matter, however, if an effort is to be made to really revive the Vernacular – to encourage the experimental exploitation of the unexplored possibilities of Vernacular expression.[1]

And in his next 'Causerie' continuing this seminal 'Theory of Scots Letters' Grieve writes: 'The Scottish Vernacular is the only language in Western Europe instinct with those uncanny spiritual and pathological perceptions alike which constitute the uniqueness of Dostoevsky's work, and word after word of Doric establishes a blood-bond in a fashion at once infinitely more thrilling and vital and less explicable than those deliberately sought after by writers such as D. H. Lawrence

[1] *Ibid.* pp. 182–3.

in the medium of English, which is inferior for such purposes because
it has an entirely different natural bias which has been confirmed down
the centuries to be insusceptible to correction. The Scots Vernacular
is a vast storehouse of just the very peculiar and subtle effects which
modern European literature in general is assiduously seeking and, if
the next century is to see an advance in mental science equal to that
which last century has marked in material science, then the resumption
of the Scots Vernacular into the mainstream of European letters, in a
fashion which the most enthusiastic Vernacularist may well hesitate
to hope for is inevitable.'[1] There then follows a purple passage in
praise of the old Scots language.

So suddenly it would seem the poet MacDiarmid turned on the
theorist in himself and made him turn in a completely new direction;
his imagination had obviously been set alight by the discovery of the
old Scots words in Wilson's *Lowland Scotch*. It was there that he found
words such as 'on-ding', 'yow-trummle', 'antrin', 'watergaw', 'weet
nicht' and the phrase 'there's nae reek the laverock's hoose the-nicht'
which he took, and worked, and subtly modified into 'The Watergaw',
although this is not to say that some of these words would not already
be known to Grieve and that Wilson's word lists acted as a memory
jogger as well as a supplier of new phrases. 'The Watergaw', although
so well known now, has to be quoted to show what MacDiarmid
achieved immediately he turned to Scots:

> Ae weet forenicht i' the yow-trummle
> I saw yon antrin thing,
> A watergaw wi' its chitterin' licht
> Ayont the on-ding;
> An' I thocht o' the last wild look ye gied
> Afore ye deed!
>
> There was nae reek i' the laverock's hoose
> That nicht – an' nane i' mine;
> But I hae thocht o' that foolish licht
> Ever sin' syne;
> An' I think that mebbe at last I ken
> What your look meant then.

The poet's imagination was obviously split wide open by the rediscovery of his mother-tongue and very quickly MacDiarmid went

    [1] 'Causerie: A Theory of Scots Letters', *Scottish Chapbook*, vol. 1, no. 8, March 1923,
p. 210.

on to produce some of the greatest short lyrics ever written in Scots and also some of the greatest written in any language in this century. But obviously this was not where the poet had intended going. The avant-garde writer must have felt very insecure writing in Scots with its century-old association with infantile versifying in the Burns tradition and no doubt the poet was very glad when his theorist self discerned the possibility that Joyce's achievement in *Ulysses* could perhaps be equalled by a Scot writing in Scots. So also he must have been supported by being able to write, as I have quoted above, 'a vast storehouse of just the very peculiar and subtle effects which modern European literature in general is assiduously seeking' and to be able to go on to write 'It is an inchoate Marcel Proust – a Dostoevskian debris of ideas – an inexhaustible quarry of subtle and significant sound'.[1]

No doubt also he was very glad to see that Gregory Smith's theory of the Caledonian Antisyzygy could be used to link his Scots poems to the avant-garde movements in European literature. Smith had suggested that Scottish literature is very varied and indeed 'almost a zig-zag of contradiction' which reflected similar contrasts shown by the Scot throughout history. To Smith 'the sudden jostling of contraries seems to preclude any relationship by literary suggestion. The one invades the other without warning'. MacDiarmid took this as an essential part of the creative dynamic of true Scottish literature and it was to be an essential theoretical support for him, particularly when he came to write *A Drunk Man Looks at the Thistle*:

> Grinnin' gargoyle by a saint,
> Mephistopheles in Heaven,
> Skeleton at a tea-meetin',
> Missin' link – or creakin'
> Hinge atween the deid and livin'. . . .

This Caledonian Antisyzygy is an interesting theory in its own right, quite apart from its importance to MacDiarmid as a theoretical support for his imagination, with, as Kenneth Buthlay has noted, roots in Coleridge's theories of the imagination, but I cannot but wonder why only MacDiarmid at that time made the breakthrough that took Scots poetry back into the mainstream of European literature, and the obvious answer is that the same could be said of this theory as Eliot said of Coleridge's distinction between Imagination and Fancy; we

[1] *Ibid.*

are here simply talking about the difference between good and bad poetry. But for MacDiarmid personally these associations with Europe and the identification of these characteristics as essentially Scottish (as they may be) were a strength to him working in the moribund Scottish tradition. And working also now to revive a tradition which he believed had been swamped under the dull, conforming sterility of modern anglicised Scotland; this again was of value to the poet who was acting in both a reactionary and a progressive manner by his use of Scots. But MacDiarmid is a born propagandist and fighter for causes, so that it came naturally to him no doubt.

But all this is also poetic equipment as what had happened, I have no doubt, was that in Coleridge's words, MacDiarmid had discovered through Scots 'the sense of novelty and freshness, with old and familiar objects; a more than usual state of emotion with more than usual order; judgment ever awake and steady self-possession with enthusiasm and feeling profound or vehement. . . . The sense of musical delight . . . with a power of reducing multitude into unity of effect, and modifying a series of thoughts by some one predominant thought or feeling.' These are well-known words but they describe perfectly for me the sense of power and freedom allied to the music etc. that MacDiarmid obviously felt when he began writing in Scots and indeed the exhilaration which so many of us have found, thanks to his example, when we have turned from our educated English to the 'disreputable' Scots. It is too bad, of course, that the unity of effect, etc., are just as hard to achieve in Scots as in English.

But although the primary impulse of Grieve towards the use of Scots, and of his commitment to a Scottish literary revival, may have been a literary one, his nationalism must be considered as another part of such an impulse. Indeed the pre-Grieve/MacDiarmid interest in the revival or the preservation of Scots, or of the Vernacular to use the term of these days at the beginning of this century, obviously also had its roots in the revival of things Scottish brought about by the revival of the national consciousness which can perhaps be seen as beginning in the eighteen-fifties and which was given a new impulse by the 1914–18 war. There was also the example of Irish nationalism and the Irish literary revival.

Grieve began his political activities as a member of the Fabian Society and of the Independent Labour Party, joining both organisations during his student days in Edinburgh. It was as an Independent Socialist that he was a Parish and Town Councillor in Montrose but he also had nationalistic beliefs and when the various small nationalist groups began to move together in 1927–28 towards forming the National Party of Scotland, Grieve was very active in encouraging the formation of the new Party; he was one of the principal speakers when the new National Party held its inaugural meeting in Stirling on 23rd June 1928. It was at this time too that Grieve began to show a real interest in the Gaelic background to Scottish culture. He was closely associated with the Hon. Ruaraidh Erskine of Marr who had been a Vice-President of the Scottish Home Rule Association as early as 1892 and who was fanatically concerned with the movement towards a Gaelic revival. Erskine advanced the slogan 'No Language. No Nation', which was obviously in tune with Grieve's own thinking as he formulated, in the *Chapbook* and elsewhere, his theories for a Scottish National literature and a Scottish literary renaissance. But by 1927 when Grieve was writing Gaelic-orientated political essays for Erskine's *Pictish Review* (1927–28) the renaissance movement had ceased, in Grieve's thinking, to be a purely literary movement and had become linked to political nationalism. It can be argued that Grieve's nationalism was yet another necessary support for his poetry, as indeed it can be argued that the whole renaissance movement was a supporting structure for his Scots poetry, but Grieve has always stood out against literature in isolation; he sees the whole nation involved culturally and at a high level; he has also been opposed to any lowering of cultural standards to meet the demands of an uneducated society. As he wrote in 'Second Hymn to Lenin':

> Nae simple rhymes for silly folk,
> But the haill art, as Lenin gied

Although nearer the beginning of the same poem he asks:

> Are my poems spoken in the factories and fields,
>   In the streets o' the toon?
> Gin they're no', then I'm failin' to dae
>   What I ocht to ha' dune.

Essentially this is a poetic voice with poetry seen as embracing the whole of life and raising life to higher levels:

> Sae here, twixt poetry and politics,
> There's nae doot in the en'.
> Poetry includes that and s'ud be
> The greatest poo'er amang men.[1]

[1] 'Second Hymn to Lenin'.

In 1927 Grieve published *Albyn: or Scotland and the Future* which can be seen as his first considered statement, in book form, of his aims for a Scottish Renaissance movement. He begins on the first page of *Albyn*:

The forces that are moving towards a Scottish Renaissance are complex and at first sight incompatible. The movement began as a purely literary movement some seven or eight years ago, but of necessity speedily acquired political and then religious bearings. It is now manifesting itself in every sphere of national arts and affairs, and it is at once radical and conservative, revolutionary and reactionary. Engaged in traversing the accepted conceptions of all things Scottish, it is in keeping that it should not have set the heather on fire. . . . The movement has had various more or less short-lived organs of its own;[1] it will undoubtedly acquire others. . . . Its inception synchronised with the end of the War, and in retrospect it will be seen to have had a genesis in kin with other post-war phenomena of recrudescent nationalism all over Europe, and to have shared to the full in the wave of Catholic revivalism which accompanied them. It took the full force of the War to jolt an adequate majority of the Scottish people out of their old mental, moral and material ruts; and the full force of post-war reaction is gradually bringing them to an effective realization of their changed conditions.[2]

He goes on to raise his slogan 'Not Burns. Dunbar' writing: 'As to Scots, here, again, its desuetude was largely due to the Reformation and to the Union with England. Its "direction" is completely at variance with the "direction" of English; and the present state of English literature on the one hand, and the newer tendencies in Europe to which London is most antipathetic on the other, considered in conjunction with the special virtues of Scots, suggests that the psychological moment for its revival has arrived and that through it lies a way for the successful re-entry of distinctively Scottish culture into the

---

[1] These short-lived organs of the 'twenties were largely edited and published by Grieve himself: *The Scottish Chapbook* (August 1922–November–December 1923); *The Scottish Nation* (May 1923–December 1923); *The Northern Review* (May 1924–September 1924). Grieve was also a very prolific contributor to other magazines and newspapers, including especially a most controversial series of articles to the *Scottish Educational Journal* (some of which were reprinted in *Contemporary Scottish Studies*, 1926) and his syndicated articles of 1927–29, written under various pseudonyms, which appeared in over thirty weekly newspapers. For further details of Grieve's journalism see Duncan Glen, *Hugh MacDiarmid and the Scottish Renaissauce*, 1964, pp. 90–104, 256–62, etc.

[2] *Albyn*, pp. 5–6.

European stream. The Burns influence has been wholly bad, producing little save puerile and platitudinous doggerel. It is necessary to go back behind Burns to Dunbar and the Old Makars – great Catholic poets using the Vernacular, not for the pedestrian things to which it has latterly been confined, but for all "the brave translunary things of great art".'[1]

And in line with his essays in the *Pictish Review* he goes on: 'The Scottish Renaissance movement is even more concerned with the revival of Gaelic than of Scots. It regards Scotland as a diversity-in-unity to be stimulated at every point, and, theoretically at any rate, it is prepared to develop along tri-lingual lines.'[2] He saw lost ground 'being rapidly recovered; efforts are being made once more to create distinctively Scottish literature comparable in artistic quality and tendencious force to the contemporary output of other European countries, and to regain the independent cultural position of Scotland in Europe; efforts are being made to create a Scottish national drama and Scottish national music – both of which Scotland alone of European countries entirely lacks, mainly because of Calvinistic repression – and all these efforts are achieving a measure of success. Scottish genius is being liberated from its Genevan prison-house. But the centralisation of British arts and affairs in London is still restricting it in ways that can only be redressed by that re-orientation of facilities which would follow the re-establishment of an independent Scottish Parliament.'[3] And Grieve ends the first Chapter of *Albyn* with the uncompromising political statement which is yet concerned to promote the cultural movement: 'The movement cannot manifest its full stature and move freely, save within that framework of a Scotland become once again a nation in every sense of the term for which it has been designed.'[4]

These ideas with which MacDiarmid created the Scottish Renaissance movement have changed the direction of Scottish poetry and indeed the cultural life of Scotland in general although obviously they could not have been so powerful an influence without the major Scots poetry of MacDiarmid behind them; the support has been a two-way thing – the movement acted as a support for the poet, and his poetry acted as perhaps *the* essential support for the movement. Both the poetry and the theoretical structure of the movement are major achievements and as David Daiches has excellently said, Grieve could have 'settled for less. He could have stayed at the head of a Scottish literary revival and become a respected Allan Ramsay type of figure . . . And

---

[1] *Ibid.* pp. 12–13.   [2] *Ibid.* p. 13.   [3] *Ibid.* pp. 14–15.   [4] *Ibid.* p. 15.

indeed he has played some of the parts played by Ramsay . . . But his driving vision of the fulfilled man in the fulfilled society – a vision which is as much responsible for his choice of language, his kind of imagery and the course of his poetic career from lyricist to discursive epic encyclopaedist as it is for his ever shifting syntheses between nationalism and communism – would not leave him alone.'[1]

But if the movement acted as a support for MacDiarmid and gave him something of a tradition to work within, he inevitably knew only too well that

> . . . poetry's no' made in a lifetime
> And I lack a livin' past;

And for long, despite the structure of a literary revival that he built up, he also knew, as he said in the same poem:

> There's nae sign o' a mate to be seen![2]

The 'mates' were to come in the 'forties and 'fifties and new disciples continue to appear although whether MacDiarmid would recognise them as 'mates' I will leave for him to say. But long before the mature appearance of such second-generation renaissance poets as Sydney Goodsir Smith, Robert Garioch, Tom Scott, T. S. Law, and Alexander Scott, MacDiarmid had largely moved away from Scots. By 1933 he was showing a theoretical interest in the English language and advocating the use of an extended English and suggesting that a 'concerted effort to extend the general vocabulary and make it more adequate to the enormous range and multitudinous intensive specialisations of contemporary knowledge is long overdue'.[3] This is, of course, a transference or extension of his use of an extended Scots, although he personally believed that he had only touched the fringe of Joycean experimentation in his Scots poems. We can only disagree and see the experimentation irrelevant beside the achievement in the poetry; the great poetry of MacDiarmid's three Scots periods: the early lyrics, *A Drunk Man Looks at the Thistle* and *To Circumjack Cencrastus*, and the poems of intellectual wisdom often centred on Langholm and its waters and woods and which, with many of the poems in *First Hymn to Lenin and other poems*, 1931, and *Scots Unbound and other poems*, 1932, were intended to be a part of the intriguing but never to be published 'Clann Albann'. For the poems of extended English which

[1] 'Hugh MacDiarmid in his Context', *Library Review*, vol. 20, no. 1, Spring 1965, p. 4.
[2] 'The Mavis of Pabal', *Collected Poems*, p. 154.
[3] 'Problems of Poetry To-day', *At the Sign of the Thistle*, 1934, p. 92. Reprinted from the *New English Weekly*, vol. 3, no. 24, 28th September 1933.

MacDiarmid referred to in the essay of 1933 we have to turn to the 1934 collection, *Stony Limits and other poems*, and to such poems as 'On a Raised Beach'. Even as it stands the *Stony Limits* collection has some Scots poems but there would have been many more as the first selection submitted to its publishers included the Scots poem 'Harry Semen' and the original Scots version of 'Ode to all Rebels' which were eventually published in 1956 in *Stony Limits and Scots Unbound and other poems*. Nevertheless there is no doubt that by the middle 'thirties MacDiarmid was turning towards English.

Contemporary with this move from Scots to English, MacDiarmid was moving from the National Party of Scotland to the Communist Party of Great Britain. In 1934 the National Party merged with the Scottish Party to form the Scottish National Party which survives to this day but when it was moving towards union with the Scottish Party the National Party expelled its more extremist members including C. M. Grieve. Grieve's expulsion seems to have been linked to his communism but, despite the publication of his 'First Hymn to Lenin' in Lascelles Abercrombie's anthology *New English Poems* in 1931, and the appearance of the collection *First Hymn to Lenin and other poems* in the same year, Grieve did not join the Communist Party until after his expulsion from the National Party. But despite this membership switch, Grieve continued to advocate a Scottish nationalism in literature and indeed politically also as his editorials in his magazine the *Voice of Scotland*, founded in June–August 1938, show. Indeed he was expelled from the Communist Party in 1938 for 'nationalist deviation', but his literary nationalism was moving increasingly towards the Gaelic background of Scottish culture. Towards, indeed, a pan-Celticism which also had associations with his communism or Scottish Workers Republicanism in that he saw the Celtic countries, or areas, uniting to form independent republics. MacDiarmid had of course written of the Gaelic Idea in the 'twenties and indeed it is to be found in his poetry, as in *To Circumjack Cencrastus* published in 1930:

> If we turn to Europe and see
> Hoo the emergence o' the Russian Idea's
> Broken the balance o' the North and Sooth
> And needs a coonter that can only be
> The Gaelic Idea
> To mak' a parallelogram o' forces

But now he seemed to be advocating it with a new involvement in the development of his poetry. There was also a link here with the East – what MacDiarmid was to caption 'The East-West Synthesis'. In 'Direadh III' written in the late 'thirties he writes:

> And think of the Oriental provenance of the Scottish Gael,
> The Eastern affiliations of his poetry and his music,
> '. . . the subtler music, the clear light
> Where time burns back about th' eternal embers,'

In the Introduction to his *The Golden Treasury of Scottish Poetry*, 1940, MacDiarmid noted Yeats's interest in the Upanishads and suggested that the movement 'back to the ancient Gaelic classics and then North to Iceland and then East to Persia and India is the course the refluence of Gaelic genius must take'. MacDiarmid has been criticised for his lack of scholarly discrimination in his advocation of this Gaelic Idea, but whilst this may be regrettable from a scholarly stance, the poet knew what he was about just as, to wave a white rag to a blue lion, Robert Graves knew what he was about in *The White Goddess*. He was still creating for himself as he said in a revealing, if bad, poem, 'The Kulturkampf':

> . . . a tradition, inspire us with faith,
> Help us to find new gods.[1]

By the late 'thirties, MacDiarmid had moved on to his very long 'world-view' epics which perhaps can be seen beginning in the three 'Direadh' poems and culminating in the massive forms of *In Memoriam James Joyce* and *The Kind of Poetry I Want*. When 'Direadh I' was printed in the *Voice of Scotland*, December 1938– February 1939, MacDiarmid wrote 'I turn from the poetry of beauty to the poetry of wisdom – of "Wisdom", that is to say, of moral and intellectual problems, and the emotions they generate.' To move into an analysis of MacDiarmid's long epics is beyond the scope of this essay but it is interesting to see MacDiarmid building for himself the new essential theoretical and personal supports as he moved into this new poetry of 'wisdom'. His working-class parents have something of the same poetic purpose as Yeats's belief in his descent from the Duke of Ormonde had for the Irish poet. It is poetic equipment put

---

[1] *A Kist of Whistles*, Glasgow, Maclellan, 1947, p. 14.

to good use as MacDiarmid also links his communism to the theories of his new poetry.

> The greatest poets undergo a kind of crisis in their art,
> A change proportionate to their previous achievement.
> Others approach it and fail to fulfil it – . . .
>
>   * * *
>
> – I am forty-six; of tenacious, long-lived country folk.
> Fools regret my poetic change – from my 'enchanting early lyrics' –
> But I have found in Marxism all that I need –
> (I on my mother's side of long-lived Scottish peasant stock
> And on my father's of hardy keen-brained Border mill-workers).
> It only remains to perfect myself in this new mode.
> This is the poetry I want – all
> I can now regard as poetry at all,
> As poetry of today, not of the past,
> A Communist poetry . . .[1]

To MacDiarmid communism means the opportunity to learn from the bottom upwards and to have the opportunity of learning. He sees it concerned with mentalism rather than materialism and so here a communist poetry is a poetry encompassing all knowledge. The poet has to know everything and be 'facing in all directions' and 'myriad-minded' and must, of course, also infuse that wisdom with the 'spiritual' light of the poetic imagination. These wide-ranging poems, with their expression of MacDiarmid's belief in an internationalised language, are a further development of the poet's life-long Joycean extension of language. It did seem, however, to some of his Scottish admirers that they were also a further abandonment of the Renaissance movement which he had built around his use of the Scots language. In reply MacDiarmid has seen these poems as a part of that movement's aim to intellectualise Scottish poetry and to break out of the anti-intellectual slough of the post-Burnsian tradition, but in reading these later, long 'world-view' poems I cannot but think that emotionally, as a poet, MacDiarmid had moved on from the need of involvement in the original movement. But emotion is almost a dirty word to the MacDiarmid of the later poetry who in *In Memoriam James Joyce* cries for a high classical poetry.

[1] *Lucky Poet*, p. 152.

> —An exacting intellectual undertaking.
> The expression to a far greater extent
> Of thought and reason than of emotion,
> And fully understanding
> The sources of its emotions and ideas,

This would seem to be a long way from the earlier self of the poet who wrote in 'Gairmscoile', printed in *Penny Wheep*, 1926:

> It's soon', no' sense, that faddoms the herts o' men,
> And by my sangs the rouch auld Scots I ken
> E'en herts that ha'e nae Scots'll dirl richt thro'
> As nocht else could – for here's a language rings
> Wi' datchie sesames, and names for nameless things.

But although MacDiarmid may have moved a long way, no great poet ever loses faith in the 'grace' of language and he is no exception for all the emphasis he has put on an intellectual approach to poetry. In a sense this intellectual stance was a self-defence reaction – a healthy but still a protective piece of poetic equipment – to the anti-intellectual state in which he found Scottish poetry and Scottish culture in general. This stance taken by MacDiarmid has been very beneficial to Scottish poetry and also, I believe, has served his own poetry very well in that, as with other of his creeds or theories, he used it to support his poetry but was not slow to ignore it when it suited his purpose to do so. As Yeats said 'passionate man must believe he obeys his reason'.

Scarlet Eminence

A STUDY OF THE POETRY OF HUGH MACDIARMID

BURNS SINGER

Physically he is a magnificent mouse of a man. I remember him best as he used to sit, sagged back in front of his fireplace, his legs plaited together and curled beneath his armchair, one hand, the left, lying indolently beside him while the right one gripped his black pipe. Then he would bend down forwards to tap out ash on the hearth and, as he did so, his head would turn sideways towards where I sat. That head looked huge. The hair curled up from it like the grey-brown smoke of a volcano and, though his expression betrayed no more than a quick slant of curiosity, the force of the man became apparent. The features were small and squeezed into the lower half of the face, the brow high and myriad wrinkled, the nose a sharp jut forwards, the eyes sunk in deep sockets as though eroded by a surfeit of sight; the whole composition denied his posture of repose. Then, at last, when he rose and walked across the room with that swift jerky gait of his, talking all the while, as though keeping time to his footsteps, in a learned staccato, one would glimpse the vigour that had written his twenty-odd books and his millions of words of invective.

By the time I met Hugh MacDiarmid he was over fifty but his physical appearance had probably changed very little since those days some twenty years before when he had published his first book of Scots lyrics, *Sangschaw*. At that time, he was already employed in the exercise of his vituperative genius. It was directed against such minor and local figures as, among others, Sir Hugh Roberton, the conductor of the Orpheus Choir. Since then he had enlarged the scope of his attacks but they were still bitter and violent. The poems of those years possessed, however, an unusual delicacy and established him as the greatest lyric poet in Lowland Scots since at least the time of Burns. The first volume and its successor, *Penny Wheep*, are both small books containing small poems that have a seriousness of intention and a sophistication of manner comparable to the best European poetry of the 'twenties. The range is limited and can be roughly defined

as lying between such charming trifles as the following poem for a
child:

> The auld men o' the sea
> Wi' their daberlack hair
> Ha'e dackered the coasts
> O' the country fell sair.
>
> They gobble owre cas'les
> Chow mountains to san';
> Or lang they'll eat up
> The haill o' the lan',
>
> Lickin' their white lips
> An' yowlin' for mair,
> The auld men o' the sea
> Wi' their daberlack hair.[1]

and the deeply significant statements of a personal or philosophic kind
which are found in others.

As an example of the more private of these manners his elegy to his
first wife [sic] deserves quotation:

> Ae weet forenicht i' the yow-trummle,
> I saw yon antrin thing,
> A watergaw wi' its chitterin' licht
> Ayont the on-ding;
> An' I thocht o' the last wild look you gied
> Afore you deed.
>
> There was nae reek i' the laverock's hoose
> That nicht – an' nane i' mine;
> But I hae thocht o' that foolish licht
> Ever sin' syne;
> An' I think that mebbe at last I ken
> What your look meant then.[2]

That the person who had died was the poet's wife [sic] is powerfully
and economically suggested by the one phrase: *'an' nane i' mine'*. The
death of a friend or even a child would hardly affect a man's home to
this extent: but his mother's house, on the other hand, would not be
thought of as 'mine' in the proprietary sense implicit in this phrasing.
The poem is thus deeply personal yet it overlooks imaginative immen-

---

[1] 'Hungry Waters' [Ed.].   [2] 'The Watergaw' [Ed].

sities hardly ever visible from previous peaks in Scots verse. From the vantage point of these verses a world is seen in which, as in Heraclitus, everything is on the point of disappearing into its opposite. It is evening, so that night is overcoming day. The ewes vibrate in the cold as spring refuses to give way to summer. The poet's home has become an exposed hovel, bleak with memories, like the deserted nest of the lark. And the whole outside world mirrors the personal calamity of a man who has lost his wife [sic]. For love, which is the supreme affirmation of life, has been altered into despair. Yet within these sad changes their reverse is already incipient. Night is answered by a promise of morning, the storm by a sign of the coming calm, and even the shivering of the sheep gives hope that summer will indeed arrive. This wavering certainty emerges from the twilight as the love and faith of the dead woman filtered through the agony of her final moments and condensed itself into a 'last wild look'. The look was as tenuous as the hope inspired by a rainbow, and much more ambiguous. Is it a belief in immortality that it means to convey? Is it just the assurance that whatever happens the poet has once been loved completely? Or is it a confirmation of his own love and the discovery that it will last as long as life? There is no hint in the poem. I believe it is all of these, and something else as well, something that cannot be explicitly stated but which is conveyed by the heavy slow majesty of the verse as it moves.

An even heavier rhythm is found in some still shorter poems of a more impersonal nature. Here the density of the Lallans vocabulary intensifies the dismal solidity of the thought. The counterpoint between objective and subjective worlds is maintained as it is throughout Hugh MacDiarmid's life's work. Objective reality is seen as reinforcing subjective tendencies in the mind of man.

> I' the how-dumb-deid o' the cauld hairst nicht
> The warl' like an eemis stane
> Wags i' the lift;
> An' my eerie memories fa'
>   Like a yowdendrift.
>
> Like a yowdendrift so's I couldna read
> The words cut oot i' the stane
> Had the fug o' fame
> An' history's hazelraw
> No' yirdit thaim.[1]

[2] 'The Eemis Stane '[Ed.].

Or is it the subjective which supports the objective? Both processes are in action. The meaning of life is hidden by the sheer mass of events, by the number of lives that must be justified, by the length of time involved; as well as being obfuscated by the clutter of personal experience, the paraphernalia of conflicting guilts.

MacDiarmid has never lost the technical delicacy which allows him to concentrate thought, fact, and emotion in a few significant and well-ordered phrases. His slow renunciation of Lallans has merely brought to a larger public this earliest gift of the gods. His elegy for the Scottish poet, John Davidson, who committed suicide by walking into the sea off Cornwall, is typical of many slender but firm lyrics written in English:

> I remember one death in my boyhood
> That next my father's, and darker, endures;
> Not Queen Victoria's, but Davidson, yours,
> And something in me has always stood
> Since then looking down the sandslope
> On your small black shape by the edge of the sea,
> —A bullet-hole through a great scene's beauty,
> God through the wrong end of a telescope.[1]

Or again, in attenuated Scots, 'Deep-Sea Fishing':

> I suddenly saw I was wrang when I felt
> That the gapin' mooths and gogglin' een
> O' the fish were no' what we should expect
> Frae a sea sae infinite and serene.
>
> I kent I'd be equally wrang if I wished
> My nice concern wi' its beauty to be
> Shared by the fishermen wha's coarser lives
> Seemed proof to a' that appealed to me.
>
> Aye, and I kent their animal forms
> And primitive minds, like fish frae the sea,
> Cam' faur mair naturally oot o' the bland
> Omnipotence o' God than a fribble like me.

The apparent modesty of this last poem is only apparent. Mac-Diarmid is not a humble man. But Auden was right: poetry is born of humiliation, and the humble man cannot be humiliated. He begins by

[1] 'Of John Davidson', [Ed.].

admitting his inferiority. After that admission he can never again be reduced to it. Repeated humiliation gives one the courage to fail. Modesty demands its modest successes. Of these last MacDiarmid has had very few. He has consistently aimed at the highest and the deepest poetry and has shown contempt for all those who are content with anything less.

This contempt is both motivation and message for the brutal severity of his pamphleteering. Communism and Scottish nationalism are the causes he has condescended to defend, but the virulence and, often, the vulgarity of his attacks on their enemies have embarrassed most other nationalists and Communists. To unite the delicacy of his best lyrics with the violence of his attempts at propaganda has been a central undertaking of his life. 'The goal is Beauty' but the only road that leads to it lies through the 'cruelty' of Lenin – a cruelty, indeed, that is greater than any Lenin ever imagined, the cold cruelty of the aesthete intent on perfection. It is this duality that has made him the greatest of Communist poets. He does not indulge in the lachrymose humanism of Neruda any more than in the rowdy optimism of Maya-kovsky. He has not time for the proletariat, 'innumerable meat without minds'. To many he will seem to show Communism at its worst, but for all of us he shows it at its truest – a merciless arrogance of the human intellect preparing to build the *perfect* society with barrowloads of corpses. 'What maitters 't wha we kill? . . .'

His first major attempt at this grotesque synthesis was published in 1926 under the title of *A Drunk Man Looks at the Thistle*. It could be argued that this 'gallimaufry' is the greatest of all Scots poems. It was assembled by the author, in conjunction with his friend, Francis George Scott, from an assortment of fragments in various metres and stanzaic forms. Connecting passages were added whenever it was absolutely necessary. This example became the type for MacDiarmid's method of composition. Much of his best work has never got beyond the stage of being 'excerpts from a long unfinished poem'. That a sustained aesthetic unity can be achieved by such methods may well seem astonishing. The poet himself has referred to one of these attempts as 'a sort of anti-poetry' that 'gaes a' airts and nane'. Yet the *Drunk Man* itself does possess unity. The thistle and moonlight, the rose and Christianity, whisky and lust, Good and Evil, whirl in their pairs or are isolated singly, as the partners in an eightsome reel meet or are separated by their energetic convolutions. The pattern changes continually, yet it is never wholly lost. For these are the eight main

D

symbols of the *Drunk Man* and MacDiarmid returns to them repeatedly, discovering new opportunities on every occasion for reaching through to a different truth, a revolutionary combination. And each discovery is expressed with the fanatical concision of direct revelation. Such a fluidity of form is common in Scottish literature. The lyrics in 'The Jolly Beggars' are connected by descriptive passages as those in the *Drunk Man* by philosophic ones. *Don Juan* too, with its virtuoso digressions from a semblance of narrative, exhibits the same asymmetry and, in doing so, fulfils Byron's claim to being 'half a Scot by birth, and bred / A whole one'. It is found in Urquhart, Sir David Lyndsay, and in the Flyting of Dunbar and Kennedy. It is the aesthetic element in the jumble of absurdities that MacDiarmid has subsumed under the term (borrowed from Urquhart and having the root meaning of asymmetry) Caledonian Antisyzygy.

The expression is clumsy. It is meant to be so. The Scots flair for pedantry is thus made implicit. These large words can be applied to scenery, the ragged useless gigantic rockscapes of the Highlands, and the almost unnatural contrast between them and the smooth smog-ridden Lowlands. The Caledonian Antisyzygy is illustrated in every branch of Scottish culture and in every phase of character. Violent, sentimental, learned, unimaginative, hyper-sensitive, the mythical Scotsman lives in a mythical Scotland, enjoying a schizophrenic isolation from his actual counterpart and the modern nation.

This mythological Scotland has as much historical documentation to its credit as most myths. 'The Scottish nation, being from the beginning always free, hath created kings upon these conditions, that the government entrusted to them by the people's suffrages might be also (if the matter required) removed by the same suffrages.' So George Buchanan, one of the greatest Latinists of the Renaissance, in the early sixteenth century. And it is certainly doubtful whether the Scots would have accepted an English king with the same grumbling timidity as the English extended to James VI of Scotland. It is a historical fact that they did not so accept the Hanoverian accession.

An intransigent people: a free people, sometimes militantly rebellious. The myth has a basis. In all Scottish institutions there is some hint of it; law, religion, education, all support the myth. But only the last is relevant to our purpose. Even now the Scottish university tries to keep its gates open to any intelligent aspirant and to furnish him with an understanding of the methods of study rather than to fob him off with a parcel of lecture notes. More important still are the elementary and secondary schools. These have existed for the past five hundred years though they are now in danger of losing their identity. It is to these schools that the distinctively popular character of Scottish literature is due. Henryson taught in one and Burns learned in another. Whereas most English and French writers belong to an upper middle-class background, the Scots can produce poets and dramatists at every social level, and have been able to do so for some centuries. Aristocrats like Lyndsay and Urquhart, plebeians like Davidson and Hogg, they were all taught to write in these country schoolrooms and they were taught together, with very little favour given to social position. Scots poetry is therefore popular, either in the sense of the Ballads or in the way of a Court literature which is much more truly popular than the current European régime of literature for the *literati*. It possesses usually a set of values that is socially valid as well as aesthetically. It is concerned with entertaining everyone or influencing everyone in a complex and various society, and to do so it must admit a non-literary dictation of literary forms.

Such a socially effective idiom is what MacDiarmid has always been looking for. He is thus related analogically, rather than linealogically, to earlier Scots poetry. The Border Ballads set out to inspire a bundle of cattle thieves to the hazards of a life of murder, robbery, and rape. The complex sonorities of Dunbar, on the other hand, were addressed to the king and his contingent noblemen. Hence the difference between these two types of verse. MacDiarmid's public is of another kind altogether. His purpose lies with 'the wisest and learnedest of mankind, who have this one great gift of reason, to answer solidly or to be convinced'. The people he wishes to influence are the scientists, administrators, and scholars of his time. In their hands lies the fate of the world and it is their present insensitivity to those diabolical and illogical influences, explicit only in art, that today endangers humanity. He is therefore anxious to persuade them of the finally objective importance of the aesthetic exploration. It would be patently ridiculous for MacDiarmid to try to convince such people in terms of poetry itself. If that could be done, if, at that level, they were sensitive, then Shakespeare and Dante would already have done the job. He therefore tries to attack them on their own ground, using poetry like a guided missile that flies over territories alien to its maker. He tries to demonstrate that there is no field of knowledge which could not be better understood if the irrational, the mystic, and the aesthetic elements were not ignored; and to demonstrate this clearly to specialised workers in each of these fields. A typical example of his attempts to impress such limited but important publics is found in his little poem, 'Thalamus'. 'Busy as any man in those regions of the brain where consciousness flourishes' (i.e. the frontal lobes) he yet proclaims that he is more interested in those older regions, like the thalamus, which govern our instinctual behaviour. He goes further, and says that these older regions are also evolving, that our emotional as well as our intellectual capacities are increasing and that we have a duty to try to develop all aspects of our psyche in symmetrical proportions:

> Let fools think science has supplanted poetry;
> Rationalism, religion. Even physically
> The older parts are more than holding their own;
> The fools are liars to their own anatomy.

An extension of this method has led MacDiarmid to try to revive the ancient concept of the poet as the universal sage versed in every subject, like an Arabian minstrel or a Celtic bard. The accumulations of two millennia of historical speculation and research are enough to knock the bottom out of any such pretensions and to explode any previous notions of heroic form. Therefore, reasons MacDiarmid, a new form must be made and its first requirement is that it should contain all knowledge. Other formal considerations, even such basic ones as unity and intelligibility, become negligible when set alongside this impossible imperative. He has tried to create a heroic form, primitive, didactic, universal. The heroes are not men, as they were in Homer. Only the fact has the heroic prerogative of victory. It overcomes theories. But these theories, like evolution, psycho-analysis, Marxism, make the facts into mouthpieces by law of the superior organisation in the consciousness. There is thus created a mythology of facts and superfacts similar to the Homeric distinction between men and the supermen whom Homer called gods.

To hanker after omniscience is not necessarily to be formless and MacDiarmid's indifference to the ordinary concepts of form has another root. He is writing poetry on the grand scale. Ideologies are part of his epic *personae*. He is therefore committed to feeling the validity of each conflicting system of beliefs within himself. He must be borne down by the whole weight of whatever truth any faith may have. But MacDiarmid has always been singularly promiscuous in matters of faith. He has espoused simultaneously the causes of Scottish Nationalism, International Communism, and Social Credit, while writing, in parenthesis and in contradiction to his own conclusions, a poetry that shows a deep understanding of Christianity. He himself regards this ideological virtuosity as one more manifestation of the Caledonian Antisyzygy.

> I'll ha'e nae hauf-way hoose, but aye be whaur
> Extremes meet – it's the only way I ken
> To dodge the cursed conceit o' being' richt
> That damns the vast majority o' men.

That, from the *Drunk Man*, is his basic definition. Later he writes: 'It is a mental counterpart of the Chinese Tin-Tang dichotomy, the peculiar beauty of which is that both parts are regarded as equally necessary, valid and to be accepted – there is no question of *triumphing* over the dark element and wiping it out as though it were an arbitrary evil – whereas the Christian doctrine insists more on the *conflict* between opposites than their sustained relationship, this conflict is supposed to be waged to an end, until evil no more remains and Saint George has killed his complementary dragon, at which point the morality play leaves off and we do not know what becomes of the victorious saint, or how he fares in the anomalous situation in which he finds himself now, with no dragon left to do battle with, and, consequently, no reason left for living, whereas the more civilised Chinese have an affection for dragons of all kinds – the profound relationship fraught with beauty and terror, which must nevertheless be entered into.'[1]

That he should quote Chinese philosophy in this context may make some readers doubt whether his Antisyzygy is truly Caledonian. But he has often laboured the close connection between Celtic art and that of the East and maintained that Scotland is intellectually closer to Far Eastern countries than to those in Western Europe. The Gael and the Chinaman, that is, can be enlisted together against the cultural axis formed by the Graeco-Roman-Christian countries, in which England is one of the senior partners. In some respects he is right. The Scots have never accepted authority, either in society or in religion, with the same placidity as most Europeans. This is particularly true of the Border Scots, where local chiefs acted as independent sovereigns right into the seventeenth century, and MacDiarmid is a Border Scot. Each man has been master of his own land and his own mind for so long that it would be an unwise king or bishop who would try to filch him of either. When MacDiarmid comes across a countryman who attempts

[1] *Lucky Poet*, pp. 371-2 [Ed.].

the usual virtues of the Englishman, he denies all blood connection
as in *A Drunk Man*:

> Nae doot they're sober, as a Scot ne'er was,
> Each tethered to a punctual-snorin' missus,
> Whilst I, puir fule, owre continents unkent
> And wine-dark oceans waunder like Ulysses.

For himself, he may have no land but he will keep a mind of his own
and continue to exhort each of his neighbours to stick independently
to what his whole conscious intelligence tells him is true. No matter
how vehemently he may disagree with Puritanism, he has a Calvinistic-
ally violent love for contradictory truths. 'Truth' here is a better word
than 'ideology', though I do not mean to imply anything that can be
tabulated by its functions or proved by experiment. It is rather our
decision to accept the evidence of such tables or demonstrations that is
meant. Anything that can be proved is not a truth in this sense because
the truth lies in our awareness of it; and that we can never prove: that
is what we are. We cannot get outside it in order to establish its
validity. We are, each of us, imprisoned in this kind of truth. That is
why this kind of truth is more assimilable into the symbolism of
geology than that of botany. We look at one another's prisons and call
them ideologies so that we can assess them historically; or we label
them 'character' and watch their social effects. There is a great variety
of such ideologies and characters to be found on the Scottish scene;
perhaps no more than elsewhere; but in Scotland each takes itself so
seriously that it refuses to exercise the tact, the *politesse*, that is always
found in great Imperial peoples like the Romans and the English.
'Each man in the name of his God', the Scots people advance savagely
against one another, every man of them determined to purify the
world and cast out the alien idols. Each man has his own orthodoxy,
his own intellectual armament and moral rearmament, and the devil
is expected, quite literally, 'to tak the hinmaist'.

> No hating by request but by oneself – vital images thrown in our
>   way by life,
> Grim selection of ideas and feelings, harsh opinions, intolerance,
>   frankness – all
> The red roaring life of Burns, Fergusson, old Scotland generally,
> Hypocrites have whitewashed, emasculating us under their thrall.[1]

[1] *The Battle Continues*, 1957, p. 33; *Lucky Poet*, p. 335 [Ed.].

The spiritual dogmatist is thus confronted by ten thousand heresies, but for the poet they are so many truths and the unique absurdity of the situation increases that number to ten thousand and one. I say 'for the poet' because the poet's method of expression is a technique for discovering these truths at the point of their appearance within himself, before they have had time to fossilise into ideologies: he can express them when they are no more than a particular movement of his blood, before they have reached the stage where he can decide whether or not to believe in them.

It was a plethora of such truths, instinct within himself, that Mac-Diarmid uncovered, revelation by revelation, in the eight main symbols of the *Drunk Man*. It is because they were each emotively present within him and each could be arrived at only after the other had been realised that his poem has the perfectly organic quality of an evolutionary sequence in biology. No matter how accidental his sudden transitions from one mood to another may seem when they are observed in isolation, they are, like genetic mutations, regulated by the fact that any accident other than the one which happened would have led to a very different result and, probably, to a dead end. The total pattern thus acquires the aspect of inevitability which makes it, for those who understand its language, a very readable and satisfying poem.

About the language of MacDiarmid's early lyrics, the *Drunk Man*, and a few of his later poems, too much has already been written. It should be enough here to say that it is a very beautiful language, handled with consummate artistry. Its notorious difficulty reflects the stupidity of its critics rather than the intentions of its creator. It is much easier to read than the Cantos of Ezra Pound and passages of *Ulysses* are linguistically less accessible. Philologically it is a synthesis of most of the spoken Scots dialects with a few odd words thrown in from the obsolete sections of the vocabulary of the medieval makars. Its defenders, including MacDiarmid, have magnified its differences from modern English in an attempt to identify it with the nationalist move-in Scottish politics. No such political entanglements are necessary to justify it. MacDiarmid had good reasons of a purely aesthetic kind for trying to rejuvenate English and his attempt was far from being an isolated experiment. Eliot, Pound, Joyce, they were all overcoming the apathetic vacuity in which the *fin de siècle* poets like Dowson and Johnson had left their native tongue. Even Kipling and Newbolt had reverted to colloquialisms in an attempt to bring this vague poetic diction down to earth. MacDiarmid's Scots is by no means so revolutionary as the English manner of his later years. In his first book, he had written: 'He was now quite certain that the imagination had some way of dealing with the truth, which the reason had not, and that commandments delivered when the body is still and the reason silent are the most binding that the souls of men can ever know. So far so good! But this left for his journalistic mind the more difficult problem of communicability.'[1] He solved that problem in the same way as many other young men have solved it, by returning to his childhood language and taking his imagination with him.

But, in recent years, he has set himself the task of writing a 'high classical poetry', 'poems *de longue haleine* – far too long to be practicable in any existing medium',

> A poetry that is – to use the terms of Red Dog –
> High, low, jack and the goddam game.[2]

And for such poetry the language of childhood is insufficient. He needs:

> A language like the magnetic needle,
> The most sensitive thing in the world, which responds alike
> To Polar light in the North, electric currents
> Flowing around the equator, the revolutions
> Of the earth on its axis, the annual course
> Of the earth round the sun, the revolution of the sun itself,
> And the mysterious processes in sun spots.[3]

A Drunk Man Looks at the Thistle is well over three thousand lines in length.

> A brain laid bare,
> A nervous system.

There is no way of doing justice to such a poem in these few words. The brain is that of a drunk man who is contemplating a thistle by moonlight. He is too drunk to get up and go home so he is left alone at the mercy of his thoughts, and these thoughts are merciless. The themes are spotlighted by gruesome jokes, or they are suddenly set ablaze in a lyric like the following translation from Blok:

> I ha'e forekent ye! O I ha'e forekent.
> The years forecast your face afore they went.
> A licht I canna thole is in the lift.
> I bide in silence your slow-comin' pace.

[1] *Annals of the Five Senses*, 1923, p. 189.   [2] *The Kind of Poetry I Want*, 1961, p. 41 [Ed.].
[3] *Ibid*, p. 28 [Ed.].

> The ends o' space are bricht: at last – oh swift!
> While terror clings to me – an unkent face.
> Ill-faith stirs in me as she comes at last,
> The features lang forekent . . . are unforecast.
> O it gangs hard wi' me, I am forspent.
> Deid dreams ha'e beaten me and a face unkent
> And generations that I thocht unborn
> Hail the strange Goddess frae my hert's-hert torn!

The thistle becomes a symbol of the human condition.

> It is morality, the knowledge o' Guid and Ill,
> Fear, shame, pity . . .
> The need to wark, the need to think, the need to be,
> And a'thing that twists Life into a certain shape
> And interferes wi' perfect liberty—

The moonlight is that Liberty. At one point the ideas of Liberty, Love, and Knowledge are all identified with one another in a remarkably incisive metaphysical image:

> The munelicht is my knowledge o' mysel',
> Mysel' the thistle in the munelicht seen,
> And hauf my shape has fund itsel' in thee
> And hauf my knowledge in your piercin' een.
>
> E'en as the munelicht's borrowed frae the sun
> I ha'e my knowledge o' mysel' frae thee,
> And much that nane but thee can e'er mak' clear,
> Save my licht's frae the source, is dark to me.

But this love knowledge is two-sided. He talks of women:

> Through a' my self-respect
> They see the truth abject
> – *Gin you could pierce their blindin' licht*
> *You'd see a fouler sicht!*

And so it goes on, every illusion breaking down under the weight of thought that the drunk man imposes on it; until finally, thought itself becomes a casualty.

> Juist as man's skeleton has left
> Its ancient ape-like shape ahint,
> Sae states o' mind in turn gi'e way
> To different states, and quickly seem
> Impossible to later men,

> And Man's mind in its final shape,
> Or lang'll seem a monkey's spook,
> And, strewth, to me the vera thocht
> O' Thocht's already fell like that!

In this situation communication becomes impossible except with the
'apallin' genius' of Dostoevsky:

> Aye, this is Calvary – to bear
> Your Cross wi'in you frae the seed,
> And feel it grow by slow degrees
> Until it rends your flesh apairt,
> And turn, and see your fellow-men
> In similar case but sufferin' less
> Thro' bein' mair wudden frae the stert! . . .

So he continues into the final squalid pessimism:

> The wee reliefs we ha'e in booze
> Or wun at times in carnal states,
> May hide frae us but canna cheenge
> The silly horrors o' oor fates.

Yet MacDiarmid is not a dispiriting poet. His fits of despair are not
the results of physical discomfort or purely personal frustration. It is
rather the sense of imminent beatitude, of a psychological and social
revolution that is just on the point of happening and that is going to
bring forth a race of men to whom our 'Heaven is just the blinterin' o' /
A snail-trail on their closet wa'.' But this celestial carrot keeps its tantalising but minute distance. There is thus an inexplicable discrepancy
between MacDiarmid's spiritual sense of the significance of life and
his accurate observation of its stupidity and pettiness. Around this
central contradiction he arranges incongruous armies of his dialectics.
'My disposition,' he has written, 'is toward spiritual issues made
inhumanly clear.'[1]

> A'thing that ony man be's
> A mockery o' his soul at last.
> The mair it shows't the better, and
> I'd suner be a tramp than king,
> Lest in the pride o' place and poo'er
> I e'er forgot my waesomeness.
> Sae to debauchery and dirt

[1] "On a Raised Beach" [Ed.].

And to disease and daith I turn,
Sin' otherwise my seemin' worth
'Ud block my view o' what is what,
And blin' me to the irony
O' bein' a grocer 'neth the sun,
A lawyer gin Justice ope'd her een,
A pedant like an ant promoted,
A parson buttonholin' God,
Or ony cratur o' the Earth
Sma' - bookt to John Smith, High Street, Perth,
Or sic like vulgar gaffe o' life
Sub speciem aeternitatis –
Nae void can fleg me hauf as much
As bein' mysel', whate'er I am,
Or, waur, bein' onybody else.

After this Scots masterpiece MacDiarmid increasingly identified spiritual issues with political ones. Both his Communism and his Nationalism increased in virulence, and his verse, for a short time, showed a marked tendency to degenerate into scurrilous epigrams without grace or gaiety. His next book, *To Circumjack Cencrastus*, contained an excellent translation from the German of Rilke and a few fine poems, written in a Scots considerably less dense than any in the earlier books. This was to mark the beginning of a trend back into English, a trend that he is in the habit of reversing with such demonstrations in virtuoso Lallans as 'Water Music' and parts of the 'Ode to All Rebels'.

With the publication of the 'First Hymn to Lenin' he emerged as a fully committed Communist poet. This was in 1931, and, in talking of the leftish poets of the 'thirties, John Lehmann has referred to this book as 'the prelude to the whole movement'. In this assessment Mr. Lehmann is mistaken. MacDiarmid was, from the beginning, a very different kind of Communist from his English juniors. In 1933 he wrote: 'Some of our younger poets – Spender, Auden, Day Lewis – are Communists, I am told. We will see what we will see. I have seen nothing so far germane to my present concern (i.e. socialist poetry). Ezra Pound's passages in defence of Douglasism are another matter, a solitary exception.'

MacDiarmid's Communism, like Pound's Fascism, had an aesthetic basis. Lenin is comparable to Rilke in the intensity, integrity, and

understanding with which he pursues an entirely different end. But no.
The ends are not so very different. They are both making things, the
one a poem and the other a social system. What matters is that both
the state and the poem should be well made, an intricate organisation
delicately balanced. MacDiarmid carries it further than this. Not only
the chiefs of state, the Lenins of the world, create a society. Every
member must be a creator and must suffer the creative agony.

> A line, a word – and emptiness again!
> The impotent desire to ken aince mair
> The shinin' presence, and the bitter sense
> O' bein' unjustly treated, wi' despair
> Cryin' 'better than see and tine, no' see ava'
>   Like maist men' – ah!
>
>   *   *   *
>
> Be this the measure o' oor will to bring
> Like cruelty to a' men – nocht else'll dae;
> The source o' inspiration drooned in bluid
> If need be, owre and owre, until its ray
> Strengthens in a' forever or's hailly gane
>   As noo save in an antrin brain.[1]

It is not out of simple sadism that the poet wishes to inflict his own pain
on the uncreative millions but because he wants them to share the
painful experience of growing up into adult human beings aware of
their ultimate limitations.

> A man never faced wi' death kens nocht o' life.
> But a' men are? But micht as well no' be!
> The ancient memory is alive to few
> And fewer when it is ken what they see,
> But them that dae fear neither life nor death,
>   Mindin' them baith.[2]

His Communism is not a simple matter of more pay for the workers
and more jobs for the boys, but a genuine ascetic religion. By forcing
society to organise itself more efficiently, much energy that is at present
wasted could be diverted to the one task that is truly human, that of
understanding, to the point of despair and beyond it, the actual extent
of what is understandable and thus to a sophisticated acceptance of
those mysteries which cannot be understood. Such an attitude towards

---

[1] "The Burning Passion" [Ed.].   [2] "Water of Life" [Ed.].

Communism could hardly have been more acceptable to Comrade Stalin than Pound's opinions to Herr Hitler.

In 1934 MacDiarmid published *Stony Limits*, the first book in which he establishes those types of versification (that lack of versification) and the concatenation of antagonistic ideas which are his most original and far-reaching contribution to English – as opposed to Scottish – poetry. Here we find the lines larded with learned allusions, inter-penetrated by a terrifying stoicism, rich with surface mines of the blackest hatred, categorical, polysyllabic, aphoristic lines following one another in ungrammatical abundance. It is a very beautiful, noble, and well-balanced book. The title poem is dedicated to Charles Doughty but I should prefer to consider another and, to my mind, better poem in which Doughty's influence is perhaps still more omnipresent. It is called 'On a Raised Beach' and it begins:

> All is lithogenesis – or lochia,
> Carpolite fruit of the forbidden tree,
> Stones blacker than any in the Caaba,
> Cream-coloured caen-stone, chatoyant pieces,
> Celadon and corbeau, bistre and beige,
> Glaucous, hoar, enfouldered, cyathiform,
> Making mere faculae of the sun and moon,
> I study you glout and gloss, but have
> No cadrans to adjust you with, and turn again
> From optik to haptik and like a blind man run
> My fingers over you, arris by arris, burr by burr,
> Slickensides, truité, rugas, foveoles,
> Bringing my aesthesia in vain to bear,
> An angle-titch to all your corrugations and coigns,
> Hatched foraminous cavo-rilieva of a world,
> Diectic, fiducial stones, chiliad by chiliad
> What bricole piled you here, stupendous cairn?
> What artist poses the earth écorché thus
> Pillar of creation engouled in me?
> What eburnation augments you with men's bones,
> Every energumen an Endymion yet?
> All other stones are in this one's haecceity it seems,
> But where is the Christophanic rock that moved?
> What Cabirian song from this catasta comes?

Whatever the reader may have made of this *hapax legomenon* of an opening, he cannot fail to realise that this is going to be a poem about stones; and that stones are as different from mankind as the vocabulary in which they are addressed differs from the speech of the average educated Englishman. This vocabulary is drawn from a dozen different specialised disciplines – geology, crystallography, neural physiology, history, art, architecture, even the theology of Duns Scotus. Each word brings with it the peculiar 'haecceity' of the subject to which it belongs so that the whole conscious mind is attacked simultaneously from a dozen different directions, and, since very few men can be expected to understand every word at first sight, the unconscious too will be called in to fill gaps. After having startled his reader into so many types of awareness, MacDiarmid goes on to compare the nervous impermanence of the human mind to the self-sufficiency of his raised beach. It, and all other geological strata, outlast the stone constructions that men may make. The strata may indeed change, their constituent particles transported, but in the end:

> There are plenty of ruined buildings in the world but no ruined stones.

The geological permanence of stones is seen as the result, the reward almost, of their placid acceptance of their fate. They accept silence with the same joyous indifference as a bird accepts its song – though, of the two, silence is undoubtedly the better song. The ambitious yearnings of humanity after immortality are contrasted to the humble stones with their more nearly immortal lifetimes.

> Impatience is a poor qualification for immortality.
> Hot blood is of no use in dealing with eternity.
> It is seldom that promises or even realisations
> Can sustain a clear and searching gaze.
> But an emotion chilled is an emotion controlled;
> This is the road leading to certainty,
> Reasoned planning for the time when reason can no longer avail.

This then is the reason that the man who understands death can also accept life. This is the end result of a disposition 'toward spiritual issues made inhumanly clear'. Politics and mysticism converge on this one statement, this command to have a kind of hopeless faith that anticipates Eliot's where: 'The love and the hope and the faith are all in the waiting.' Yet MacDiarmid is never quite so 'thoroughly dry and small' as Eliot. He contemplates the stones again and is forced to exclaim:

> This is no heap of broken images.
> Let men find the faith that builds mountains
> Before they seek the faith that moves them.

By the exercise of such faith they will be able to live in spiritual independence of one another, each creating his own life's work, his own mountain, careless of what any other man might think of it.

> Great work cannot be combined with surrender to the crowd
> – Nay, the truth we seek is as free
> From all yet thought as a stone from humanity.

Yet this truth is not a hidden truth, an underground stream that squeezes a few occasional drops of its sanctifying liquors through a fissure in the rocks. Our difficulty in approaching it is the product of our fear.

> Truth is not crushed;
> It crushes, gorgonises all else into itself.

The truth is in the rock itself.

> Do not argue with me. Argue with these stones.

But you will lose the argument, for the stones, like the poet, keep 'a mind as open as the grave'.

> 'Ah!' you say, 'If only one of these stones would move
> – Were it only an inch – of its own accord.
> This is the resurrection we await,
> – The stone rolled away from the tomb of the Lord
> I know there is no weight in infinite space,
> No impermeability in infinite time. . . .'

Here, at last, is 'the Christophanic stone that moved'. Its existence is a sign of the ultimate infinity of human nature. Surrounded by the love of Christ the stone is cut off from the laws of its own kind as it would be in an infinite space-time continuum where no gravitational forces were operative. This brilliant image for the love of God does not impress the man who devised it. He looks again at the stones, and denies the miracle:

> Detached intellectuals, not one stone will move,
> Not the least of them, not a fraction of an inch.

The Christian myth is mere myth. And then the poem ends in a final incandescense of polysyllables.

In spite of this fanatical stoicism, MacDiarmid's autobiography, *Lucky Poet*, is a hastily built haystack of verbiage chiefly concerned with complaints about his bad luck and full of attacks on the human categories (literary men, Englishmen, Scotsmen, non-literary men, etc.) he regards as responsible for it. Yet, although it is often infantile and usually ungrammatical, it is a magnificent book, its frequent vulgarities somehow subordinated to a complex myth that can be recognised more easily than it can be identified.

> – And all this here, everything I write, of course
> Is an extended metaphor for something I never mention.

This 'something I never mention' is the same as Wittgenstein's experiences, 'whereof one cannot speak'. It explains why the word 'silence' is central to MacDiarmid's conception of poetry, why the *Drunk Man* ended with that silence:

> . . . whom nocht in man or Diety,
> Or Daith or Dreid or Laneliness can touch,
> *Wha's deed owre often and has seen owre much.*

and why, at a critical point in his later poem, *In Memoriam, James Joyce*, he writes:

> . . . Hölderlin sought,
> And often miraculously found,
> The word with which silence speaks
> Its own silence without breaking it.

It is because such silence is omnipresent, cradled within and stretching beyond all his ranting, his exhibitionism, his passion for facts, that MacDiarmid is a poet: but it is because so many of the 'silly horrors o' oor fates' are brought into contact with this healing and justifying silence that he is a great poet.

Stony Limits is the transitional book. From then on MacDiarmid's ideas, though remaining in antagonism, become increasingly systematic, while his verse forms loosen. There is no attempt, in most of his recent poetry, to construct verse in any ordinary sense of the term. Long prose passages, transcribed from the work of writers like Martin Buber and Leo Shestov, are liberally inserted. The division of these passages into lines serves as an additional, and very flexible, method of punctuation, altering the emphasis of the original to suit the requirements of the poet. This seems, to me at least, to be a perfectly justifiable device, and when it is supported, as it sometimes is, by a subtle ear for strange and forceful rhythms, it can lead to poetry every bit as delicate as the more pretentiously complex stanzaic forms of most modern verse.

MacDiarmid's fundamental forms are not, however, stanzaic. They are dictated by the sequence of ideas. All kinds of ideologies are used and a variety of facts is subsumed under each of them. These ideologies are inter-connected, often by simple apposition as two geological strata of very different periods may be found to outcrop side by side in the landscape. Administrative decentralisation is thus compared to the division of a diseased personal psyche under analysis and is regarded as having the same liberating effect. Each theory, the social and the psychological, is a metaphor for the other.

But MacDiarmid is a practical poet, a propagandist at the spiritual level, and for this a nexus of practical propositions is necessary. Like most of us he considers that the world is in a very bad way and likely to destroy itself: but, unlike the majority of his own Communist friends even, he has no complete faith in any partial or political solutions. It is his reiterated belief that a psychological revolution is necessary if mankind is not to commit suicide. He goes further and states his conviction that such a revolution is already taking place: 'A new mutation is occurring in the "soul" of man, as a result of which his consciousness will be so enlarged as to be capable of conceiving and pursuing new ends commensurate with his technical mastery of means.' Such a change has already been envisaged by Gerald Heard in *The Ascent of Humanity*: 'Man's own self-consciousness alone decides whether he will mutate and the mutation is instantaneous; as a result of this mutation the barrier between consciousness and the unconscious will disappear, we shall consciously realise our oneness with life as a whole with which the unconscious is already continuous, though the fact is at present hidden from us, and our enlarged consciousness will give us direct insight into the nature of reality.' It is obvious that this cannot be effected by any mere improvement in the techniques of scientific verification or any increase in their scope. Such a linking of conscious and unconscious knowledge is to be found only in the 'artist's diseased nervous system'. 'Just as man the Pagan concentrated upon the truth or sureness of his foot and man the Christian upon the virtue or strength of his arm, so it has been left to modern man to develop that beautiful precision of the eye, that instinct for the right thing which is the property of the artistic genius rather than of thought

E

or moral character.' It is the artist alone who can throw a rope to the unconscious wisdom of the individual and the race, and thus begin to bridge our unconscious repressions. This leads to the metaphysics of Shestov. 'The whole art of philosophy should be directed towards freeing us from the "good and evil" of cooks and carpenters, to find that frontier beyond which the might of general ideas ceases.' And the same goes for 'good and bad' in art. General ideas of form are no help. The aggressive 'formlessness' of his poetry has, therefore, a formal significance.

> . . . beyond the four dimensions of space-time
> There is a fifth dimension, individuality, . . .
> Here empty space as well as the space-time continuum disappear.
> The individual discontinuum
> Becomes established as the physical principle
> Of this world, and the five-dimensional aspect is introduced.
> Homogeneity, causality, probability disappear.
> In a universe without emptiness events do not happen
> Because other events happen before.
> Within its five dimensions
> Forces influence each other elastically.
> There is no logic,
> No determinate sequence,
> Only tendencies.[1]

A poem is a 'tendency' toward verbal form. Instead of facetious verbal ambiguity MacDiarmid tries to reach through to 'the ageless ambiguity of things' and refuses to reject any one truth because its linguistic opposite is also a truth.

To try to classify him, to make an estimate of his stature, to nibble away his pointless eccentricities and decide what there is of lasting value in his work, would be a job for a hero who was also a sage. In Scots he has been generally accepted as forming one of the triumvirate, Dunbar-Burns-MacDiarmid, which rules over poetry. Neither of the others was of comparable intellectual stature and his technical mastery of many verse forms is as complete as theirs. Yet there is a lack of warmth in most of his poetry, a lack of those simple irrational sympathies known as love and charity. His emotions seem to follow an intellectual party line so that, when he says he loves, he has always such good reasons for doing so that one feels he is more in love with his

---

[1] *In Memoriam James Joyce*, p. 99. [Ed.].

train of thought than with any chance object that might get in its way. The curses of Dunbar have a touch of camaraderie and joy: those of MacDiarmid are pure hate, like Hitler's. The social exuberance of Burns is always tinged with respect and gratitude, no matter how scathingly comic he may be: MacDiarmid, equally exuberant, can never overcome his contempt – for it is essentially a self-contempt.

His English, as well as his Scots, poems express the spiritual austerity of a man who refuses to give vent to his kinder impulses, but they are still more difficult to judge since they have never been published in their final form. Immense chunks occasionally appear but they are only fragments, ragged as shrapnel, of a much larger poem that has not yet got into print. Much of his earlier work is no longer available so that it would seem high time that a *Collected Poems* was produced.[1] His work needs to be read in mass, as it does not depend for its effect on a happy coincidence of phrases but upon the 'speculative stamina' with which he blazes new trails of thought. His faults are almost as great as his virtues. Few men have ever written so badly as MacDiarmid at his worst, but fewer still have equalled him at his best. But his is a new kind of poetry. (That is why it is possible to deny that it is poetry at all.) And the world is not so rich in new things that it can afford to dispense with

> A poetry like the barrel of a gun
> Weaving like a snake's head.
>
> A poetry that can put all its chips on the table
> And back it to the limit.
>
> A poetry full of the crazy feeling
> That everything that has ever gone into my life
> Has pointed to each successive word
> And I couldn't have failed to write it if I'd tried.[2]
>
>   *   *   *
>
> A poetry at the worst adept
> In the artful tessellation of commonplaces
> Expressed with so exact a magnificence
> That they seem – and sometimes are – profound.[3]

[1] Published in 1962 [Ed.].   [2] *Lucky Poet*, p. 166 [Ed.].
[3] *The Kind of Poetry I Want*, p. 26; *Lucky Poet*, p. 120 [Ed.].

Hugh MacDiarmid's Early Poetry

DAVID DAICHES

The long overdue collected edition of Hugh MacDiarmid's poetry recently [1962] published by Macmillan in New York (it is Scotland's bitter shame that she has had to wait for America to produce a collected edition of her greatest modern poet) opens with the poem 'A Moment in Eternity', which originally appeared in his *Annals of the Five Senses* (1923) and was later included in *To Circumjack Cencrastus* (1930). Anyone who comes to this poem from the Scots lyrics in *Sangschaw* or *Penny Wheep* might well be surprised at what at first sight looks like its conventional English romantic imagery. The poem is frankly mystical, an account in terms of imagery largely of light of an intimate revelation of God and Eternity.

> And again the wind came
> Blowing me afar
> In fair fantastic fires,
> –Ivies and irises invading
> The upland garths of ivory;
> Queen daisies growing
> In the tall red grass
> By pools of perfect peace;
> And bluebells tossing
> In transparent fields;
> And silver airs
> Lifting the crystal sources in dim hills
> And swinging them far out like bells of glass
> Pealing pellucidly
> And quivering in faery flights of chimes;
> Shivers of wings bewildered
> In alleys of virgin dream;
> Floral dances and revels of radiance
> Whirling in stainless sanctuaries;
> And eyes of Seraphim,
> Shining like sunbeams on eternal ice,

> Lifted toward the unexplored
> Summits of Paradise.

'Transparent', 'dim', 'crystal', 'faery', 'virgin dream', 'radiance', 'stainless', 'Seraphim', 'eternal ice' – this seems like a curious combination of Vaughan and Blake and Shelley and even Milton, worlds apart from, say,

> An' the roarin' o' oceans noo'
> Is peerieweerie to me:
> Thunner's a tinklin' bell: an' Time
> Whuds like a flee.

Yet this early poem of MacDiarmid's is not as far removed from his later work as one might imagine. The difference lies in the degree of verbal realisation of the subject, not in the nature of the subject itself. In 'A Moment in Eternity' MacDiarmid is seeking for words to contain an experience whose reality is wholly independent of the poem; the poem attempts to clothe the experience, and the comparatively facile eloquence which results is an eloquence of expression – the poet wears his words as indications of the nature and importance of his experience, as a high-ranking officer wears appropriate uniform and insignia or as peers wear robes at a coronation. The result is not ineffective, yet not wholly satisfactory either, because the imagery is not *special* enough, it does not fully contain the utter individuality of that complex of thought and feeling which prompted the poem.

Take, by contrast, the little 'Ex Vermibus' from *Sangschaw*:

> Gape, gape, gorlin',
> For I ha'e a worm
> That'll gi'e ye a slee and sliggy sang
> Wi' mony a whuram.
>
> Syne i' the lift
> Byous spatrils you'll mak',
> For a gorlin' wi' worms like this in its wame
> Nae airels sall lack.
>
> But owre the tree-taps
> Maun flee like a sperk,
> Till it hes the haill o' the Heavens alunt
> Frae dawin' to derk.

What explodes this poem into its unique comic-yet-serious meaning is the brilliant transition from the visual to the aural to the visual again by means of which the wriggling worm becomes in the bird the actual trills of song first as expressed in splendidly turned crotchets and quavers ('mony a whuram', 'byous spatrils'), then as notes to the ear, and finally as light-giving sounds that illumine Heaven. This, too, is in its way a mystical poem, but here MacDiarmid has found the appropriate kind of language for his kind of mysticism – or perhaps we might say that he has by now developed that kind of response to language which enables him to see the experience potential in the words. He wrote in *Lucky Poet* of 'the act of poetry being the reverse of what it is usually thought to be, not an idea gradually shaping itself in words, but deriving entirely from words'. This is a deliberate over-simplification, but it provides an important clue to what is going on in this poem. The vision, which moves from worm to bird-with-worm to note to sound to illuminated Heaven, is not an 'idea' clothed in language: it is the total realisation in language of what cannot exist outside this particular realisation.

Of course, something of this sort can be said of any successful poem. But the process of verbal realisation in MacDiarmid demands special attention, for he has created his own language as few other poets have done – not invented it, but out of English and Scots, out of modern Scots dialects and mediaeval Scots literary vocabulary, created a language which, at its best, is at one with his version of experience. 'Ex Vermibus' begins with an almost casual familiarity, the poet addressing the bird as he approaches it with a special worm:

> Gape, gape, gorlin',
> For I ha'e a worm
> That'll gi'e ye a slee and sliggy sang
> Wi' mony a whuram.

'Now there's a fine worm for you, birdie', one might say. The tone is familiar, humorous, interested. 'I ha'e a worm / That'll gi'e ye a slee and sliggy sang.' 'Now *that*'ll really make you sing', is the rough prose equivalent, but then what becomes of the splendid 'slee and sliggy sang' with its *conspiratorial* suggestion – the poet and the bird are now working together to produce something quite remarkable. We are prepared now for something more than the poet approaching the bird with a fine wriggling worm hoping that the worm will make the bird sing particularly well. We are prepared not only for that translation of the wriggling of the worm into the wriggling of the notes and the trilling of the sound (*quavering* quavers, one might say), but also for that odd mixture of comradeship and impersonality in the poet's relation to the bird, quite different from Burns's attitude to the mouse or from anything in the Scottish animal-poetry tradition. The poet's involvement in the bird's singing success grows out of the language. It seems at first that the little poem is simply going to play some tricks with language, assimilating the worm to the song through the inter-mediary of the wriggle. (The place played in the poem by the progres-sion 'slee and sliggy sang' – 'mony a whuram' – 'byous spatrils' – 'airels' warrants a long discussion in itself: if only all discussion of the possibilities of Lallans in modern Scottish poetry were linked to con-crete examples like this!) But the linking of the material and the spiritual, of a greedy bird and a vision of Heaven, is much more than a trick of language. It is an aspect of the mystic's habit of seeing eternity in a grain of sand, of refusing to accept the normal categories that isolate the material from the spiritual and the trivial from the over-whelmingly important. The worm become song turns into a spark that sets Heaven ablaze – and it is not a flash in the pan, but a blaze that lasts 'frae dawin' to derk'. A verbal joke becomes a striking poem: I can think of no more immediately convincing illustration of how MacDiarmid makes language work in his Scots poems from *Sangschaw* to *A Drunk Man Looks at the Thistle* than this wonderful little lyric.

Something like this happens in nearly all of MacDiarmid's early short poems in Scots. It is misleading to talk simply, as so many critics have done, of the beauty and tenderness and delicacy of these poems and then proceed to wonder what happened to these qualities in Mac-Diarmid's later poetry. These poems properly read will take us to the heart of MacDiarmid as a poet and enable us to see both the achieve-ment of this early phase of his career and his later need to make a different kind of verbal attack upon experience. The shortest poems are often the most revealing. Consider 'The Bonnie Broukit Bairn', with its deliberate bringing together of astronomical myth, colloquial violence, and sudden flash of impatient insight:

> Mars is braw in crammasy,
> Venus in a green silk goun,
> The auld mune shak's her gowden feathers,
> Their starry talk's a wheen o' blethers,
> Nane for thee a thochtie sparin',
> Earth, thou bonnie broukit bairn!
> – *But greet, an' in your tears ye'll drown*
> *The haill clanjamfrie!*

The modulation of the language more than corresponds to the progression of the mood and the emergence of the insight – it positively
creates them. The phrase 'a wheen o' blethers' suddenly transmutes the
splendidly dressed planets to a group of stairhead gossips, and the
turning away from them towards the earth, humanised by the diminu-
tive in 'thochtie' and by the rising tenderness of the apostrophe, 'Earth,
thou bonnie broukit bairn', leads at last to that wonderful putting of
the other planets in their place that is achieved by that splendid phrase,
'the haill clanjamfrie'. Or consider the choice of Scots words in 'The
Watergaw' through which a sense of wonder and foreboding is dis-
tilled and observe how the colloquial and proverbial 'there was nae
reek i' the laverock's hoose' mediates between the strangeness of
nature and strangeness of human relations. Or take 'Au Clair de la
Lune', that uncanny sequence of lyrics where once again (and this is
particularly noticeable in 'Moonstruck') the strangeness, the reality
and the power of the experience are determined by the vocabulary
and by the manipulation of the movement, speed and length of the
lines. Perhaps the most remarkable example of all is 'The Eemis
Stane':

> I' the how-dumb-deid o' the cauld hairst nicht
> The warl' like an eemis stane
> Wags i' the lift;
> An' my eerie memories fa'
> Like a yowdendrift.

> Like a yowdendrift so's I couldna read
> The words cut oot i' the stane
> Had the fug o' fame
> An' history's hazelraw
> No' yirdit thaim.

Criticism stands powerless before this miracle of verbal choice and
placing. The unexpectedness yet, once expressed, the extraordinary
rightness of the comparison of the world in the cold harvest night to
an 'eemis stane' wagging in the sky (and how much is lost by translating the phrase 'wags i' the lift', how uniquely expressive is 'how-dumb-
deid o' the cauld hairst nicht', and how pallidly rendered by 'insecure
stone' is 'eemis stane'!) makes the poem almost a miraculous work of
nature rather than a contrived work of art. The beautifully controlled
rise of emotion caught by the repetition of 'like a yowdendrift' leads

the poem effortlessly to a new and strangely moving use of the image of the eemis stane, which now becomes a worn tombstone with its inscription obliterated by moss and lichen, 'the fug o' fame an' history's hazelraw'.

If we say that there is a mystical centre in these poems and point out that time and again MacDiarmid shows himself to be obsessed with attitudes to time and eternity, this does not mean that this is an 'other worldly' poetry which soars off into the empyrean and leaves all common dailiness of human life behind. Far from it: there is nothing of Shelley but quite a bit of Blake in MacDiarmid, and his vision comes from proper realisation of the ordinary. The little poem 'Country Life', with its contrast between the life of nature outside and the homely domestic interior (an old Scottish tradition this, but here used in a new way), is really made of the same materials as his more visionary poems, the only difference being that it doesn't push through to the vision but is content to state the contrast with a compelling simplicity, the very precision of the contrasting images suggesting, though not developing, some of the implications of the contrast:

> Ootside! . . . Oootside!
> There's dooks that try tae fly
> An' bum-clocks bizzin' by,
> A corn-skriech an' a cay
> An' guissay i' the cray.
>
> Inside! . . . Inside!
> There's golochs on the wa',
> A cradle on the ca',
> A muckle bleeze o' cones
> An' mither fochin' scones

This, I think, for all its brevity and simplicity, is a better poem than 'I heard Christ Sing', with its more lax vocabulary and its echoes of the 'nineties.

God, Christ and Eternity figure frequently in these poems, but though the traditional themes of Christian religious poetry can be found here again and again there is at work in the treatment of them a rock-like apprehension of the sheer stubbornness of life and indeed of the whole universe – what I can only describe as an inspired *coorseness* – that is bound up both with MacDiarmid's sensibility and with his language. One sees it in 'The Sauchs in the Reuch Heuch Hauch' with its deadly last stanza:

> There's no' a licht that the Heavens let loose
> Can calm them a hanlawhile,
> Nor frae their ancient amplefeyst
> Sall God's ain sel' them wile.

One sees it, too, in the end of 'Crowdieknowe':

> Fain the weemun-folk'll seek
> To mak' them haud their row
> *– Fegs, God's no blate gin he stirs up*
> *The men o' Crowdie knowe!*

and in 'The Frightened Bride':

> Seil o' yer face! Ye needna seek
> For comfort gin ye show yer plight.
> To Gods an' men, coorse callants baith,
> A fleggit bride's the seilfu' sicht.

The poems in *Penny Wheep* continue many of the same methods and themes. In a poem such as 'Cloudburst and Soaring Moon' we see that ability to use natural scenery in order to give meaning to a human situation while at the same time (as in Chinese classical poetry and the economical Japanese verse forms of the *tanka* and *hokku*) doing it all by simple juxtaposition, that is such a characteristic part of Mac-Diarmid's early talent:

> Cloodburst an' soarin' mune
> And 'twixt the twa a taed
> That loupit oot upon me
> As doon the loan I gaed.
>
> Noo I gan white an' lanely
> But hoo I'm wishin', faith,
> A clood aince mair cam' owre me
> Wi' Jock the byreman's braith.

This is one of the simpler examples of this particular technique; one can see clearly just what is going on here. A more complex welding of nature, mood and glint of insight that transcends both, is in that brief but finely wrought poem 'Somersault', where the Scots words achieve an effect of enormous precision and at the same time of enormous suggestiveness:

> I lo'e the stishie
> O' Earth in space
> Breengin' by
> At a haliket pace.
>
> A wecht o' hills
> Gangs wallopin' owre,
> Syne a whummlin' sea
> Wi' a gallus glower.
>
> The West whuds doon
> Like the pigs at Gadara,
> But the East's aye there
> Like a sow at the farrow.

The similes of the last stanza startle us by their apparent incongruity, and the shock of attention that results provides that combination of cosmic geography and a sense of the earthyness of physical life – the midden heap linked to the stars, and *both equally there* – that is at the core of so much of MacDiarmid's poetry.

Sometimes the fusion of language and experience fails and Mac-Diarmid has to fall back on a tame gnomic remark, as at the end of 'Parley of Beasts':

> It's fain I'd mell wi' tiger and tit,
> Wi' elephant and eel,
> But noo-a-days e'en wi' ain's sel
> At hame it's hard to feel.

These last two lines, with the inversion having no other function than to assist the rhyme, fall curiously flat (there is no question here of the idea of the poem 'deriving entirely from words'). In his later poetry MacDiarmid develops a quite different way of handling the discursive poem of ideas, pushing past words towards the total rhythm of the meaning, oblivious of any incidental bathos or awkwardness, because he knows where he is going, the power of the whole deriving not from an instantaneous fusion of words and experience but from the cumulative pressure of thought and feeling in action. Until he developed this, he found difficulty in crossing from the visionary to the didactic; that interesting but not wholly successful poem 'Sea-Serpent' gives clear evidence of this. Yet that deservedly popular short lyric, 'Wheesht, Wheesht', which is not one of the visionary lyrics but a coolly objective statement of a situation, has the beautiful clarity and concentration, as well as the uncanny rightness in the choice of Scots words, that we find in what I call the visionary lyrics. A comparison of this poem with Robert Graves' 'Down, Wanton, Down' will show MacDiarmid's extraordinary delicacy of feeling and language.

At the very time when he seemed to be resisting the urge to write longer poems – *Penny Wheep* includes the little poem, 'To One Who Urges More Ambitious Flights', which contains the line 'Wee bit sangs are a' I need' – MacDiarmid was working out a technique of the long poem considered as a poem-sequence in which incidental short lyrics could take their place enriched by their context. In 1926, the same year that saw the publication of *Penny Wheep*, appeared *A Drunk Man Looks at the Thistle*, his masterpiece in a *genre* which if he did not actually invent, he certainly developed in a new way.

> A amna' fou' sae muckle as tired – deid dune.
> It's gey and hard wark coupin' gless for gless
> Wi' Cruivie and Gilsanquhar and the like,
> And I'm no juist as bauld as aince I wes.
>
> The elbuck fankles in the coorse o' time,
> The sheckle's no' sae souple, and the thrapple
> Grows deef an dour: nae langer up and doun
> Gleg as a squirrel speils the Adam's apple.
>
> Forbye, the stuffie's no' the real Mackay . . .

This is the opening of *A Drunk Man*, with its splendid rendering of fatigue and a sense of the passing of time anchored to the realities of contemporary Scottish life both by its setting and by the sudden increase in the colloquial tone in 'Forbye, the stuffie's no' the real Mackay'. The slow movement of the first line, with the dead fall of its last two words, captures the moment of utter tiredness that invites drunkenness, and this is both personal to the speaker and symbolic of the state of Scotland. But it does more than this: it is the precise equivalent, in terms of the placing and meaning of this line in the poem, of Dante's

> Nel mezzo del cammin di nostra vita
> Mi ritrovai per una selva oscura,
> Che la diritta via era smarrita.

But in MacDiarmid's lines the allegorical and symbolic elements are totally subsumed in a real contemporary world of commonplace experience. MacDiarmid, too, was 'nel mezzo del cammin' when *A Drunk Man* appeared, and the poem is something of a testament. It is not, however, presented as a formal vision, but is allowed suddenly to open out before us as though we have pushed open the door of a pub and found ourselves inside with the speaker. This *placing* of the reader in the poem is achieved partly by the quietly conversational opening in which the writer confronts the reader as though the two had always been together. And then the matter-of-fact reference to 'Cruivie and Gilsanquhar and the like' shrugs the social context into the poem in a way which takes for granted our knolwedge and acceptance of it. The last line of the opening stanza gives the first casual suggestion of the speaker's resigned awareness that he has lost his youth – 'And I'm no juist as bauld as aince I wes'. This leads into the next stanza, where a rising elegiac note is brilliantly developed in a colloquial Scots language with reference to the tiring of the drinker's elbow and the stiffening of his wrist in the course of years of boozing. Who but MacDiarmid could have sounded the true mediaeval 'ubi sunt' plangency in such everyday – indeed, such 'low' – imagery?

> The elbuck fankles in the coorse o' time,
> The sheckle's no' sae souple, and the thrapple
> Grows deef and dour: nae langer up and doun
> Gleg as a squirrel speils the Adam's apple.

Note, too, how the poet will not allow himself the self-indulgence of remaining long in this elegiac mood, the brisk and humorous imagery of

> nae langer up and doun
> Gleg as a squirrel speils the Adam's apple

breaking in to suggest a short ironic laugh – ironic, yet amused (there is an engaging suggestion of the poet being amused by his own simile here). This in turn leads to reflections on the price of whisky having gone up and the quality down, which provide the introduction of one of the poem's main themes – the state of Scottish civilisation:

> It's robbin' Peter to pey Paul at least . . .
> And a' that's Scotch aboot it is the name,
> Like a' thing else ca'd Scottish nooadays
> – A' destitute o' speerit juist the same.

The pun on 'speerit' links the state of Scotch whisky to the state of Scotland.

Thus in five beautifully manœuvred stanzas MacDiarmid has moved us from confronting a tired man in a pub to confronting questions about civilisation. A wry parenthesis follows, in which he justifies this method: now for the first time he appears as a poet confronting the reader, no longer simply as a drinking companion drawing the reader into a pub conversation:

> (To prove my saul is Scots I maun begin
> Wi' what's still deemed Scots and the folk expect,
> And spire up syne by visible degrees
> To heichts whereo' the fules ha'e never recked.
>
> But aince I get them there I'll whummle them
> And souse the craturs in the nether deeps,
> – For it's nae choice, and ony man s'ud wish
> To dree the goat's weird tae as weel's the sheep's!)

There is now an 'I' and a 'they'. The poet has clearly emerged as the satirist. But where does the reader stand at this point? Is he with the poet, or is he one of 'them'? MacDiarmid wants to keep the reader's position uncertain for as long as possible, for it is only by allowing the reader to feel that he makes a 'we' with the author and then suddenly shocking him into seeing himself as one of 'them' that he can achieve the special kind of shock treatment which is an important part of his satirical method. Is the poet enlisting the emotional support of professional Scotsmen in deploring the decline of things Scottish? If the reader is fooled into thinking this, he has not long to wait before being disillusioned, for the attack on the professional Scot flashes out in the immediately following stanzas and we are startled into the realisation that all the standard and respectable Scottish attitudes are part of the decline that has been talked about. This technique of getting the reader (as he thinks) on the poet's side and then hitting out hard and suddenly at the position the reader thinks he now shares with the poet is very common in MacDiarmid's poetry; it is a satirical device he has made peculiarly his own – a new twist to Baudelaire's 'hypocrite lecteur', who becomes not 'mon semblable, mon frère', but *'leur* semblable, *leur* frère'.

The Burns cult is the symbol of the false Scottish feeling that is such a central target for MacDiarmid, and the relatively broad satire of its handling is an indication of how natural a target it is:

> Croose London Scotties wi' their braw shirt fronts
> And a' their fancy freen's, rejoicin'
> That similah gatherings in Timbuctoo,
> Bagdad – and Hell, nae doot – are voicin'
>
> Burns' sentiments o' universal love,
> In pidgin' English or in wild-fowl Scots, . . .

The attack, of course, is not on the sentiments themselves, but on the sentimentality, hypocrisy and routine platitudinousness of these proceedings. Similarly the comic-satiric treatment of the international aspect of these gatherings –

> You canna gang to a Burns supper even
> Wi'oot some wizened scrunt o' a knock-knee
> Chinee turns roon to say 'Him Haggis – velly goot!' –

is not of course aimed at the Chinese or any other foreign nation; the target is the bogus internationalism associated with annual spoutings about 'A man's a man for a' that'.

The speaker in the poem, it must be remembered, is both dead tired and somewhat drunk. This device serves a similar purpose to the dream allegory in mediaeval literature; a drunk man, like a dreaming man, has his own logic, and his thoughts and feelings can be developed in a sequence which may at first sight appear totally disordered but which in fact has a true order of its own which is part of the poetic pattern of the whole. Thoughts about the Burns cult lead to reflections on hypocrisy in modern life and comparisons of Burns's fate to Christ's before the poet pulls himself up by recalling his own state:

> But that's aside the point! I've got fair waun'ert.
> It's no' that I'm sae fou' as juist deid dune,
> And dinna ken as muckle's what I am
> Or hoo I've come to sprawl here 'neth the mune.
>
> That's it! It isna me that's fou' at a',
> But the fu' mune, the doited jade, that's led
> Me fer agley, or 'mogrified the warld.
> – For a' I ken I'm safe in my ain bed.
>
> *Jean! Jean!* Gin she's no' here it's no' *oor* bed,
> Or else I'm dreamin' deep and canna wauken,
> But it's a fell queer dream if this is no'
> A real hillside – and thae things thistles and bracken!

This interesting transitional passage reveals the poet as now outside the pub – on a moonlit hillside – and provides the first knowledge of his wife back at home, that Jean whose name and presence act as a kind of anchor, bringing the poet back again and again from fancy to the homely realities of everyday life until the remarkable ending, where, after the beautiful concluding lyric on silence ('yet ha'e I Silence left, the croon o' a'') with the poet's last rising cry, 'O I ha'e Silence left', her dry realism rounds the poem off:

> – 'And weel ye micht,'
> Sae Jean'll say, 'efter sic a nicht!'

It is Jean's words echoing in his own mind, not her physical entry into the poem, that provides this comment, for the poet's sense of his wife is a force in the poem that breaks through intermittently to provide a variety of effects.

But this is to anticipate. After the moment of half-waking on the hillside, as it were (and what a host of archetypal associations *that* brings in!), the poet proceeds to develop his earlier train of thought, still rather staggeringly, for

> It's hard wark haud'n by a thocht worth ha'en'
> And harder speakin't, and no' for ilka man;
> Maist Thocht's like whisky – a thoosan' under proof,
> And a sair price is pitten on't even than.

But the weaving quality of the thought is necessary for this kind of poem; it enables the poet to move easily between the commonplace realities of modern Scotland and of his own daily life and varying kinds of speculative reaching out or of sudden lyrical intensity. The sharpness of the satire can be set against the moments of self-doubt. Most satirical poets (Pope, for example) feel the necessity of maintaining the pose of complete confidence in their own rightness and moral superiority if they are to have a position from which their satire can be effectively launched. MacDiarmid does something more difficult: he allows the objects of his scorn to destroy themselves by the way they appear in his lines, and than at intervals shows us himself groping towards a philosophy. This visible process brings the reader into a special kind of relationship with the poet, quite different from the kind of relationship which, say, Pope establishes in the 'Epistle to Dr. Arbuthnot' by enabling the reader to identify himself with the recipient of the letter, Pope's intimate friend and thus one of the elect. In

MacDiarmid's case the poet commands further assent by the integrity
with which he displays his own uncertainties:

> I'll ha'e nae hauf-way hoose, but aye be whaur
> Extremes meet – it's the only way I ken
> To dodge the curst conceit o' bein' richt
> That damns the vast majority o' men.
>
> I'll bury nae heid like an ostrich's,
> Nor yet believe my een and naething else.
> My senses may advise me, but I'll be
> Mysel' nae maitter what they tell's. . . .
>
> I' ha'e nae doot some foreign philosopher
> Has wrocht a system oot to justify
> A' this: but I'm a Scot wha blin'ly follows
> Auld Scottish instincts, and I winna try.
>
> For I've nae faith in ocht I can explain,
> And stert whaur the philosophers leave aff,
> Content to glimpse its loops I dinna ettle
> To land the sea serpent's sel' wi' ony gaff.

This leads to a cry for water (has he stumbled into a stream, or is
his mouth dry from too much alcohol, or does he want to water the
Waste Land of modern Scotland?) which at once modulates down to
the matter-of-fact and the domestic again:

> Water! Water! There was owre muckle o't
> In yonder whisky, sae I'm in deep water
> (And gin I could wun hame I'd be in het,
> For even Jean maun natter, natter, natter). . . .

(That 'even Jean' is deft: it prevents the reference from being surly and
from in any way endangering the solidity of this relationship: she is
clearly a very special woman, but *even* she natters.) The domestic
imagery of this stanza moves naturally to thoughts of 'the toon that
I belang tae', which shares in the common drouth:

> And in the toon that I belang tae
> – What tho'ts Montrose or Nazareth? –
> Helplessly the folk continue
> To lead their livin' death! . . .

F

'What tho'ts Montrose or Nazareth?' This links up with the preceding
references to Christ, and at the same time provides one of those
periodic expansions of context by means of which MacDiarmid links
Scotland to the world and makes his poem a poem about civilisation
and about the whole question of the possibilities of redemption in the
world past and present as well as a poem about the state of his own
country. There follows the first of the inset lyrics, a finely localised
account of the poet in the pub based on the Russian of Alexander
Blok. Though this was obviously written separately, its insertion into
A Drunk Man at this point provides a moment of lyrical concentration
which lights up the whole context. It is about the relation of drink
and the Muse, about the poet's necessity to seek for something beyond common experience in the very midst of common experience.
The pub itself is situated in the midst of all the symbols of domestic
routine:

> And heich abune the vennel's pokiness,
> Whaur a' the white-weshed cottons lie;
> The Inn's sign blinters in the mochiness,
> And lood and shrill the bairnies cry.

But there is also moonlight on the lochan:

> And on the lochan there, hauf-herted
> Wee screams and creakin' oar-locks soon'
> And in the lift, heich, hauf-averted,
> The mune looks owre the yirdly roon'.

The pub mediates between domesticity and moonlight, as it were, and
itself provides rough society and private mystery: on the note of
private mystery the lyric ends:

> My soul stores up this wealth unspent,
> The key is safe and nane's but mine.
> You're richt, auld drunk impenitent,
> I ken it tae – the truth's in wine!

We then turn to the poet again, staggering about among the thistles
on the Scottish hillside under a Scottish moon:

> The munelicht's like a lookin'-gless,
> The thistle's like mysel',
> But whaur ye've gane, my bonnie lass,
> Is mair than I can tell.

This has almost parodic overtones of the conventional Scottish song in the Burns tradition ('my bonnie lass'). But in fact MacDiarmid is taking up the theme of the preceding lyric – the vision seen in the glass of whisky – and developing it into a search for identity:

> A man's a clean contrairy sicht
> Turned this way in-ootside,
> And, fegs, I feel like Dr. Jekyll
> Tak'n guid tent o' Mr. Hyde. . . .

The thistle seems to threaten him, he is aware of his own unshaven and semi-drunken condition, there is a roaring in his ears – then suddenly the poet falls into another lyric (again 'freely adapted' from Alexander Blok) in which feelings of foreboding and even of terror are turned to another anticipation of the coming of the Muse, the 'strange Goddess' both 'forekent' and unimaginable. Then he turns on her in a violent colloquial outburst:

> Or dost thou mak' a thistle o' me, wumman? But for thee
> I were as happy as the munelicht, . . .

Moonlight plays on the next few stanzas, which slowly settle down into a more regular (but never wholly regular) metrical beat as the poet reflects on 'the need to wark, the need to think, the need to be' that constrain a man; and now he can use the thistle and moon images in a new way:

> For ilka thing a man can be or think or dae
> Aye leaves a million mair unbeen, unthocht, undune,
> Till his puir warped performance is,
> To a' that micht ha' been, a thistle to the mune.

The immediate scene now weaves in and out of the lines – the hillside, the thistles and bracken, the moonlight – as the poet tries to force it into a meaning by contemplation ('And yet I feel this muckle thistle's staun'in' / Atween me and the mune as pairt o' a Plan) and as he does so the very quiddity of the thistle takes hold of him and provokes new insight:

> I never saw afore a thistle quite
> Sae intimately, or at sic an 'oor.
> There's something in the fickle licht that gi'es
> A different life to't and an unco poo'er.

A short lyric on 'the Gothic thistle', from the Belgian poet George Ramaekers, effectively concentrates this moment of vision before the poet shrugs it off with

> But that's a Belgian refugee, of coorse.
> *This* Freudian complex has somehoo slunken
> Frae Scotland's soul – . . .

The Scottish thistle is wilder than Ramaekers', and in any case 'To meddle wi' the thistle and to pluck / The figs frae't is *my* métier'. An adaptation of a poem on the octopus from the Russian of Zinaida Hippius presents the thistle-octopus as a monstrous threat and at the same time the poet's own soul, and the notion temporarily unhinges him, so that he is lost on the ebb and flow of his own thoughts –

> The munelicht ebbs and flows and wi't my thocht.

Then, cutting across this ebb and flow, comes the sudden awareness that there are many people who have no doubts or hesitances, who know what is important to them, and write about it. It is a great splash of comic irony:

> And O! to think that there are members o'
> St. Andrew's Societies sleepin' soon',
> Wha to the papers wrote afore they bedded
> On regimental buttons or buckled shoon,
>
> Or use o' England whar the U.K.'s meent,
> Or this or that anent the Blue Saltire,
> Recruitin', pedigrees, and Gude kens what,
> Filled wi' a proper patriotic fire!

These people, so confident in their routine reactions, have in a sense chosen a better part:

> Nae doot they're sober, as a Scot ne'er was,
> Each tethered to a punctual-snorin' missus,
> Whilst I, puir fule, owre continents unkent
> And wine-dark oceans waunder like Ulysses. . . .

The poet then breaks into a short lyric ('suggested by the German of Else Lasker-Schüler') in which moonlight, the thistle, and the poet's soul are presented as in complex and disturbing counterpoint. A shift in rhythms and stanza form then brings in a passage which makes a transition from the thistle to the bagpipes –

> Your leafs
> Mind me o' the pipes' lood drone
> – And a' your purple tops
> Are the pirly-wirly notes
> That gang staggerin' owre them as they groan.

The language and the thought, moving faster as it were to the music of the pipes, present a brief version of the Caledonian Antisyzygy with comic anecdote and ideas side by side ('Grinnin' gargoyle by a saint') before we reach four stanzas which reflect briefly on the Scottish educational system (explaining how a village drunk can bring in so many 'foreign references') and then break down in temporary confusion:

> Guid sakes I'm in a dreidfu' state.
> I'll ha'e nae inklin' sune
> Gin I'm the drinker or the drink,
> The thistle or the mune.

The moments of semi-drunken confusion in the poem serve as effective transitions; when the image on the screen comes back into focus, as it were, we are somewhere else – but where we are is always related to the main theme and purpose of the work as a whole. We move, then, to a short section in two-line stanzas on celebration in Scotland:

> Drums in the Walligate, pipes in the air,
> Come and hear the cryin' o' the Fair.
> A' as it used to be, when I was a loon
> On Common-Ridin' Day in the Muckle Toon.

Things are different now; yet the poet's vision of some splendid celebration has grown stronger and wilder:

> But I'll dance the nicht wi' the stars o' Heaven
> In the Mairket Place as shair's I'm livin'.

But the cosmos is too grandiose: the nostalgic mood with which the section opens returns at the close of it in a more limited human context:

> Devil the star! It's Jean I'll ha'e
> Again as she was on her weddin' day . . .

This moving to and fro between the cosmos and the particularised moment of individual experience – between Blake and Burns, one might say – is an important feature of the poem, and one of Mac-Diarmid's characteristic devices. This note rises in the powerful lyrical interlude that follows:

> Nerves in stounds o' delight,
> Muscles in pride o' power,
> Bluid as wi' roses dight
> Life's topplin' pinnacles owre,
> The thistle yet'll unite
> Man and the Infinite!

The individual is a microcosm of the universe:

> Lay haud o' my hert and feel
> Fountains ootloupin' the starns
> Or see the Universe reel
> Set gaen' by my eident harns, . . .

This vision is linked with the thistle; yet another look shows that 'the howes o' Man's hert are bare, / The Dragon's left them for good'; the thistle has fled to become, 'rootless and radiant', a Phoenix in Paradise, and we are left gaping at vacancy:

> There's nocht but naethingness there,
> The hole whaur the Thistle stood, . . .

A shift of rhythms helps to modulate from elegy into self-mockery, as the poet addresses himself as a 'thistleless fule', and then another shift brings three stanzas of deliberately self-conscious speculation about what poets and artists can achieve in such a world. The wildness that always lies near the surface in this poem breaks out for a moment in the poet's half-ironic, half-defiant assumption of a pose of traditional bardic dignity (the language is in fine contrast to Milton's account of the poet 'with all his singing robes about him'):

> — Crockats up, hair kaimed to the lift,
> And no' to cree legs wi'!

The wildness then swings the poem into an almost hysterical short lyric of departure and discovery – 'We're ootward boond frae Scotland. / Guid-bye, fair-ye-weel; guid bye, fare-ye-weel' which comes near to dissolving everything in 'coutribat and ganien' before the screen clears again and we see the poet meditating on the relation between mind and body. Jean here plays her mediating part, anchoring the poem again in a physical relationship which is at the same time more than physical. This leads in to a group of related lyrics on love and sex and the combined lusts, fears, jealousies and mysteries that are involved in marriage, to culminate in the brilliant and well-known 'O wha's been here afore me, lass'. A pause after the striking conclusion of this lyric is followed by some wry reflections on women and child-birth, which brings the poet round to the birth of Christ, touched on first with a shrugging irony:

> Wull ever a wumman be big again
> Wi's muckle's a Christ? Yech, there's nae sayin'.

The Christ child is all very well, but ordinary births and ordinary bairns are different:

> Christ had never toothick,
> Christ was never seeck,
> But Man's a fiky bairn
> Wi' bellythraw, ripples, and worm-i'-the-cheek! . . .

Moonlight, thistle, child-birth combine in the poet's mind in tormented speculation which dissolves in a wild jig:

> O Scotland is
> THE barren fig.
> Up, carles, up
> And roond it jig. . . .
>
> A miracle's
> Oor only chance.
> Up, carles, up
> And let us dance!

But Burns has degenerated into the kailyard, Dunbar has been discarded; Scotland had taken the wrong road. A four-line stanza with five-stressed lines brings in this sterner tone, moving with a deliberate tiredness. The lesson is – and the poet's voice turns momentarily to that of the preacher now –

> to be yersel's,
> Ye needna fash gin it's to be ocht else.
> To be yersel's – and to mak' that worth bein', . . .

Whatever Scotland is, she is not England; with implicit echoes of

the Rose as used in so much English poetry (such as 'Go, lovely rose')
the poet turns to explain his quarrel with England:

> I micht ha'e been contentit wi' the rose . . .

The quarrel is in fact less with England than with the Scots for grovel-
ling before the richer country and for ignoring the strengths of their
own culture. The movement of the verse becomes less bland:

> I micht ha'e been contentit – gin the feck
> O' my ain folk had grovelled wi' less respec', . . .

This leads to an attack on the 'drumlie clood o' crudity and cant' and
to another lament over Scotland:

> Eneuch! For noo I'm in the mood,
> Scotland, responsive to my thoughts,
> Lichts mile by mile, as my ain nerves,
> Frae Maidenkirk to John o' Groats!

He turns again to Cruivie and Gilsanquhar in the pub: inquires as to
what are the prophets and priests and kings of Scotland 'and Cruivie'll
goam at you, Gilsanquhar jalouse you're dottling'!' The lines shorten
as he contrasts his own concern with his country with their com-
placency, their rude health with his 'gnawin' canker'. The language
becomes bitter and colloquial –

> Guid sakes, ye dinna need to pass
> Ony exam. to dee. . . .

The poet's predicament is the theme of the succeeding group of
lyric passages which move, as so often in *A Drunk Man*, between
metaphysical speculation and the familiar realities of daily experience.
The thistle in the moonlight takes on ever changing shapes and
meanings:

> The munelicht is my knowledge o' mysel',
> Mysel' the thistle in the munelicht seen, . . .

Gropings after self-knowledge, speculations on the relation between
love and lust (Jean flits in and out again), thoughts on human destiny,
lead back to the thistle, on whose significance the poet muses in a grave
and slow-moving passage in six-line stanzas before turning to a ballad
measure in which, giving now a quite new significance to the Rose, he
writes a symbolic lyric on the General Strike:

> I saw a rose come loupin' oot
> Frae a camsteerie plant. . . .

This is the precise equivalent of Yeats's 'A terrible beauty is born', but quite differently done. Scotland's self-torture is both beautiful and bitter: the Devils admire the technique of crucifixion of this silly Christ:

> Like connoisseurs the Deils gang roond
> And praise its attitude,
> Till on the Cross the silly Christ
> To fidge fu' fain's begood!

The unexpected word 'connoisseurs' breaks into the colloquial Scots here with extraordinary effect, and the word is repeated with increasing irony in the next two stanzas.

What, then, is the Thistle? The long passage in fast moving octo-syllabic verse that follows wrests all possible meanings out of the Scottish national plant, and as the meanings proliferate the poet's drunkenness is used as a means of explaining the ever expanding images:

> Gin I was sober I micht think
> It was like something drunk men see!

Whisky and theology move together with sex and mystical vision in a drunken dance of moods and ideas which bring together most of the recurring motifs in the poem. This sequence ends with a sudden sobering:

> Aye, this is Calvary – to bear
> Your Cross wi'in you frae the seed,
> And feel it grow by slow degrees
> Until it rends your flesh apairt,
> And turn, and see your fellow-men
> In similar case but sufferin' less
> Thro' bein' mair wudden frae the stert!

A wild focussing of the poet's fiercely colloquial language and a mingling of religious and domestic imagery provides a startling two-stanza interlude:

> I'm fu' o' a sticket God.
> THAT's what's the maitter wi' me.
> Jean has stuck sic a fork in the wa'
> That I row in agonie. . . .

The poet then returns to his meditations on Scotland's destiny which in turn flows into a 'Letter to Dostoevsky' in which Scotland appears both as a particular region of the world with its own special history and topography and a symbol of something universal and eternal:

> And as at sicna times am I,
> I wad ha'e Scotland to my eye
> Until I saw a timeless flame
> Tak' Auchtermuchty for a name,
> And kent that Ecclefechan stood
> As pairt o' an eternal mood. . . .

The Russian-Scottish juxtaposition is employed as a catalyst to project this counter-pointing of time and eternity, locality and universality, which is at bottom a poetic testament of MacDiarmid's kind of Scottish nationalism.

The lyric which follows is a moving appeal to Jean to illuminate through her love his own identity and the true nature of his Scottishness, after which the poet returns to brooding over the thistle and its possible meanings. The verse now becomes ever more flexible, the lines contracting or expanding as the thought and emotion demand. As the emotion steadies the verse jells again, as it were, so that we get a section in neatly turned four-line stanzas in which the irony is relatively straight-forward: this includes the parody of the famous lines from Home's *Douglas*:

> My name is Norval. On the Grampian Hills
> It is forgotten, and deserves to be. . . .

The poet then returns to Dostoevsky in a lyric whose rising elegiac rhythms draw the whole poem into a plangent sense of loss which yet, somehow, is related to a sense of hope:

> The wan leafs shak' atour us like the snaw.
> Here is the cavaburd in which Earth's tint.
> There's naebody but Oblivion and us,
> Puir gangrel buddies, waunderin' hameless in't.
>
> The stars are larochs o' auld cottages,
> And a' Time's glen is fu' o' blinnin' stew.
> Nae freen'ly lozen skimmers: and the wund
> Rises and separates even me and you.

> I ken nae Russian and you ken nae Scots.
> We canna tell oor voices frae the wund.
> The snaw is seekin' everywhere: oor herts
> At last like roofless ingles it has f'und,
>
> And gethers there in drift on endless drift,
> Oor broken herts that it can never fill;
> And still – its leafs like snaw, its growth, like wund –
> The thistle rises and forever will! . . .

This seems to me to be the true emotional centre of *A Drunk Man*. Yet MacDiarmid cannot allow himself such a simple slogan as 'The thistle rises and forever will' without raising the counter-statement. His nationalism does not go in for crude sloganising. So:

> The thistle rises and forever will,
> Getherin' the generations under't.
> This is the monument o' a' they were,
> And a' they hoped and wondered.

Here the thistle is a gravestone as well as a symbol of hope, and we are left to make what we will of the conflicting meanings. The poem then plunges into another lively ironic account of the barren civilisation of modern Scotland.

The Scots are as good as anybody else at laying flattering unctions to their souls. 'Fier comme un Ecossais' is a description they like to cherish. MacDiarmid exposes it by repeating it three times in the midst of a short ironic lyric which reveals the hollow centre of the modern Scot – and of much more than the Scot – as Eliot does in 'The Hollow Men' but more succinctly:

> The wee reliefs we ha'e in booze,
> Or wun at times in carnal states,
> May hide frae us but canna cheenge
> The silly horrors o' oor fates.

The poet returns to the thistle, pursuing its twisted snake-shape to a host of further implications. And the rose? Whatever his quarrel with the thistle, it is not to the rose that he will turn:

> And let me pit in guid set terms
> My quarrel wi' th'owre sonsy rose, . . .

Good or bad, the rose 'ootside me lies'. The final dismissal of the rose precedes a final endeavour to *place* Scotland:

> He canna Scotland see wha yet
> Canna see the Infinite,
> And Scotland in true scale to it.

All very well, but as images of Scotsmen crowd in, from John Knox to Harry Lauder, the poet is moved to protest:

> Mercy o' Gode, I canna thole
> Wi' sic an orra mob to roll.

The poet now conducts a 'dialogue of one'. His other voice refuses to allow him to repudiate 'this huge ineducable / Heterogeneous hotch and rabble'. It tells him somewhat portentously:

> A Scottish poet maun assume
> The burden o' his people's doom,
> And dee to brak' their livin' tomb.

The ironic voice replies:

> And I look at a' the random
> Band the wheel leaves whaur it fand 'em.
>   'Auch, to Hell,
> I'll tak' it to avizandum.' . . .

The poet will go back to Jean, anyway –

> She'll ope her airms in welcome true,
> And clack nae mair aboot it.

In the coda (as it might be called) the poet looks up in wonder at the stars and feels his heart and brain 'toomed'. In the superb concluding lyric he falls back on silence, the ultimate eloquence:

> Yet ha' I Silence left, the croon o' a'.

> No' her, wha on the hills langsyne I saw
> Liftin' a foreheid o' perpetual snaw.

> No' her, wha in the how-dumb-deid o' nicht
> Kyths, like Eternity in Time's despite.

> No' her, withooten shape, wha's name is Daith,
> No' Him, unkennable abies to faith

> – God whom, gin e'er He saw a man, 'ud be
> E'en mair dumfooner'd at the sicht than he.

> – But Him, whom nocht in man or Deity,
> Or Daith or Dreid or Laneliness can touch,
> *Wha's deed owre often and has seen owre much.*

> O I ha'e Silence left,
>   – 'And weel ye micht,'
> Sae Sae Jean'll say, 'efter sic a nicht!'

We are left in the end with the forthright voice of womanly common sense, anchoring the whole poem in that domestic reality that it has kept returning to.

I make no apology for having devoted most of my space to *A Drunk Man*. It is not only MacDiarmid's finest sustained performance but also the greatest long poem (or poem-sequence) in Scottish literature and one of the greatest in any literature. It is hardly less than miraculous that in an age when Scottish culture is so confused and adulterated a poem, with this kind of originality, this kind of integrity, and this kind of technical brilliance has been written. It would be pleasant indeed to think that this extraordinary achievement marks the opening of new creative possibilities for Scottish literature, but it would be quite unrealistic to make the claim. It is over thirty-five years since *A Drunk Man* was written, and what other Scottish poet has come within a hundred miles of this kind of greatness? MacDiarmid created his own Scottish Renaissance by sheer force of creative personality. His particular brand of what I can only call trans-humanism, which cuts across all accepted political, social and moral attitudes in its almost mystical search for whatever is fully realised, truly itself, whether it is a community or a stone, is the clue to the apparent contradictions in his thought and, more significantly, to the way he uses language. MacDiarmid's synthetic Scots works in his poetry as no other language could work because his imagination works linguistically; for him, the proper naming of things is the revelation of their real meaning in experience. He is first and foremost a poet, and he is always less effective when he adopts any other role. His greatest work was produced in the 1920s and 1930s. I know he does not like people to say this, and I know too that some of his more recent work has remarkable qualities. But after one has re-read carefully all his published poetry, one is left in little doubt that (as with Wordsworth, though without anything like such a definite decline) the greatest is on the whole the earlier. Such a judgment sounds, however, grudging in the face of such real genius. Let us remember that when we talk about MacDiarmid's 'greatest' work we are using the word in its proper sense, not journalistically. Dunbar, Burns and MacDiarmid are the great Scottish trio. Let pedants wrangle over which of these deserves the precedence; there can be little doubt that MacDiarmid is the greatest miracle.

A Critical Note on
A Drunk Man Looks at the Thistle

JOHN C. WESTON

Christopher Murray Grieve first found it useful to write under his now common pseudonym in 1922, four years before he published *A Drunk Man Looks at the Thistle* (November 1926). He had formerly written poems in English and had been publicly unfriendly to the literary revival of the vernacular. He was urging, as he has continued always to urge, the modernising and Europeanising of Scottish life, to which the old couthie Scots poetry of the worst of Burns and since, he felt, was detrimental. Now he had modified his views about the native language and literature, had found a remarkable new voice in some lyrics in Scots he had written, and was coming to believe that the Scots language and literary tradition could be extended to express the real concerns of modern life. He needed a new name to disguise his apparently inconsistent views, perhaps to cover his reputation in an experiment which might fail, to allow Grieve the editor of anthologies and periodicals to print and praise MacDiarmid the new Scots poet, and perhaps to gratify those strange yearnings of a divided culture which have led so many Scots to write under assumed names. Characteristically avoiding all halfway houses, he engaged himself totally in his new campaign to bring mind to Scots literature by enlarging the language, that is, by reviving dead and dying words from medieval court poems and old popular speech and by dealing with themes and subjects other than patriotism and nostalgia for a rural past common to poetry in Scots at the time. MacDiarmid was almost alone. He had to combat a native culture profoundly provincial and anti-intellectual, especially as that culture was associated with poetry in Scots. The most common poems in Scots were like the opening of 'Hame', which Grieve himself printed in the second of his poetry annuals *Northern Numbers* (1922), the same year he began his Scots language campaign. Here is the opening of the poem:

> God bless our land, our Scotland,
> Grey glen an' misty brae,

The blue heights o' the Coolins,
　The green haughs yont the Spey,
The weary wastes on Solway,
　Snell winds blaw owre them a' –
But aye it's Hame, lad,
Yours an' mine, lad,
　– Shielin' or ha'.

Its' Hame, it's Hame for ever,
　Let good or ill betide!
The croon o' some dear river,
　The link o' ae braeside.

This mindless, sentimental poetry in Scots explains not only the vehemence of his satire on St. Andrew's societies and Burns clubs in *A Drunk Man* but the manner and matter of the poem, highbrow in the extreme, as far removed as possible from the kailyard, or often popular in form and images but applied ironically and unexpectedly to sacred or intellectual topics. He wanted his Scots medium packed with foreign words and unfamiliar names, every page echoing passages from the most advanced, at times avant-garde literature of Europe. He wanted to be shocking in his emancipated irreverence to all the thoughtless sensibilities of his countrymen. Since he wanted a full display of Scots language and Scots attitudes, he used a thoroughly familiar type, like Tam o' Shanter, on his way home from a tavern at midnight, and, going beyond Tam, but still very Scottish, fallen by the hillside road, blind drunk and talking to himself. He would begin at comfortable, familiar levels but soon take the reader on the familiar road of his medium to unexplored regions where he would 'souse the craturs in the nether deeps' (ll. 21–6). This medium and character were to exploit all the modern currents of thought to develop a complicated universal vision of mankind's development. The whole thing was to be a tour de force in what was least expected of a vernacular poet. He had tried something of this kind, a very modern use of Scots, in three philosophical, mystical pieces of about 75 to 140 lines concerning supersensory perception, the unity of all things, and the goal of world history ('Ballad of the Five Senses', 'Sea-Serpent', 'Bombinations of a Chimaera'), themes he had earlier incorporated into his English poem 'A Moment in Eternity' (August 1922). The first of these longer poems in Scots, a poem of 118 lines first published under the repellent title 'Braid Scots: an Inventory and Appraisement' (later shortened a bit and retitled 'Gairmscoile'), clearly shows his movement away from the single, isolated lyric and the interests which led him to his long masterpiece: here he argues for national atavism in life and poetry, for primitive feeling as the basis of life and the subject of the greatest poetry, for the Scots language, even those lost words whose meanings depend on sound alone, as best expressing the national experience. But this poem is obviously fragmentary and was perhaps abandoned in favour of *A Drunk Man*. All four of these longer poems were reprinted from magazines with his beautiful Scots lyrics in two collections (September 1925, June 1926).

Before the publication of the second collection of lyrics, he had begun *A Drunk Man*. As could be expected he kept Scotland aware of his endeavours by sending to the *Glasgow Herald* literary press releases in the form of advance puffs and excerpts. His intentions in his new poem are made quite clear in these important descriptions written while he was composing it: 'a long poem . . . split up into several sections, but the forms within the sections range from ballad measure to *vers libre*. The matter includes satire, amphigouri, lyrics, parodies of Mr. T. S. Eliot and other poets, and translations from the Russian, French, and German. The whole poem is in braid Scots, except a few quatrains which are in the nature of a skit on Mr. Eliot's "Sweeney" poems, and it has been expressly designed to show that braid Scots can be effectively applied to all manner of subjects and measures' (17th December 1925). In another announcement he presents these additional views: 'It is a complete poem . . . deriving its unity from its preoccupation with the distinctive elements in Scottish psychology which depend for their effective expression upon the hitherto un-realised potentialities of Braid Scots; . . . it is divided into various sections, affording scope for a great variety of forms. . . . The intention here has been to show that Braid Scots is adaptable to all kinds of poetry, and to a much greater variety of measures than might be supposed from the restricted practice of the last hundred years. The poem is therefore designed as a contribution to the movement for the revival of Braid Scots which is being promoted by the Burns Federa-tion, and to the Scottish literary Renaissance movement which is seeking to re-establish the distinctively Scottish contribution in the literature of Europe' (13th February 1926). From some interesting fragments of letters recently published we learn that the poem had grown from 600 lines in February to over 4000 lines in August and had been excised by more than one-third for publication in November

G

but had always been considered by the poet as 'really one whole' (J. K. Annand, ed., *Early Lyrics of Hugh MacDiarmid* [Akros Publications, 1968], pp. 14–16).

On the basis of MacDiarmid's intentions as expressed in these early releases and of the new information establishing the poem's slow growth, I believe that MacDiarmid began writing it sometime in 1925 (line 290 was written then, anyway) and up through the early part of the next year thought of it primarily as a demonstration piece of Scottish literary expansionism, a star witness in his case for Scots intellectual poetry, but that as he progressed he came to realise that he had a great poem in itself. The original purpose still shows through in its shrill intellectuality and flashy learning, for example the ostentatious assertion in footnotes of translation directly from Russian (ll. 169, 241, 353) when in reality the source is English, a language to be eschewed according to the original purpose of the poem. But we should, of course, recognise that this swaggering display of learning is, coincidently or not, also a feature of MacDiarmid's later 'poetry of fact'. In any case, by August, writing in a letter to a friend about the poem still in progress, he is clearly aware that his poem had transcended polemics: 'It's the thing as a whole that I'm mainly concerned with, and if, as such, it does not take its place as a masterpiece – *sui generis* – one of the biggest things in the range of Scottish literature, I shall have failed.' A month after the publication of the long poem, he wrote to the same friend: 'I set out to give Scotland a poem, perfectly modern in psychology, which could only be compared in the whole length of Scots literature with Tam o' Shanter and Dunbar's Seven Deidly Sins. And I felt I had done it by the time I had finished despite all the faults and flaws of my work' (*ibid.*, pp. 15–16).

Thus slowly expanded and then just before publication severely excised, the resulting long poem forms more of a unity than most non-narrative long poems, like Pound's *The Pisan Cantos*. This sense of unity is all the more impressive in an undivided poem (undivided except for rows of periods and changes of type face and verse form), to which the poet refused to provide handrails, as he defiantly asserts to philistines in his Author's Note. Its unity derives most obviously from its form, an interior monologue in which the Drunk Man speaks, somewhat as does Prufrock in his 'Love Song', sometimes to himself, sometimes to the reader, sometimes in fantasy to others, like Jean (his wife), Burns, Dostoevsky, the people of Glasgow, but always, unlike Prufrock, from a physical situation of which the reader is repeatedly reminded by a pattern of returnings. The Drunk Man begins by speaking of his psychic and drunken condition and habits, and then after his comic attack on Scottish life and address to Burns, he establishes the scene by speculating about where he is: sprawled, he thinks, on a hillside, he knows not how, among thistle and bracken under the full moon (ll. 93–104). To reinforce this physical situation and to give it additional particularity, he explicitly describes it again, after a personal creed and a series of related lyrics, from a new viewpoint: the Drunk Man sees himself as a museum display, a mock-up of a scene of Scottish life in 1925, 'Mounted on a hillside, wi' the thistles / And bracken for verisimilitude' (ll. 285–6). In the meantime we have learned about his drinking companions Cruivie and Gilsanquhar (l. 3), about his wife Jean (l. 101), that he is in his present talkative state by having drunk too much that night (ll. 162, 277–9), that he lives in Montrose (l. 166), but most important that he is looking repeatedly at and sometimes talking to a great thistle plant in the moonlight (ll. 221–2, 233–4, 256–8). Various actions seem to take place during the course of the poem: he gets the hiccups (ll. 233–6), a wind roars in his ears (ll. 240, 372, 867, 1443), he hears the yowling of a cat (ll. 565–7), he has an erection (ll. 591–4), a storm passes over (ll. 1244–5), he gets thirsty (l. 1380). We are constantly reminded of the presentness and particularity of the dramatic situation by such temporal and spatial pointing words as, 'there' (l. 509), '*yonder* whisky' (l. 162), '*this* yella licht' (l. 667), the 'munelicht . . . / E'en *nou*' (ll. 1903–5). We keep coming back to the physical, dramatic situation, the *Drunk Man actually looking at the thistle*, as it changes in his mind to all the sublime or grotesque visions and hallucinations of similitudes, yoked by wonderful violence to the thistle, which constitute a good part of the poem. The title is dryly downright in its accurately describing what the poem is about on its most obvious formal level.

But the Drunk Man not only looks at the thistle and sees it metamorphose endlessly; he 'graipples' (l. 2208) with it. The poem is about the Drunk Man's struggle with the thistle, and this symbolic conflict provides a thematic unity to correspond to the dramatic unity given by the moonlit, thistle-observing situation. For the thistle represents, not only the traditional Scotland or Scotsmen, but in MacDiarmid's private symbolism, the divided nature of himself, the Scot, and of all mankind, a division which must be exploited, engaged, harmonised. The blossoms represent, like the moon toward which they extend, our spiritual, idealist, romantic aspirations; the roots, our animal and fleshly ties;

the disorderly growth of foliage and thorns between represents the contradictory elements of life which must be possessed or integrated without conflict all at the same time (ll. 2350–3), MacDiarmid's interpretation of the variously applied notion of the Caledonian Antisyzygy, which is, of course, the phrase G. Gregory Smith invented to characterise his formulation of opposites in the Scottish character (*Scottish Literature*, 1919, p. 4). Sometimes the Drunk Man becomes the thistle, gets inside his symbol (for example, ll. 2172–80); similarly the thistle is compared to images of engulfing and entrapping, like monsters – a dragon (l. 508) or leviathan (l. 486) or octopus (ll. 353–64) – or like a spider web (l. 2212). The thistle possesses the Drunk Man, which means that man is caught in his contradictory divided nature. The speaker tries to rise above the thistle, but the thistle continues to baffle him, to hold him earthbound and thus exhaust him, as shown by the repeated plea, 'Shudderan thistle, gie owre, gie owre' (ll. 699, 1442). The speaker longs to 'win free' or 'clear' of his thistleness (ll. 528, 1876), which means that he wants to achieve a momentary state of pure mind leading to mystical awareness (ll. 1903–24) or collectively with all men to the apotheosis of human development, when all men lose their identity and attain collective freedom and Godhead (ll. 1959–67, 2497–511, 2548–83). But one can 'win free' only by accepting the thistle or one is left thistleless with only a hole where it was (ll. 510, 2079–88), which means that in our ideal aspiration we condemn the other half of life only at our peril and that one must progress by uniting contraries in endless individual struggle rather than by Platonic spiritualisation: each man must realise his *whole* self by developing his own eccentricity (ll. 1415–36, 1876–9), Scotland must progress by using the contrary qualities of its Scottishness not by striving toward some universal goal (ll. 2017–19), and all mankind progresses toward the apocalyptic moment of freedom by achieving its collective nature in undirected individual and national self-realisation.

The simplest practical lesson of the poem, to put it in isolation too simply, is *to be oneself*, a phrase with variations which is repeated for emphasis, but perhaps too much (ll. 147–8, 745, 1434–6, 1820, 1829–1832). One must realise one's own individual essence through experiencing all life without an extrinsic goal, not in an existential sense because the experience does not seem to create the essential self, which is prior to experience as potential but hidden without it. There may be closer analogues to this theory of individual self-realisation through full experience, and MacDiarmid had earlier urged as a slogan of his

Scottish literary revival 'the *Nietzschean* "Become what you are"' (*Scottish Chapbook*, vol. 1, no. 8, March 1923, p. 214), but it seems to me to be strikingly close to Goethe's romantic view in *Faust*. But more certainly the Drunk Man's general view of history can be taken as a Romantic alternative offered, point for point, to the views of Oswald Spengler's *The Decline of the West*, published a few years before and explicitly condemned in this poem (ll. 349–52): Spengler presents history, in a view quite antithetical to the Drunk Man's, as deterministic cycles of large cultures, a view in general opposed to progress of all mankind and to the historical efficacy of individual endeavour; and in regard to twentieth-century Western civilisation, opposed to art, philosophy, psychology, and religion as out of harmony with the tendency of the age.

The poem is obviously not narrowly derived from a few literary sources. MacDiarmid clearly picked up a number of ideas and attitudes from the Russian apocalyptists and antirationalist mystics, particularly Dostoevsky, Vladimir Solovyev, and Leon Shestov (as Kenneth Buthlay has already noted in *Hugh MacDiarmid*, Writers and Critics Series, 1964, p. 47). Perhaps a future scholarly sorting out may show something like this: from Dostoevsky, an interest in the unconscious (ll. 1765–76), the concept of national destiny in uniting the human race (ll. 1651–8), the necessity of debasing oneself in squalor and suffering to achieve one's individuality and humanity (ll. 1801–28); from Solovyev, the view of history that God is slowly realised in man as he proceeds toward the apocalypse, when the process is complete (ll. 1990–7); from Shestov, a hostility to philosophical schemes in favour of will and experience (ll. 129–48) and a belief that meaningful perception begins when logical inquiry leaves off (ll. 153–6). In general he adapts the Christian views of the Russians to his own humanistic-mystical vision, while keeping the Christology only as figure and symbol. With flexibility he rejects anything which is uncongenial to his view, like Dostoevsky's political submissiveness and Solovyev's ideas of the anti-Christ and of the Fall's breaking a pre-existent unity with God. This eclecticism results not, I think, from a systematic selection from an exhaustive reading in each of the authors of interest, but from a more casual use by a busy journalist of congenial ideas found in a vast but spotty and permiscuous reading, sometimes at second hand, usually in English translation. If we consider these selective adaptations with the interest MacDiarmid shows in a wide variety of ideas, for instance in Melville's religious questing in *Clarel* (ll. 1659–70), we will realise that the poem results from a unique, imaginative synthesis of diverse literary elements, to speak only of the considerable bookish aspect of the poem, of course. The main unifying and most original idea is MacDiarmid's quite individual interpretation of Gregory Smith's Caledonian Antisyzygy, mentioned before, or as he put it later, in a definition of the term inevitably too simple (*Voice of Scotland*, vol. 3 [1946], no. 2, p. 27): 'a capacity to entertain at one and the same time without conflict two or more opposite and irreconcilable opinions'.

This struggle with the thistle in which the Drunk Man attempts to entertain opposites and irreconcilables as necessary in the economy of the world has two stages, one in which he develops its implications as to his own history and the other as to the history of mankind. Consequently there are two central sections in the poem, one, after the introduction (ll. 1–120), about the Drunk Man's individual predicament (ll. 121–810) and the other, after a brief sequence on men and women (ll. 811–1003), about the process of mankind's development (ll. 1004–2243). Near the end of this long section on progress comes the ideological climax of the poem, when the Drunk Man affirms his belief in man's past and future progress in quite explicit and pointed terms: 'The thistle rises and forever will' (ll. 2230–5). But this leaves Scotland and the personal problem of the Drunk Man unprovided for. What is Scotland's role and Scotland's drunken poet's role in the cosmic economy?

These topics receive comment in the next section (ll. 2244–658), where after the poet seems to accept his role as a voice of an independent Scottish nation, synthesising contraries in a universal scheme, he, like a medieval dream allegorist, has a vision of the Great Wheel (ll. 2419–613), which is explicitly offered as an inevitable summary and a true conclusion to what has gone before (ll. 2420–6). It shows allegorically the development of man in universal history toward the apocalypse, the synthesis of all men, and of events beyond. The Drunk Man is depressed enough by the slow general progress in an indifferent world toward this goal (ll. 2587–95), but when he sees the lack of independent movement at all in the lesser wheel of Scotland, with its crazy and embarrassing cast of characters, he protests (l. 2614), in one of the funniest but bitterest passages of the poem, that he cannot abide his company. Then ensues the tragi-comic discussion with another part of himself, who tells him that Scots have always hated change and new ideas but that he must either die to break their living tomb – as many Scots poets have done before – or renounce his Scottishness. This is the dramatic climax of the poem (after l. 2646). The thematic climax came before when the Drunk Man affirmed his faith in mankind in general. Now he must choose whether or not to put that general faith into action by dying for the ineducable Scots. The Drunk Man after a pause, in some confusion, marked by the shattering of the neat triplets and whole lines, refuses to make a choice, and then with an ambiguous attitude toward the weary but glorious progress of mankind, cuts off his agony of decision by calling out like a child for Jean, who will he knows comfort him. Here there appears a row of asterisks, the only such structural signal in the poem.

The poem could be over, for the Drunk Man's refusal to choose is final. And we may note that he is quite sober now (and that, incidentally, the progress of sobering from the drunken opening is another structural aspect of the poem). But there remains a brief section (ll. 2659–), a quiet coda, a dense and intense close of two lyrics, ending with a sudden, bathetic snap of the fingers: first a lyric about the emptiness caused by his struggle to remain whole and earthbound in spite of his ideal longing and second another on Silence, which I take to be a humanistic affirmation, an elegy to the collective dumb experience of all mankind. In the last line and a half, MacDiarmid causes Jean's retort to turn it all into a joke, to bring the whole poem back to earth, away from the heavens and the prophetic future to the hillside in Montrose. This ending to a great Scottish poem is appropriate to Scotland, whose literature, it has often been noted, abounds in flashing shifts of sensibility, in grotesque combinations of lofty idealism and low realism, of delicate fantasy and coarse earthiness. And the sudden shift at the end is only the last instance of an important formal method of the poem, the unexpected juxtaposing of opposite viewpoints and tones without transition. And this method, of course, is an instance of the form echoing the sense, for the most important idea in the poem also relates to bringing together opposites, of struggle toward spirit through flesh, of uniting the roots and the blossoms of the thistle by the counterdirected foliage in between.

The Symbolism of
A Drunk Man Looks at the Thistle

RODERICK WATSON

MacDiarmid's long poem tends to swallow critics. No short account can do justice to its energy and fluidity, while within its deceptively familiar colloquial stance there lie philosophical depths of considerable profundity. In exploring these the critic finds himself more and more involved in digressions into the likely influence of, say, Denis Saurat's philosophy of the 'Actual', or Shestov's opposition to dogma in any form. Thus the first clear outline (so necessary to the essay) is soon lost in explication and MacDiarmid has once more kept his promise to whummle us in the nether deeps. Perhaps the complete answer, although inelegant, will be a 'reader's guide to *A Drunk Man*'. The present essay, however, can have no such pretensions, but must attempt, instead, to see the poem as a whole by noting only its basic images and intentions, and by trying, along the way, to place them in relation to MacDiarmid's previous and subsequent development. The way in which these basic symbols are inter-related will also establish something of the poem's fundamental unity, despite its apparently free and furious progress. It will be helpful to begin with a brief look at the provenance of the poem, and then at the drunk man himself and the nature of his intoxication.

The roots of *A Drunk Man* can be found in the overtly philosophical or metaphysical interest which so characterises MacDiarmid's English verse of the early 'twenties – the 'Sonnets of the Highland Hills', or 'A Moment in Eternity', for example, and the prose of the 'psycho-logical studies' in *Annals of the Five Senses*. Although the prose of *Annals* is markedly abstract and 'intellectual' in its outlook, it provides a striking and valuable correlative to the intense and fluctuating cere-bral states which it sets out to describe. The poetry of this period, however, is not so successful, and it relies overmuch on personified abstractions such as 'Time' and 'Death', and on an imagery that is more decorative or inflated than fully functional. With his 'discovery' of Scots in 1922, however, MacDiarmid's poetry achieved the organic vitality which had hitherto escaped it, and he went on to use this characteristically concrete and domestic imagery with great success in the lyrics of *Sangschaw* and *Penny Wheep*. The 'metaphysical' interest remains in these collections, however, in what has been called their 'cosmic' outlook, and in particular, in the overtly discursive poems, 'Ballad of the Five Senses', 'Bombinations of a Chimaera' and 'Sea-Serpent'. The dramatic and speculative content of these last three poems clearly points the way to *A Drunk Man*. A brief example from 'Sea-Serpent' will suffice, for there will be occasion to refer to these lines again later.

> Round the cantles o' space Leviathan flickered
> Like Borealis in flicht
> Or eelied thro' the poorin' deeps o' the sea
> Like a ca' o' whales and was tint to sicht,
> But aye in its endless ups-and-doons
> As it dwined to gleids or walloped in rings
> God like a Jonah whirled in its kite
> But blithe as a loon in the swings.[1]

The 'voice' of these lines is characteristically within the Scottish tradition, and they demonstrate, in miniature, most of the qualities which MacDiarmid found within that tradition and used to such good effect in *A Drunk Man*. These can be summarised as follows: a down-to-earth familiarity with both physical and spiritual matters; a dramatic and characterful utterance; what Gregory Smith described as the sense of movement produced by the Scottish 'zest for handling a multitude of details', and, finally, what he also referred to as a 'medieval' freedom 'in passing from one mood to another', a freedom which he took to be typical of the 'Caledonian Antisyzygy'.

Following the success of his first poems in Scots, MacDiarmid began to identify himself and his work more and more with the nature of the Scottish sensibility, and with the expressive potential which he believed Scots to offer to the writer. Thus, by 1923, he is confidently defining and theorising about the character of the 'true' and the 'false Scot'. He associated these figures with the qualities of 'Faustian' and 'Apollonian' man, as defined by Spengler in the second volume of *The Decline of the West*. MacDiarmid aligned himself unhesitatingly with the 'true Scot'. He tells us that this 'Faustian' mind is 'dominated by

---

[1] *Collected Poems* (hereafter cited as *C.P.*), p. 34.

the conception of infinity, of the unattainable, and hence is ever questioning, never satisfied, rationalistic in religion and politics, romantic in art and literature – a perfect expression of the Scottish race.'[1] He also identified this restless, contradictory sensibility with Gregory Smith's definition of the Caledonian antisyzygy, and he went on to claim a further affinity between it and the dynamic psychologies evinced and explored in the works of Dostoevsky. By these means MacDiarmid was eager to refute what he believed to be the widely held misconception of the Scot as a dogmatic, practical and 'canny' individual. His hatred of the 'music-hall Scot', and his mercurial pursuit of unattainable questions both reappear as overt themes in *A Drunk Man*.

These, then, very briefly, are some of the factors which had a bearing on the writing of *A Drunk Man*. In considering the poem I want to begin by studying the author's basic creative premise, and the character which he created in order to realise it.

THE DRUNK MAN

MacDiarmid's stance throughout his long poem is quintessentially Romantic. The drunk man begins with himself, and only from there does his chosen field of attention move to Scotland and the Scots, and from there, still further, to a philosophical examination of all human life. His scope may be no less than cosmic, but the poem's structure and progress emphasises that all speculation starts from and returns to his own condition. He is not a solipsist, however, but rather a man who believes that his own organism contributes to and reflects something of the pattern of the universe, be it ever such a small part of the organic whole.

> Lay haud o' my hert and feel
> Fountains ootloupin' the starns
> Or see the Universe reel
> Set gaen' by my eident harns[2]

His position is, in fact, exactly similar to that which MacDiarmid ascribed to 'Mrs. Morgan' in his short story, 'The Never-Yet-Explored':

> It was necessary that she . . . make the coldest effort to regard her own organism as merely one among others. Her physical-intellec-

---

[1] 'A Theory of Scots Letters', *The Scottish Chapbook*, vol. 1, no. 8, March 1923, p. 214.
[2] *C.P.*, p. 80.

tual being was the sensorium of Nature, but it was also one thing among natural things whose number was legion. It was the mirror in which she viewed the world, the part most necessary for her to know and work upon . . .[1]

The drunk man sets no boundaries to the movement of his thought, and his interest moves freely from his own psychology, to politics, to metaphysics. Indeed, this is no more than a logical progression for him – three stages along the expanding cone of his attention. Even the processes of rational thought itself are only another such stage to him, and are finally expendable:

> Reason ser's nae end but pleasure,
> Truth's no' an end but a means
> To a wider knowledge o' life
> And a keener interest in't.[2]

In this belief the drunk man resembles another character described in *Annals*. The protagonist of 'A Four Years' Harvest' longed for just such a 'wider knowledge'. Like the drunk man he started from himself, and he, too, suspected that he might have to abandon the methods of the intellect in the end:

He started anew from himself around an anthropomorphic universe, and went in search of a larger self which was the reflection and confirmation of his own . . . an impulse this deeper than all philosophy . . . but, just because it lay so deep, it conflicted with another tendency equally ingrained in him, the impulse of revolt against 'the pale cast of thought', the feeling that if he could only escape from his mind's anticipations he should find himself face to face with things as they really were.[3]

The longing for such transcendence, for other – and further – modes of being or knowing, recurs constantly throughout *A Drunk Man*, and it is sustained precisely *because* the protagonist believes that he will never attain them. That is, it is based on his intimation that 'A'thing that ony man can be's / A mockery o' his soul at last'.[4] In one of the poem's finest passages, for example (the section called 'A Stick-nest in Ygdrasil'), the drunk man relentlessly and courageously insists on the fact of this mockery, and on the relative unimportance

---

[1] *Annals of the Five Senses*, Montrose, 1923, pp. 154–5.   [2] *C.P.*, p. 81.
[3] *Annals*, p. 69.   [4] *C.P.*, p. 111.

of man in the face of the infinite universe. Human life is only one facet
in the teeming pattern of Creation and it is dwarfed as easily by the
depths of the microcosm within himself as it is by the vast spaces of
the galaxy:

> O hard it is for man to ken
> He's no' creation's goal nor yet
> A benefitter by't at last –
> A means to ends he'll never ken,
> And as to michtier elements
> The slauchtered brutes he eats to him
> Or forms o' life owre sma' to see
> Wi' which his heedless body swarms,
> And a' man's thocht nae mair to them
> Than ony moosewob to a man
> His Heaven to them the blinterin' o'
> A snail-trail on their closet wa'![1]

It is from this apprehension of infinity that the poet begins his
examination of himself and Scotland. It is against this void that he
recognises 'the irony / O' bein' a grocer 'neth the sun',[2] and from such
knowledge he must go on to confess that 'Nae void can fleg me hauf
as much / As bein' mysel', whate'er I am.'[3] In the attempt to know and
be himself, he will 'waunder like Ulysses', 'owre continents unkent /
And wine-dark oceans'. The poem charts his odyssey from cheap
whisky to silence.

The command to 'be yourself' recurs throughout the poem, even
although, in the last analysis, the only goal which the drunk man
endorses is the certainty that nothing *can* be attained. The poet values
the effort, however, even if he despairs of its end:

> . . . manifest forevermair
> Contempt o' ilka goal.
>
> O' ilka goal – save ane alane;
> To be yoursel', whatever that may be,
> And as contemptuous o' that,
> Kennin' nocht's worth the ha'en,
> But certainty that nocht can be,
> And hoo that certainty to gain.[4]

[1] *C.P.*, p. 113.   [2] *Ibid.* p. 111   [3] *Ibid.* p. 112.   [4] *Ibid.* p. 120.

In this way he recognises 'the abyss', and consigns himself to it, even if it is 'bottomless'.

Thus the drunk man is, indeed, a 'true', or 'Faustian' Scot – 'dominated by the conception of infinity, of the unattainable, and hence ... ever questioning, never satisfied' – and through him, MacDiarmid sets out to explore both his own deepest nature and the nature and characteristics of the Scottish sensibility. Therefore the cry to 'be yourself!' has political as well as personal application,[1] and although MacDiarmid's quest is for ultimate self realisation ('romantic in literature'), it does not obviate a pragmatic desire for self-government in his country ('rationalistic in politics'). What may have seemed to be a paradox in the 'true' Scot's make-up is thus resolved, and it should be emphasised that such mobility is typical of the poem. To summarise: the drunk man cannot, or will not, make permanent distinctions between his own spiritual condition and the condition of his nation, and thus Scotland in 1926 is as much his own personal 'waste land', as it is the country he loves. The specific symbol for this ambiguous relationship of personal/national sterility or pride, is, of course, the thistle.

In the Author's Note to the first edition of *A Drunk Man*, MacDiarmid warned his readers that 'drunkenness has a logic of its own', and this must be remembered (if it is not immediately obvious), in any discussion of the poem's structure and organisation. More significantly, however, it is drunkenness that allows MacDiarmid to liberate his protagonist's sensibility under the Dionysian and prophetic spell of a divine inebriation. By this means the poet rings the most abrupt and vivid changes on fantasy, delusion, revelation, vision, obsession, hallucination and free association. He presents his hero *in extremis*, and in the grip of heightened and unnatural states of awareness which vary from despair to farce with violent, and at times almost hysterical, changes of mood and style. The mode is quintessentially that of Expressionist art, and so it is not surprising that the drunk man, like the Expressionist artist, should undertake an odyssey into the labyrinth of his own consciousness in search of something more than a merely subjective revelation:

> Man's mind is in God's image made,
> And in its wildest dreams arrayed
> In pairt o' Truth is still displayed.[2]

[1] In *Chapbook* MacDiarmid pointed out that '*Soyons nous-mêmes*' was the slogan of the Belgian literary revival.   [2] *C.P.*, p. 142.

And in a more carnal context, he observes that:

> It's queer the thochts a kittled cull
> Can lowse or splairgin' glit annul.
>
> Man's spreit is wi' his ingangs twined
> In ways that he can ne'er unwind.[1]

Like the two characters from *Annals* mentioned above, the drunk man looks at the world in the mirror of his own mind, and he expects to see in it 'a reflection and confirmation' of himself. In pondering on his 'wildest dreams', God's mind, man's image, his spirit and his belly, the drunk man considers the mystery of Creation itself. In his intoxication, however, and governed by the continual flux of – distorted – sensation and memory, 'Truth' appears to him as some elusive monster, a whale, or a minotaur, which he pursues until he is exhausted:

> . . . till at last
> His brain inside his heid is like
> Ariadne wi' an empty pirn,
> Or like a birlin' reel frae which
> A whale has rived the line awa'.[2]

Thus the complementary factor to the drunk man's intense and spiritual longing for some 'wider knowledge', is the fevered excitation of an over-active and intoxicated mind, and a resulting exhaustion which is yet without rest.

The protagonist's drunkenness allows him expressive, as well as imaginative, licence. MacDiarmid was greatly helped in this respect by the fact that the Scots tradition in literature is so particularly suited to the speaking voice. The energy of the language is perfectly fitted to the vigour of the poet's imagination, and it is difficult to conceive the one without the other. Thus, at his best, MacDiarmid achieves that fusion of 'passionate thinking' which leads towards metaphysics, as described by Sir Herbert Grierson in the work of Donne. In the following lines, for example, MacDiarmid poses a serious ontological question, and yet it is made concrete, vivid and wryly humorous by the image of the cat's eyes, and by the familiar ease imparted by the Scots tongue:

> Darkness comes closer to us than the licht,
> And is oor natural element. We peer oot frae't
> Like cat's een bleezin' in a goustrous nicht

[1] *C.P.*, p. 83.   [2] *Ibid.* p. 113.

(Whaur there is nocht to find but stars
That look like ither cats' een)[1]

This speculative bent is typical of the way that MacDiarmid's mind
constantly turns towards what he called 'the "eternal" questions', an
orientation which he admired greatly in the work of Vladimir Solovyov. The interest shows itself clearly in the main symbols of *A Drunk
Man*, and perhaps the simplest introduction to the body of the poem
can be made through an examination of these images and what they
signify.

The three central images of the poem are immediately connected
with its theme and setting, namely, the thistle, whisky, and woman.
For the purposes of explication it will be convenient to suggest that
each of these symbols has a second part, or counter-part, associated
with it, and this leads to the grouped pairs of thistle and rose, whisky
and moonlight, woman and sea serpent. It will become apparent,
however, that these groupings are not stable, and that in keeping
with the mobile character of the poem, some of the symbols inter-
change in value and effect.

THISTLE : ROSE

For MacDiarmid the thistle's nature is supremely ambiguous, and he
chooses it as a symbol both for his own (Scottish) character, for the
state of Scotland, and, latterly, for the condition of all created things.
Gregory Smith noted that the thistle produces both thorns and the
softest thistledown, but MacDiarmid restates its contradictory quality
by contrasting the plant's ugly spikes with the flower – the rose – at
its crown. Accordingly, he conceives the thistle as a symbol of duality,
containing a promise of the ideal in its flower, and the promise of its
failure in the thorns. He also holds this to be the historical and spiritual
condition of all Scots.

Few Scots will deny the dour attractiveness of their national plant,
and certainly its mottoes are proud and stirring words – '*Nemo me
impune lacessit*' / 'Wha daur meddle wi' me?' The heraldic stance is
familiar in its arrogance, and yet, at the same time, beneath the daunt-
less words there is the suggestion of an underlying insecurity. – The
condition is particularly Scottish, and it has been realised in several
of the magnificent failures of Scottish history. (The fate of the 1715

[1] *Ibid.* pp. 131–2.

rebellion provides a striking example.) Living in Montrose in the
1920s, MacDiarmid was particularly concerned to combat this penchant
for defeat from within, and his first task was to define it properly.
Thus, in *A Drunk Man* he despairs at the sight of a familiar historical
process being re-enacted in the failure of the General Strike of May
1926:

> Syne the rose shrivelled suddenly
> As a balloon is burst;
> The thistle was a ghaistly stick,
> As gin it had been curst.
>
> Was it the ancient vicious sway
> Imposed itsel' again,
> Or nerve owre weak for new emprise
> That made the effort vain,
>
> A coward strain in that lorn growth
> That wrocht the sorry trick?
>
> *   *   *
>
> The dream o' beauty's dernin' yet
> Ahint the ugsome shape.
> – Vain dream that in a pinheid here
> And there can e'er escape!
>
> The vices that defeat the dream
> Are in the plant itsel',
> And till they're purged its virtues maun
> In pain and misery dwell.[1]

Although he related this section specifically to the General Strike, it
is clear that MacDiarmid is also referring to the general principles
which lie behind the continual failure of man's idealism in all its
manifestations.

The 'vices that defeat the dream' are also within himself, and the
drunk man struggles to overcome them. Even at its best, the heraldic
pride of the thistle can all too easily lead to the rigid, cerebral and life
denying aggrandisement of Calvinism. Thus the drunk man feels that
it is the thorns of Christ's suffering on Calvary which attract him
(and the Scot), and not the rose of His love:

[1] *C.P.*, pp. 104–5.

> The language that but sparely flooers
> And maistly gangs to weed;
> The thocht o' Christ and Calvary
> Aye liddenin' in my heid;
> And a' the dour provincial thocht
> That merks the Scottish breed
> – These are the thistle's characters[1]

The thistle is skeleton and waste land, it is everything that frustrates the drunk man's hopes, both from within and without himself. He struggles desperately to overcome it, and to overcome himself, with the cry 'Yank oot your orra boughs, my hert!', and yet it is so inseparably a part of himself and of his Scottishness that he is bound to fail. To destroy the plant entirely would be to destroy all meaningful identity.

If the thistle seems to frustrate his ideals, however, it also embodies them in its flower. The rose is the ideal which the mind can imagine and for which the spirit yearns, but the thorns are the reality of the flesh's limitations. Thus the drunk man experiences an endless cycle of attraction and repulsion, hope and despair, which finally resolves itself into a dynamic and dialectical process. Thus the thistle appears as Ygdrasil, no less than the tree of life itself with the stars in its branches; and then it shrinks to a dried herring. At all times it is finally a puzzle:

> And still the puzzle stands unsolved.
> Beauty and ugliness alike,
> And life and daith and God and man,
> Are aspects o't but nane can tell
> The secret that I'd fain find oot
> O' this bricht hive, this sorry weed,
> The tree that fills the universe,
> Or like a reistit herrin' crines.[2]

It is not without significance that the imagery of rose and thorns should have distinctly religious connotations, for the Christian ethos contains a similar dynamic between the rose of God's love (the ideal enlightenment pursued by Dante), and the thorns of Christ's suffering for that love, thorns woven into a prickly crown intended to mock His presumption. MacDiarmid recognises the affinity, but he is more

---

[1] *Ibid.* p. 106.   [2] *Ibid.* p. 109.

H

concerned with the suffering Christ within himself and the pain of the ideal for which he longs. ('Aye, this Calvary – to bear / Your Cross wi'in you frae the seed, / And feel it grow by slow degrees / Until it rends your flesh apairt.')[1] The gesture is closer to Byron than to St. Augustine.

As the poem progresses, the rose comes more and more to symbolise an almost unbearably intense desire for self transcendence. The drunk man's focus becomes entirely metaphysical as he struggles with the agony of his insight into the awful depths of Eternity, and yet he still takes pride in the spiritual presumption which suggests that he may yet encompass its essence:

> – And pridefu' still
> That 'yont the sherp wings o' the eagles fleein'
> Aboot the dowless pole o' Space,
> Like leafs aboot a thistle-shank, my bluid
> Could still thraw roses up
> – And up![2]

The thistle is always there, however, to frustrate man's longing, as it 'braks his warlds abreid and rives / His Heavens to tatters on its horns'.[3]

The process of aspiration and frustration is endless, and the drunk man comes to see it as the final condition of all existence. Thistle and rose are complementary opposites within a single unity, they are flesh and spirit, or Yin and Yang[4] upon whose continuing succession all Creation depends:

> Yet still we suffer and still sall,
> Altho', puir fules, we mayna ken't
> As lang as like the thistle we
> In coil and in recoil are pent.
>
> And ferrer than mankind can look
> Ghast shapes that free but to transfix
> Twine rose-crooned in their agonies,
> And strive agen the endless pricks.
>
> The dooble play that bigs and braks
> In endless victory and defeat
> Is in your spikes and roses shown,
> And a' my soul is haggar'd wi't. . . .[5]

---

[1] *C.P.*, p. 117.   [2] *Ibid.* pp. 130–1.   [3] *Ibid.* p. 114.
[4] 'A black leaf owre a white leaf twirls', *ibid.* pp. 109, 115.   [5] *Ibid.* pp. 119–20.

As he is caught on 'the great wheel' of this succession, we can understand the desperate desire for rest and release which the drunk man
expresses at various points throughout the poem.

The combination, and reconciliation, of opposites through their
immediate juxtaposition is central to MacDiarmid's conception of
antisyzygy as a characteristic of the Scottish sensibility. In this respect
MacDiarmid follows the observations of Gregory Smith, but the poet
takes Smith's definition and makes it into a general philosophical
principle of being which the professor would never have proposed.
MacDiarmid's principle is embodied in the symbol of the thistle and
its dual nature. It is also demonstrated in the dialectical process of the
poem itself, with its many contradictions and swift reversals of mood
and pace. In every way, the thistle is rooted at the heart of the poem.

The longing for transcendence evinced by the drunk man has
already been discussed, as well as its symbol, the rose. The urge
reappears, however, in different forms, throughout MacDiarmid's
work. It recurs in *A Drunk Man*, for example, when the protagonist
is vouchsafed several tantalising glimpses of a mysterious and beautiful
woman. The same desire in later poems drives the poet to call for no
less than the 'impossible song', and, in another context, for the 'seamless garment'. The logic of the impossible song is particularly relevant
to the paradoxical nature of the thistle and MacDiarmid's vision of the
endless opposition contained within it. A brief example will suffice:

> Let all men laugh as at a child
> Crying broken-hearted for the moon –
> Fit cause for manly laughter!
> God Himself would needs have smiled
> If He had ever heard such wild
>   Nonsense from Nazareth – if not Calvary!
>
> The child is right and must not be
> Consoled until the world ends
> Nor eat nor sleep but night and day
> Cry on unceasingly.
> In any other child I see
>   A monstrous brat of death, not life.[1]

If life is a condition of continual and creative opposition, then Mac-
Diarmid embraces the process of striving, rather than the hope of

[1] 'The Impossible Song', from *Second Hymn to Lenin and Other Poems*, London,
1935; *C.P.*, p. 309.

attaining any stable goal. (For anything that a man can attain is only
'A mockery o' his soul at last'.) Exactly the same dedication to a life
of continual pursuit serves as the central theme of his next long poem,
To Circumjack Cencrastus. It is only with this mobility that the poet
feels he can come to grips with the world serpent, and face the unknow-
able immensities of the universe. The motivation, however, the pursuit
of the rose in all its forms, remains the same.

WHISKY : MOONLIGHT

Both whisky and moonlight serve as elements which transmute reality
for the drunk man, and their function is most important in the poem.
In the subjective, unsteady and internally focussed state of intoxication,
the drunk man's sensations and memories are subject to continual
change, distortion and interpenetration. Under the eerie moonlight the
exterior landscape seems to be similarly uncertain and fluid, and, taken
together, both elements serve to place the protagonist in a supremely
subjective, not to say hallucinated, state. In this aspect the moonlight
is specifically associated with his drunkenness ('This munelicht's fell
like whisky noo I see't''),[1] and with the shifting, shape-changing
condition which he experiences:

> That's it! It isna me that's fou at a',
> But the fu' mune, the doited jade, that's led
> Me fer agley, or 'mogrified the warld.[2]

The moonlight is also associated with a new and more penetrating
knowledge of himself: 'The munelicht ebbs and flows and wi't my
thocht',[3] and, 'The munelicht is my knowledge o' mysel''.[4] This
discovery is perfectly in keeping with the drunk man's subjective
exploration, and with his refusal to distinguish between internal and
external states. Thus it is that the deceptive light on the hillside around
him calls the whole nature of his understanding of reality into question;
just as his drunkenness brings him to doubt the verity even of sober
experience:

> Or am I juist a figure in a scene
> O' Scottish life A.D. one-nine-two-five?
> The haill thing kelters like a theatre claith
> Till I micht fancy that I was alive!

[1] *C.P.*, p. 72.   [2] *Ibid.* p. 66.   [3] *Ibid.* p. 76.   [4] *Ibid.* p. 96.

> I dinna ken and nae man ever can.
> I micht be in my ain bed efter a'.
> The haill damned thing's a dream for ocht we ken,
> – The Warld and Life and Daith, Heaven, Hell ana'.[1]

According to Yeats in his book *A Vision* (and to many more orthodox theosophists), the astrological period of the full moon is the time of greatest subjectivity. MacDiarmid concurs with this general identification, for he associates the moonlight with that complete freedom of possibility which we normally expect only from the imagination. The drunk man longs to achieve the liberation which the fickle light seems to lend to the objects around him, giving them 'a different life . . . and an unco poo'er'. He is frustrated, however, by his anticipation of his wife's scorn, and of his own literal-minded and prickly Scottish traits. These combine to thwart the uninhibited lunar influence:

> Or dost thou mak' a thistle o' me, wumman? But for thee
> I were as happy as the munelicht, withoot care,
> But thocht o' thee – o' thy contempt and ire –
> Turns hauf the warld into the youky thistle there,
>
> Feedin' on the munelicht and transformin' it
> To this wanrestfu' growth that winna let me be.
> The munelicht is the freedom that I'd ha'e
> But for this cursèd Conscience thou has set in me.[2]

In the above passage it is the thistle – and all it represents – which stands between the moon and the drunk man. This juxtaposition is repeated throughout the poem, and we can recognise it as a symbolic re-statement of the protagonist's basic dilemma. Man is capable of almost infinite aspiration, but no more than a limited achievement can ever be his: 'Till his puir warped performance is, / To a' that micht ha' been, a thistle to the mune.'[3] Representing 'all that might-have-been' in these lines, the moon has taken on something of the aspect of the ideal rose, and it will be remembered that in 'The Impossible Song', MacDiarmid expresses the same longing in terms of a child 'crying broken-hearted for the moon'.

There exists an important and intimate relationship between the effects of moonlight and whisky, and the appearance of the mysterious lady in several infrequent, but intense visionary moments. This figure

---

[1] *C.P.*, pp. 72–3.   [2] *Ibid.* p. 71.   [3] *Ibid.* p. 72.

is yet another manifestation of MacDiarmid's ideal longing, and it is appropriate that she is associated with our enigmatic and traditionally feminine satellite. This 'silken leddy' will be described in the following section, but for the moment, it should be noted that most of the major symbols so far discussed can now be seen to interpenetrate. Thus the rose, moonlight, the effect of whisky, and the visionary girl, all, at times, present an intimation of the ideal. The very images of the poem change roles and appearances in a way which is itself characteristic of the effects of the deceptive light and an intoxicated eye.

SEA SERPENT : WOMAN

MacDiarmid uses the imagery of sea serpent and woman to convey those 'antrin' lichtnin's', the deeper insights into the nature of reality, which come occasionally to the drunk man. The sea serpent appears infrequently and in various guises, and his role is more fully realised later, of course, as Cencrastus. Nevertheless, his early sightings in *A Drunk Man* are an important part of the poem.

MacDiarmid first described the sea serpent in the poem of that name published in *Penny Wheep*. In these verses he attempts to define the monster's elusive nature by using a continuing succession of different images. Thus, for example, it is described as a Leviathan, then it seems like a school of whales, or like the Aurora, and now it coils in a snake-like form. The effect of this is to emphasise the creature's continual movement, and to ascribe to it the power of seeming constantly to change its shape. Such complexity symbolises the infinite change and multiplicity of the created world, and yet, at the same time, the serpent maintains a unified and coherent, though almost incomprehensible, being. Thus it is 'the single movement o' life', as God first conceived it, and this is 'a movement that a'thing shares'.[1] In keeping with his view of existence as a various, but organic whole, MacDiarmid attempts to comprehend the serpent in its entirety, and hence gain an insight into ultimate metaphysical reality. The attempt was to become the prolonged pursuit of *To Circumjack Cencrastus*, but in *A Drunk Man* the serpent is still an elusive, and at times a frightening mystery. An inkling of the monster is all he asks for: 'Content to glimpse its loops I dinna ettle / To land the sea serpent's sel' wi' ony gaff.'[2]

Although it rests in no one particular spot, or shape, the serpent omnipresent ('It fits the universe man can ken / As a man's soul fits

[1] 'Sea-Serpent', *C.P.*, p. 35.   [2] *Ibid.* p. 68.

his body'),[1] and the drunk man has intimations of its protean presence, even at the most unlikely moments. Its mystery swims, for example, in his drinking crony's eyes:

> And in Gilsanquhar's glower I saw
> The taps o' waves 'neth which the warld
> Ga'ed rowin' like a jeelyfish[2]

He is acutely aware that he is exploring the 'flegsome deeps' of the mind, where monsters may, indeed, lie; depths familiar to Dostoevsky, where —

> ... frae depths
> O' an unfaddomed flood
> Tensions o' nerves arise
> And humours o' the blood
> – Keethin's nane can trace
> To their original place.[3]

Such regions are not comfortable, and, indeed, in a moment of terror he feels himself touched by the serpent, which embraces him like an octopus, and lies cold, like a snake, against his heart. He recoils from this monster only to discover that it is inextricably within himself, and that what he has, in fact, encountered is the inconceivable strangeness of his own soul:

> In mum obscurity it twines its obstinate rings
> And hings caressin'ly, its purpose whole;
> And this deid thing, whale-white obscenity,
> This horror that I writhe in – is my soul![4]

In a later passage, the drunk man visualises the manifold serpent as candelabra and octopus, uniting both the heights and the depths, and in a gloriously confident mood this time, he rejoices that both are contained within himself:

> A mony-brainchin' candelabra fills
> The lift and's lowin' wi' the stars;
> The Octopus Creation is wallopin'
> In coontless faddoms o' a nameless sea.
> I am the candelabra, and burn
> My endless candles to an Unkent God.
> I am the mind and meanin' o' the octopus
> That thraws its empty airms through a' th'Inane.[5]

---

[1] 'Sea-Serpent', *C.P.*, p. 33.   [2] *Ibid.* p. 115.   [3] *Ibid.* p. 122.
[4] *Ibid.* p. 75.   [5] *Ibid.* p. 131.

In accepting the awesome presence of the octopus he celebrates the infinitude of mystery and potential which is to be found in his own being, every bit as much as it is in the stars.

In keeping with its nature, and with the mobility of the poem's imagery, the sea serpent takes on, at times, the form of the scaly thistle, and under the moonlight the thistle in turn becomes serpent, Leviathan, and even many-branched Ygdrasil, armed like a candelabra! Thus the thistle partakes of Creation's mystery as well, and in pursuing an understanding of his Scottish stock, the drunk man sometimes finds himself following the serpent in yet another guise:

> Grugous thistle, to my een
> Your widdifow ramel evince
> Sibness to snakes wha's coils
> Rin coonter airts at yince,
> And fain I'd follow each
> Gin you the trick'll teach.[1]

The moon is also caught up in this endless metamorphosis, and it, too, is specifically associated with the power of the enigmatic Leviathan, pursued, this time, by a drunken Ahab:

> – The mune's the muckle white whale
> I seek in vain to kaa!
>
> The Earth's my mastless samyn,
> The thistle my ruined sail.[2]

When he is weary of his fevered brain, and exhausted by his longing for the rose, the drunk man takes solace in thoughts of his wife Jean, and he remembers how much he has discovered about himself in her, and other lovers' arms. He also experiences those moments of insight when the 'silken leddy' seems to offer him hints of a still 'deeper knowledge' of his nature. Thus in both her aspects – real and ideal – womankind is the guardian of many of the mysteries which the drunk man longs to understand.

The silken leddy first appears to him on a moonlit night while he is drinking in the tavern. Moving 'dimly like a dream wi'in', she brings him echoes of 'white clints slidin' to the sea', and 'the horns o' Elfland'.[3]

---

[1] *C.P.*, p. 139.   [2] *Ibid.* p. 91.

[3] These lines echo Keats: 'the foam / Of perilous seas, in faery lands forlorn'. It is significant that the 'Ode to a Nightingale' also describes a moment of insight while in a trance-like state. Compare 'Was it a vision or a waking dream?' with '(Is it a dream nae wauk'nin' proves?)'.

Under her strange influence the drunk man becomes aware of a new potentiality within himself, and even the whisky in his hand – hitherto 'the vilest "saxpenny planet"' – becomes a sun:

> I ha'e dark secrets' turns and twists,
> A sun is gi'en to me to haud,
> The whisky in my bluid insists,
> And speirs my benmaist history, lad.

From his own furtherest history he is brought to the deeps of the sea, and there the mystery of the sea serpent itself is reflected in her eyes:

> And owre my brain the flitterin'
> O' the dim feathers gangs aince mair,
> And, faddomless, the dark blue glitterin'
> O' twa een in the ocean there.[1]

The silken leddy appears again as 'The Unknown Goddess', a mysterious presence whose coming the drunk man expects and yet dreads. At this point in the poem he is exhausted and without hope because he feels that all his dreams are dead. When she appears to him, however, he experiences within himself the birth pangs of all that might yet be. He finds this to be utterly strange – a 'face unkent' – and he sees the generations of the future (which symbolise the as yet unrealised potential of the present) becoming one with the goddess, who has herself been delivered from his own deepest heart. It is a moment of terror and ecstasy:

> Ill-faith stirs in me as she comes at last,
> The features lang forekent . . . are unforecast.
> O it gangs hard wi' me, I am forspent.
> Deid dreams ha'e beaten me and a face unkent
> And generations that I thocht unborn
> Hail the strange Goddess frae my hert's-hert torn! . . .[2]

Both the passages discussed above (referring to the silken leddy) are based on English translations which Babette Deutsch and Avrahm Yarmolinsky made of two Russian poems by Alexander Blok. Blok wrote many poems about such visionary encounters with a 'beautiful lady'. He identified her with the religious philosopher Solovyov's visions of Sophia, who is the wisdom of God, personifying the pact of love which exists between the Creator and the created world. In 'The

[1] *C.P.*, p. 70.   [2] *Ibid.* p. 71.

Stranger', however (titled 'Poet's Pub' in the *Collected Poems*), Blok's
vision is more realistic and ironic than in his earlier, more mystical
verse. Nevertheless, its association with Sophia, and hence with the
Ideal, remains relevant to MacDiarmid's purpose in including the
silken leddy in the poem. In 1923, for example, he had published a
'Hymn to Sophia', and this poem makes clear his feelings towards
'the eternal feminine', and also acknowledges a debt to Solovyov's
belief that both man and the material world are embarked on a physical
and spiritual evolution towards the condition of Deity. It is in Sophia
that the physical and the spiritual worlds fully realise themselves and
meet in a final and perfect unity:

> As the whole Earth with straining hearts
>   Towards thee we draw.
>
>   *   *   *
>
> Yet will creation turn to thee
>   When, love being perfect, naught can die,
> And clod and plant and animal
>   And star and sky,
>
> Thy form immortal and complete,
>   Matter and spirit one, acquire,
> – *Ceaseless till then, O Sacred Shame,*
>   *Our wills inspire!*[1]

Such a longing for physical and spiritual transcendence is completely in keeping with the desire for the rose seen throughout *A
Drunk Man*. In the urge to Sophia, however, it takes a more detailed
and specifically philosophical form. Nevertheless, the connection
between the silken leddy, Sophia and the rose can only be reinforced
by MacDiarmid's 'Hymn to Sophia', and by the evidence it gives of
his early interest in Solovyov's thought. A further connection can be

---

[1] 'Hymn to Sophia: the Wisdom of God', *The Scottish Chapbook*, vol. 1, no. 12, July
1923; *C.P.*, p. 235. Solovyov's evolutionary doctrine appears in *A Drunk Man* in the
following lines:

> Sae God retracts in endless stage
> Through angel, devil, age on age,
> Until at last his infinite natur'
> Walks on earth a human cratur'
>
>   *   *   *
>
> Sae man returns in endless growth
> Till God in him again has scouth.
>
>   (*C.P.*, p. 128.)

made. The 'Sacred Shame' of the 'Hymn', for example, is created by a recognition of the terrible discrepancy between man's spiritual potential and his present low state. This shameful recognition urges him to aspire to higher things. In exactly the same way, the thistle is the drunk man's sacred shame, and an all too intimate knowledge of its grisly character is what drives him to escape from its pricks and to seek the rose instead.

The 'eternal feminine' figure reappears in the poem as the moon: 'The Mune sits on my bed the nicht unsocht, / And mak's my soul obedient to her will',[1] and again, as that strange bride, the virgin whore who recalls us to the profound mysteries of origin, inheritance and regeneration:

> And on my lips ye'll heed nae mair,
> And in my hair forget,
> The seed o' a' the men that in
> My virgin womb ha'e met. . . .[2]

On the same theme, the image of Mary recurs in *A Drunk Man*, to haunt the protagonist with the mystery of her part in the birth of Christ – that supremely spiritual being, who was yet realised in the flesh.

Jean may not offer him the terrors of the 'unknown goddess', but still she brings the drunk man to a devastatingly clear realisation of his own frailties, for all his metaphysical aspiration:

> Said my body to my mind,
> 'I've been startled whiles to find,
> When Jean has been in bed wi' me,
> A kind o' Christianity!'

> To my body said my mind,
> 'But your benmaist thocht you'll find
> Was "Bother what I think I feel
> – Jean kens the set o' my bluid owre weel,
> And lauchs to see me in the creel
> O' my courage-bag confined".' . . .[3]

Yet the drunk man respects the value of the bond between a man and a woman. He sees it as an important stage in the proper and full

---

[1] *C.P.*, p. 76.   [2] *Ibid.* p. 85.   [3] *Ibid.* p. 83.

realisation of the self, and then of mankind, and, finally, as yet another
aspect of his metaphysical love affair with all creation.

> I dinna say that bairns alane
> Are true love's task – a sairer task
> Is aiblins to create oorsels
> As we can be – it's that I ask.
>
> Create oorsels, syne bairns, syne race.
>
>   *   *   *
>
> And nae Scot wi' a wumman lies,
> But I am he and ken as 'twere
> A stage I've passed as he maun pass't,
> Gin he grows up, his way wi' her! . . .
>
>   *   *   *
>
> He's no' a man ava',
> And lacks a proper pride,
> Gin less than a' the warld
> Can ser' him for a bride![1]

CONCLUSION

Thus the drunk man returns, by a different route, to the theme 'be
yourself', and, indeed, it might be said that the entire poem is created
by the argument with himself which the pursuit of this goal entails.
In the final analysis it is the drunk man's personality which informs the
poem, the 'true Scot', 'dominated by the conception of infinity', and
in perpetual pursuit of the unattainable. Even when the question of
his national identity has been resolved (or at least set aside), the drunk
man is still driven to try to transcend the physical and spiritual conditions of 'being' itself.

In keeping with this Herculean task, MacDiarmid recruited Nietzsche
to his purpose, and cited his command to 'Become what you are' as a
slogan for the Scottish literary revival and for the rediscovery of a
national identity.[2] Indeed, the characteristics of the 'Faustian' sensibility as defined by Spengler, are very similar to the dynamic 'Dionysian'
qualities first described by Nietzsche in *The Birth of Tragedy*. Furthermore, the 'Dionysian' mode, with its delight in Heraclitean energy,
contrast, conflict and the bringing together of opposites, has much in

---

[1] *C.P.*, p. 97.
[2] 'A Theory of Scots Letters', *The Scottish Chapbook*, vol. 1, no. 8, March 1923.

common with the principle of antisyzygy which stands at the heart of MacDiarmid's poem, and is embodied in the dual nature of the thistle itself. The thistle contains both thorns and rose, matter and spirit inextricably inter-twined and engaged in a constant and fruitful conflict, and this, finally, is the drunk man's condition. The exhilarating movement of MacDiarmid's imagination, and the interpenetration of the images and symbols which he uses, combine to give a unique pace and a fluid coherence to the struggle.

The freedom for which the drunk man longs is that of the liberated imagination itself, and anything else, for such a spirit, is an almost literal imprisonment, as he makes clear in the following passage. He begins by claiming that a morality based on shame, fear, and all the inhibitions of the Scottish thistle, is what interferes with his search for 'perfect liberty'. In the next stanzas, however, his focus shifts to man's more general condition, and he rebels against the limitation which even 'the need to be' imposes on him. Thus the final shackle is his own mortality, and he writhes in anguish within his condition as man, a divided being whose spirit is bound to flesh, and whose flesh is imbued with spirit, a being who conceives of a perfect God in order to mock his own imperfection.

> It is morality, the knowledge o' Guid and Ill,
> Fear, shame, pity, like a will and wilyart growth,
> That kills a' else wi'in its reach and craves
> Nae less at last than a' the warld to gi'e it scouth.
>
> The need to wark, the need to think, the need to be,
> And a'thing that twists Life into a certain shape
> And interferes wi' perfect liberty –
> These feed this Frankenstein that nae man can escape.
>
> For ilka thing a man can be or think or dae
> Aye leaves a million mair unbeen, unthocht, undune,
> Till his puir warped performance is,
> To a' that micht ha' been, a thistle to the mune.
>
> It is Mortality itsel' – the mortal coil,
> Mockin' Perfection, Man afore the Throne o' God
> He yet has bigged himsel', Man torn in twa
> And glorious in the lift and grisly on the sod! . . .[1]

– The lines define the thistle's nature within the drunk man, and it is from this condition that he undertakes the journey whose process is the poem.

These, then, are some of the elements from which the poem and the exploration of the drunk man's nature is constructed. In the end, one can only confess to how much else these notes have missed out in what has been, for the most part, an approach to the 'metaphysics' of the poem. If I have pursued this – 'the star' – then the humour, the obscenity, the lyrical beauty and the wealth of special reference must not be forgotten, nor that typically contradictory impulse when the drunk man cries:

> Devil the star! It's Jean I'll ha'e
> Again as she was on her weddin' day . . .

Hugh MacDiarmid and the Colloquial Category

MATTHEW P. McDIARMID

The *academic* critic, when he operates as such, is a historian. He is aware, or should be aware, that practical appreciation is a creative act and is therefore best performed by the poet. What he most usefully offers, or seeks to offer, is the enlightenment of fact, the illuminating comparison or generalisation that claims to have such a basis. The heroic effort of Hugh MacDiarmid to write a Scots poetry that exhibits a fully modern personality, and makes the same kind of appeal to literary sensibility as the best pieces of English poetry make, is a proper subject for his commentary. He can try to state what those limitations of the Burnsian tradition in verse were from which MacDiarmid sought to escape, and with his statement pose a little more clearly the questions of the nature and degree of that escape. That at least is what this writer will attempt here.

It seems to him that understanding of the twentieth-century experiment in Scots verse requires an understanding of the eighteenth-century one – that this was an experiment and one of the most interesting in literary history most critics seem to be unaware. The practice and commentary of the older poets unreservedly accepts one opinion, that the poetic uses of Scots must be prevailingly colloquial, with all the peculiar advantages and disadvantages that this implies. The interest of their experiment is that it created the only thorough-going colloquial poetry that literature knows. It was a breakaway from the tradition of formal, sophisticated expression and allowed its poets to present ordinary nature with a vigour and faithfulness that the contemporary English poets, for example, simply did not have the means of imitating. Wordsworth tried to imitate it but was soon compelled to resume the customary literary personality. It is in this respect of a truly popular mode of expression that Chesterton's famous line says no more than truth: 'We are the people of England, and we have not spoken yet.'

But the disadvantages were severe. A sophisticated and sensuous play of language, such as characterises the English and Continental poets (who are playing, as it were, to an audience of tradition-trained critics), and such as characterised the older Scots poets, the makars, was prohibited or at least greatly limited by this popular poetic language. Foreign critics like Auguste Angellier, Friedrich Brie, and Mario Praz, find some kind of folk *ethos* in all Scots writing. Edwin Muir casts about for such epithets as 'homely', 'realistic', 'materialistic', 'democratic', and so forth. And no doubt some such ethos has always dictated a more direct and less complex kind of utterance – the difference between Henryson and Chaucer, the comic difference between Burns's 'A man's a man for a' that' and Schiller's unimaginable version of this, 'millions embrace'. But only a wilfully blind eye could make our twentieth-century apologists insist, as they sometimes do, that Scots poetic diction always instinctively rejected the complex and the sensuous. Only for the déclassé Scots medium of the eighteenth century was it out of character to be sophisticated.

'Out of character' is the key phrase. Ramsay, Fergusson and Burns – even the last-mentioned, though his experience was most suited to the language – are poets acting a part, keeping strictly to a kind of working-class *persona*. Burns may know all about Rousseau's sentimental doctrine of the good instincts and the Man of Feeling, but he has to present it as a piece of homespun philosophy, 'The heart ay's the part, ay, / That makes us right or wrang'. All of these poets read and admired the glittering satires of Pope, or the smooth-turned elegies and pastorals of Gray and Shenstone, or the idealising description of Goldsmith, but they avoided these forms and styles of expression as alien to the social role dictated by their medium. It is in this respect, as much as any real difficulty of speech, that English can be said to have 'gravelled' Burns. They instinctively and deliberately kept to forms more dramatically appropriate to a peasant's or low-class townsman's experience – the comic tale like 'Tam o' Shanter', the realistic pastoral like Fergusson's 'Farmer's Ingle', the Ode on country life like Ramsay's version of Horace, the festive description like 'The Jolly Beggars'. It is an odd procedure, whereby the educated reader gets a sophisticated pleasure from the liberties allowed by the artistic convention of a folk *persona*. For it too is a convention.

And the experiment might have rested there, but for one very important innovation by Burns, who has often been unjustly criticised for only doing better what the more original and more sophisticated Fergusson had already done. When he turned finally to song-writing he knew that so far as his own work was concerned, he had exhausted all other possibilities of his colloquial medium – except for the serious narrative poem of country-life, and the fairy-tale that Hogg was to develop. His song-writing was not a turning back but an advance. He could maintain his principle of a folk-decorum – what he called the 'essential' 'dash of the Doric' – and yet develop a more various and more specifically poetic personality than his familiar, discursive verse had yet presented. The songs are folk-songs, and yet it is in them that we are most purely conscious of him as the poet *simpliciter*, least conscious of him as the peasant poet. It was, in fact, along this line of lyric development that Hugh MacDiarmid would initially try to advance as a Scots poet and something more.

The universality of Burns's art is not questioned by this description, rather it is explained; but it does mean that for full appreciation of him we have to give up our normal nationless and classless habit as good readers. And we would not wish always to have our approach defined in this way. We would expect poetry also to cultivate a *general persona*, of the free kind that MacDiarmid describes as his ideal, 'mind out for a lark', that is, mind rejecting set stances, rôles, contexts. Of course, it must select one for any given purpose of subject-matter, but it will prefer the one that gives greatest freedom; and that will be one that is neither obtrusively colloquial nor obtrusively literary – what Dante calls the *vulgare illustre*. And if a choice has to be made, it will prefer the *illustre*, as Milton did, since that will let the writer rise to the height of whatever culture he has. The sheer impropriety of certain Milton-sounding stanzas, excellent in themselves, in 'The Cottar's Saturday Night', shows that the context of Burns's colloquial Scots simply did not allow him to say all that he wanted to say, and could have said. Milton could safely 'fall', as in the 'Blind mouths' passage in *Lycidas*, but Burns could not rise. By and large, the more impersonal literary manner allows the poet to be most freely himself.

Does MacDiarmid achieve the freedom from social context that racy description, 'mind out for a lark', demands? His most important predecessor in experimenting with a Scots freedom, Lewis Spence, flourished the slogan, 'Back to Dunbar'. What Dunbar would have made of this ghost of himself heaven knows. Spence's aureate diction only proves that he had read Dunbar, not that he was a poet. Beside Spence, Marion Angus and Rachel Annand Taylor pleasantly elaborated ballads and lyrics about the loves of very literary lads and lasses, that had a romantic sensuousness which certainly belonged more to

I

pure poetry than ploughman poetry; but at best these were mere imitative refinements on the old themes and old forms. The sensuousness that Edwin Muir had missed in Burnsian and post-Burnsian verse had been supplied, but there was no escape from the traditional context.

Sangschaw, MacDiarmid's own wood of birds (1925), made the escape. Faintly folksy, Kailyard notes can be heard in it at times, as in the somewhat sentimental close of 'The Watergaw' ('An' I think that mebbe at last I ken / What your look meant then'), and the conventionally, if splendidly, picturesque 'Crowdieknowe', with its 'trashy bleezin', French-like folk'. But it is only a poet, to be appreciated simply as a poet, and not a Scots performer, who talks to us in lines like these:

> Their starry talk's a wheen o' blethers,
> Nane for thee a thochtie sparin',
> Earth, thou bonnie broukit bairn!

or in these:

> An' the roarin' o' oceans noo'
> Is peerieweerie to me:
> Thunner's a tinklin' bell, an: Time
> Whuds like a flee.

Reading such verse one does not have to concern himself unduly with thoughts of the poet being Scots, with a Scots theme in a Scots context. It is simply great verse; it is free mind, free expression. Another piece that entirely transcends categories is 'Empty Vessel'.

Yet even this perfection can be thought limited, from the viewpoint of our definition of poetic freedom, 'Mind out for a lark'. There is firstly too little mind in it. We are being asked excessively to think with our senses, and though this is freedom on one side, it is restriction on another. Also, though this is independently perfect verse, reflection tells us that it is only its perfection that blinds us momentarily to its traditional connections. The 'mysteries, infinitudes', that MacDiarmid says he wished to inject into Scots verse are not absolutely novel. They are conscious refinements of certain ballad effects, verses like these from 'Tamlane':

> About the middle o' the nicht,
> She heard the bridles ring,
> The lady was as glad at that
> As any earthly thing.

What has happened is that just as the Augustan and sentimental vogue for the realistic pastoral gave Scots colloquial poetry its opportunity once before, so now the current vogue of 'pure poetry' allowed the revivers of Scots to develop and refine traditional features of style. A quotation in *Sangschaw* from Housman, whose cultivation of the poetic thrill owes so much to the ballads, makes the sympathy clear to us. But still more revealing is MacDiarmid's confessed admiration about this time for Paul Valéry. I need only render two sayings of Valéry from his *Variété* to pinpoint what MacDiarmid is attempting: 'At last we have a century when has appeared the will to isolate poetry finally from every other essence but itself', and, 'There is a fine part of the soul that can enjoy without comprehending'. The early MacDiarmid writes pure poetry. Later he will wish, unfairly, to say poor poetry. So much misleading talk has been heard about *Sangschaw* and *Penny Wheep* restoring ideas to Scots poetry. Ideas were precisely at this stage, what it avoided. One can only say that he successfully brought it into line with a European fashion of sensibility that was luckily sympathetic to its traditional genius.

But if MacDiarmid's early poetry is not quite so significant of revolution as has been claimed, it has at least, in the lyrics, freed the Scots poet from his folk *persona*. And in his next volume, *A Drunk Man Looks at The Thistle*, a further degree of freedom is achieved in his discursive writing. I say 'degree', because the manner of pure poetry is continued in much of it, and a style that un-self-consciously presents his individual, modern, intellectual personality is never fully developed. The traditional class character of modern Scots poetry is never wholly forgotten.

It is still 'soon', no sense', that seeks to 'faddom the herts o' men' in the version of the Russian of Alexander Blok that he calls 'Poet's Pub': 'a silken leddy darkly moves' with no more specific motive than to put a dream in the poet's drink. And in a very important respect the moonlit Thistle symbolises Valéry's doctrine of aspiration to pure spirit, pure mind; symbolises it in its despair of realising itself. Valéry's theme and much of his indirect, suggestive technique are easily identified in the most haunting of its lyrics, 'O Wha's The Bride'. The 'gudeman' of this lyric demands an impossible perfection or purity of experience, and is told that he must content himself with the limited, impure but kindly knowledge of the senses, the flesh.

The reader will have noticed again that, though we are aware of a modern poet's consciousness working intensely and freely on its matter, the 'mysteries and infinitudes' are conveyed by exploiting folk connotations, and above all that the tones (if not the overtones) are colloquial. This marvellous poetic 'gallimaufry', to use MacDiarmid's own word is, of course, intentionally pitched in the colloquial key. The poet has:

> . . . heard God passin' wi' a bobby's feet
> Ootby in the lang coffin o' the street.

In Scots poetry it is still impossible to call God a policeman.

In brief, MacDiarmid, in his most ambitious poem, may write a more overtly poetical poetry than the Burnsian and post-Burnsian school attempted, and even when exploiting folk connotations free himself from the folk-image of the poet, but his technique and style offer no serious contradiction to the eighteenth-century opinion that modern Scots poetry must be, in the main, a colloquial poetry.

That this became his own conscious conclusion is nowhere stated but the fact is patent that after *A Drunk Man* Scots is a dwindling element in MacDiarmid's work. And it seems significant that its decline coincides with his rejection of the ideals of 'pure poetry', and with his pursuit of a 'poetry of thought and fact' opposed to what he now called his 'irresponsible lyricism'. For his new kind of poetry English became increasingly his medium. One would have supposed that there was enough thought in *A Drunk Man*, but it is admittedly thought of a kind that does not require exact statement and develops no argument; it explores impressions, aspirations, not doctrines; it gives no clear pictures.

Where Scots recurs, for the last time considerably, in the Hymns to Lenin, the tone is again colloquial, but now only matter-of-factly colloquial – as in 'The Seamless Garment', where he brilliantly suggests the genius of Lenin's dialectic and Rilke's philosophic verse by images that his cousin in the Langholm weaving shop might be supposed able to grasp.

The vogue for a Communist poetry had again seemed to give his colloquial medium a congenial task, but it was at the expense of that freedom from class context that his earlier poetry had won for the image of the poet himself. There is no vital difference, in that respect, between this Scots verse and Burns's conversational epistles to other peasant-poets. MacDiarmid is indeed unique among West European poets in trying to write a genuinely working-class poetry – a fellow Communist like Louis Aragon addressed himself strictly to the intelligentsia and surrendered nothing of his literary personality. Perhaps he could not resist the temptation to make a traditional use of his medium in a situation, that of the class-conscious 'thirties, that seemed expressly to invite it.

In the present writer's opinion his greatest verse was yet to come, verse such as we find in 'On A Raised Beach', but it was not Scots verse, thoroughly Scots as its rhetoric and sentiment are.

We have had two Renaissances of the Scots Muse, and there is no reason why, thanks to Hugh MacDiarmid, there should not be a third. When it comes it will be owing to the same kind of shift in contemporary viewpoint and sensibility as encouraged the not wholly dissimilar experiments of Burns and MacDiarmid, and its scope will be determined by the same stubbornly popular genius of the Scots tradition.

The Golden Lyric

AN ESSAY ON THE POETRY OF HUGH MACDIARMID

IAIN CRICHTON SMITH

I

When one discusses the poetry of Hugh MacDiarmid one is forced to make an evaluation of the importance of ideas in poetry or to put it another way to discuss how ideas are related if at all to poetry. Now it is quite clear that a poem is not simply a system of formal ideas. Poetry is not a putting of an idea into verse. It is not enough to have an idea and then to put that idea into verse form. The classic case of a poem built up on an idea is the *De Rerum Natura* of Lucretius. Nevertheless it could be argued that the parts of Lucretius's poem which are the best poetry are those which deal not simply with ideas in the abstract but rather with death faced without hope.

The logic of poetry is not the logic of a Kant or a Hegel. It is not a question of proving anything in the sense that one proves something in geometry, for instance. Nor should one expect from a poet or any artist a purely logical mind (however much an artist may be betrayed into hankerings after this).

What ideas as such has a poet ever bequeathed to the human race? Wordsworth was possessed to a certain extent of ideas and made an attempt to create a system of thought in relation to poetry but Coleridge showed without much difficulty that the basis of his ideas was demonstrably false and removed from reality. It is not the case that country people have purer feelings than city people. It is an education to see how Coleridge demolishes Wordsworth's painfully created structure. For to think is very difficult: to think originally is so difficult that the few who have achieved it can be counted in the hundreds. What poet has shown a power of clear thought? And if he could think clearly, what value would this have for his poetry? If we want logic we should go to a logician. If we want sociology we should go to a sociologist. If we want politics we should go to a politician. That is not the poet's job.

It is a well-known fact that scientists, outside their own chosen field, have opinions which are trivial in essence. Bertrand Russell has a passage where he says that if you were to ask a scientist for his ideas on anything outside his own chosen field his supposed power of thought would collapse, revealing only personal emotive flickers, not dignified enough to justify the name of ideas. In this impotence outside their own work they are like other men. Their power of thought serves them little: and in fact many of them may even be more stupid and removed from reality than common people without their ability. It may be that Russell himself sometimes shows this idealistic stupidity.

Nevertheless it is true that poets have often felt the need to write about ideas. They are impelled to this by a feeling of helplessness. They feel perhaps that their poetry isn't changing the world, and they had possibly expected in their youth that this might happen. Mac-Diarmid himself says at one point that if the common people – the masses – do not know his poetry, then he has failed. They feel that art is not accomplishing anything. They look out into the world of action and they feel a certain envy. No-one seems to be listening to them. Pure aesthetic creations are not being valued. The Lenins of this world are the important people. And therefore they feel that they must introduce Thought into their work. Surely people will read their work if it is permeated with Thought, with Ideas.

This argument however seems essentially false. Thought put into poetry does not necessarily make good verse. It is not from Thought alone that poetry begins. And furthermore if only one idea is being promulgated then the poetry becomes propaganda. Yeats says that a quarrel with oneself makes poetry but a quarrel with others makes rhetoric. This is true. It is true because the level on which the poet works must not be exclusive. Any thinking person who has thought long and deeply – or even felt long and deeply – must realise that no one dogma is sufficient to interpret for us the meaning of the universe (if it has a meaning). A poet knows this better than anyone else. Another thing that Yeats said was that man can embody truth but not know it. One way of interpreting this might be that a poet could write about a man who believes he has the truth: to claim that he knows the truth himself would be ludicrous. Now it is true that the movement of MacDiarmid's verse recognises the difficulty of arriving at the truth. In *A Drunk Man Looks at the Thistle* he hopes that he will be preserved from those people who think they know the truth and are possessed of it. He says that sometimes he bursts out laughing when he remembers how small and trivial he himself is when set against the scale of the universe. One knows perfectly well what he is talking about. He is talking about the self-satisfied Scotsman whom he ridicules in the *Drunk Man* by pitching him out into the stars to show him how unimportant he really is. One can see why in Scotland above all MacDiarmid might time and again break himself against this colossal pride and ignorance. And to be fair to him, he writes most often from this stance.

There are times too, however, when MacDiarmid gives the idea that he himself knows the truth and that his ideas are essentially right. In this perhaps he is being infected by his Scottish environment and the stubborn blind unbreakable Scottish will. For the question is this: if people are not convinced by these ideas logically and in prose why should they be convinced when they are put into poetry and their rigour is gone?

However MacDiarmid's favourite method seems to be a dialectic one. He may have learned this from a study of Communism but he was talking about Hegel before Communism came into his poetry. In this method he veers from one idea to its opposite. And very often he comes down on neither side.

An example of this kind of argument occurs in the section of the *Drunk Man* when one verse says:

> I'm no' like Burns, and weel I ken,
> Tho' ony wench can ser',
> It's no' through mony but through yin
> That ony man wuns fer. . . .

and a good many verses later:

> He's no' a man ava',
> And lacks a proper pride,
> Gin less than a' the warld
> Can ser' him for a bride!

It would be pointless to single out all the instances of this kind of movement in his poetry. It is the most pronounced movement of his verse, the way in which he constructs a poem, especially his poems of ideas. Sometimes this dialectic can become almost ridiculous, for example:

> Ah, Lenin, you were right. But I'm a poet
> (And you c'ud mak allowances for that!)
> Aimin' at mair than you aimed at
> Tho' yours comes first, I know it.
>
> An unexamined life is no worth ha'in'.
> Yet Burke was richt; owre muckle concern
> Wi' Life's foundations is a sure
> Sign o decay; tho' Joyce in turn
> Is richt, ... etc etc[1]

Now clearly the dialectical movement in poetry is not uncommon and can be very exciting. However if the poem remains on *the level of the idea* no final result can ever be arrived at. And often one feels with MacDiarmid that in fact he does not resolve his poems as poetry. The ideas are built up in a staggering profusion, like an insane stair, and no resolution seems to be possible.

In one of his poems – the famous 'The Seamless Garment' – what in fact is achieved by the poem as such? It is true that it is finely conversational. He is explaining to a mill hand in terms of what the mill hand can understand what Lenin was like. He says that the weaver is at home with the loom and Lenin was at home with working class life. His knowledge of the working class had become second nature to him. Similarly with Rilke. Rilke too had created a seamless garment. MacDiarmid asks the weaver whether he turns out good or shoddy clothes. He says that the worker would not want to go back to the old days and the old machines. He says that machinery has improved but man has not. He says that the threads lie hundreds to the inch (in the same way as communists to the cell – which is not really a very good simile but probably just as good as some of C. Day Lewis's). The poem ends with MacDiarmid saying that what he wants is integrity too. Now all this is very well but it is really a very lame conclusion for such a poem, painfully built up. Is this all then? Is MacDiarmid just ending with a prayer and recognition of his own impotence? The poem has not been resolved in terms of poetry though the ideas move beautifully.

If we turn to another poem to find a typical dialectical movement one would perhaps turn to a poem like the 'Easter Rising'. In this poem Yeats recognises that dedication to an ideal can make a stone of the heart: but at the same time this dedication can make men heroic. Even the refrain is ambiguous, 'A terrible beauty is born'. Is there really a pun on the word 'terrible'? The poem in spite of its dialectic however does give an impression of attaining a poise which holds within it all the various possibilities inherent in it and in the argument. These men might have been ridiculous: on the other hand they might have been heroic. Great actions may really be brought to birth by fools, by clowns. Or was it a great action after all?

All this is true. But the poem does not convince us by its ideas. It convinces by its language, its pathos and its music, by the feeling that the whole of Yeats is concerned in this poem and not just his mind. One feels that for Yeats this event was a human event. It has not only changed these men: it has changed Yeats. It will possibly change us. But it will not change us simply because of the ideas. It will change Yeats because he is humanly shocked into a state in which these ideas become real for him. They will make a human change in him, not simply a mental one. One feels with MacDiarmid's poem and with much else of his poetry of ideas that in fact he himself is not changed humanly. He has only seen with his mind, not felt with his heart. 'O wae's me on this weary wheel.'

Now the course of MacDiarmid's progress can be charted fairly clearly. The first two or three books are books of lyrics mainly. Then there is the long poem *A Drunk Man*, on the whole successful because the dialectic there is freshly felt and at the same time the dialectic suits the drunk man (who is of course MacDiarmid himself to a great extent since, in spite of the left-handed tribute that MacDiarmid pays to Scottish education, what Scot would be able to quote T. S. Eliot (among many others) as well as translate from the Russian at this time?) Then after that we have *To Circumjack Cencrastus*.

Now this poem begins by using the image of the snake but it is not long till the snake image disappears. In the previous poem the thistle by a series of almost miraculous images, both grave and gay, with pathos and bravado, held the poem together: the snake does not hold its successor together. The poem itself is a ragbag of ideas. It contains a lot about MacDiarmid himself and the beginnings of his hatred of employers. Parts of this poem – especially towards the end – are very bitter and personal. It is clear that from this poem onwards however MacDiarmid is going to be more and more concerned with ideas for their own sake. But there is one astonishing brilliance in the poem and that is the really fine translation of Rilke's Requiem to Paula Moder-sohn. (MacDiarmid often refers to Rilke in his poetry: and yet in many ways the poets are very different.)

After *To Circumjack Cencrastus*, we are well on the way to the kind of poetry we get in *In Memoriam James Joyce*, though here and there in the stony waste we get some marvellous things like 'On a Raised Beach', 'The Little White Rose', parts of the 'Lament for the Great Music', 'At My Father's Grave', the savage 'At the Cenotaph' and the marvellous bit from the poem on Glasgow beginning 'Where have I seen a human being looking . . .', and many more.

Having read the whole of MacDiarmid's poetry as far as I was able to I have now come to the conclusion that MacDiarmid did take a wrong turning when he began on his poetry of ideas. At one time I did not believe this because I felt that cleverness and intelligence were very important. I still believe this but on the other hand I would not give them the high position that I once did. Now I believe there were a number of reasons for MacDiarmid to take this turning. The first reason was that he is naturally a very intelligent man. I do not mean by this that he is a great thinker for clearly this would be wrong, and he wouldn't claim this himself. I believe that a poet by definition cannot be a great thinker. However he clearly has a restless inquiring mind. He has also always been a great lover of books as he mentions in his autobiography. Therefore it was natural that he be led towards ideas and an investigation of them.

Secondly I believe that after the creation of his lyrics MacDiarmid, with that curious distrust that poets have about the value of something simply because of its smallness, felt that he ought to move on to more 'serious' work. This I believe to have been a profound error, not the fact that he should have moved on, for perhaps he could not prevent himself from doing this, but the fact that he should think a poetry of ideas must necessarily be a more 'serious' poetry. I believe that 'The Watergaw' is in every way far more serious than anything he produced on the basis of ideas alone. These long poems may be intellectually exciting but they are not serious. They do not confront us with serious things. They do not, I think, react on us as whole human beings. Their explorations are not deep enough. This may seem a very odd thing to say when the present writer admits that there are great stretches of them that he cannot understand. Nevertheless Mac-Diarmid was making the assumption that by injecting ideas into his work he would become serious. What poems could be more serious than Blake's lyrics (a poet I will return to later) and yet are they full of ideas in any detachable sense?

A mention of Hegel, a reference to Einstein, an allusion to a book here and there, does not make a poem serious. In fact MacDiarmid is here showing a snobbery, a kind of aristocracy. A third reason I think was that he was running out of Scottish material. After all MacDiarmid undoubtedly has genius. To be born in Scotland and to be a genius might seem an ironical joke. What is there in Scotland for a poet after a while? Very few human beings of consequence. A blankness without a public. And rather than write poems about Glencoe, etc., etc., Mac-Diarmid was driven towards a poetry of ideas, since no human poetry was for him possible at that stage. Let it not be thought that the present writer is passing judgment on MacDiarmid at this point. His reasons and compulsions for doing what he did appear almost inevitable but not perhaps with the inevitability of the poetic impulse. Again I think he must have been influenced by Burns and the disastrous post-Burns era. The kind of poetry written then had little or no intellectual content. Very well then, MacDiarmid must have thought, let us inject intellectual content into it. It is true that Burns's poetry had little intellectual content. However it has human content. It is not because of lack of intellectual content that Burns's poetry often fails but rather because the human content is falsified. 'Holy Willie's Prayer' is a great poem because it is exactly observed: 'The Cotter's Saturday Night' is poor because the human content is false. In the poem Burns was not telling the truth. Intellectual content would not have saved it.

Finally MacDiarmid must have been influenced by poems like *The Waste Land* and the wanderings of Ezra Pound. MacDiarmid often refers admiringly to Eliot in his work ('Eliot, a good Scots name' he says at one point) and elsewhere he remarks that *A Drunk Man* is a better poem than *The Waste Land*. One does not want to venture into these wastes now: to distinguish which is the better would be very difficult. Rather however one can in MacDiarmid's poetry notice the same tricks as in Eliot and Pound, the references to abstruse facts, the in-group authors, the quotations fitted into the text, and counter-pointing. This seems to work in *A Drunk Man* but in later poetry the stretches become more and more arid, 'a moment of joy is harder and harder to get'. Perhaps they come closer really to the Cantos of Pound which are practically incomprehensible.

To put the point bluntly as possible I would give away whole swaths of MacDiarmid's later work for 'The Watergaw' alone, which seems to be a poem about human beings at a human crisis however it was conceived whereas practically everything in the later books can be got equally well from their sources if one wants to read them.

II

It may be strange to say this but when I read MacDiarmid's poetry at length I often think of that essay which Eliot wrote on Blake. One might wonder what Blake had to do with MacDiarmid or what the point of the comparison is. Now in this essay Eliot maintained that Blake had been led astray by a hotch-potch of ideas which are completely uninteresting in themselves. It might be interesting for someone to take this comparison between Blake and MacDiarmid further (the present writer doesn't have the detailed knowledge for it).

It is sufficient to say that here are two poets – Blake and Mac-Diarmid – who both begin with lyrics of a certain kind, that is, lyrics which contain a fusion of the intellect and feeling which is highly unusual and at times hallucinatory. Both poets go on to write long poems based rather insecurely on systems which are fairly private (even MacDiarmid's communism doesn't seem to be all that orthodox). Both have little to do with the classical tradition (it is interesting that MacDiarmid very seldom refers to the Greeks and Trojans from whom so many poems have been quarried but rather goes back to Celtic sources.) Blake too does not seem interested in a classical tradition but goes back to sources found nearer home. Both are radical in their views though they have the basic aristocratic attitude of poets. They write about freedom and the spirit of man in chains.

Another similarity which I wish to stress for a particular reason is that neither had a university training. Now let no-one under any circumstances believe that I consider a university training obligatory for a poet. Nothing could be further from the truth. In fact I would be more likely to believe the contrary. On the other hand I often feel that in comparison for instance with the mind of Eliot the mind of Mac-Diarmid is untrained, and sometimes it seems to me irresponsible. Eliot's critical work of course is far superior to MacDiarmid's, such as it is. No, what I am saying is this: I cannot see any justification for MacDiarmid's writing most of his later work in verse form. Eliot too had certain things he felt like saying but he developed a prose style for them. I am not saying that all of Eliot's work or indeed much of Eliot's work outside his purely literary criticism is of much value, but at least he made the distinction between the things he could say in prose and the things he could say in poetry. I feel that MacDiarmid might have done better to make the same distinction.

If this comparison with Blake be accepted on a certain level it will be seen that there is a certain progress in the work of each of them.

Now MacDiarmid became a Communist of a particular kind in his career. It may be for all I know that there are signs of Communistic thinking at the end of *To Circumjack Cencrastus* when he attacks his boss on a personal level, and he may well have been forced into it by his later personal sufferings (and here may one say how much one admires the kind of personal integrity that MacDiarmid has shown?) and also by what he saw around him in the 'thirties especially. He wasn't the only one to be attracted by such a system in the 'thirties though I do not think that MacDiarmid could be systematised for long.

However I do not think that MacDiarmid is a Communist in any ordinary sense of the word. True, he writes in approval of certain of Lenin's actions, and in these poems a certain inhumanity emerges. But that MacDiarmid has much in common with the 'masses' I do not believe. How can one prove this, that MacDiarmid is not a Communist? There is only one test. When is his poetry at its best, at its most complex in a good way? MacDiarmid may think he is a Communist but I think on the other hand that his imagination betrays him.

I would suggest that excluding his early work up to the *Drunk Man* the burden of MacDiarmid's imagination does not emerge in his Communist poems nor on the whole do they convince me imaginatively in any way. For after all the poems about Lenin are very often more about himself than they are about Lenin and more about the integrity which will allow him to make good poetry than they are about politics. I would suggest that the burden of MacDiarmid's imagination in his later work can be found where he writes about exclusiveness and not where he writes about involvement with humanity. I am thinking in particular about 'On a Raised Beach' which seems to me his finest achievement after *A Drunk Man*, a poem about stones and an appalling apartness. It is in this kind of conscious loneliness that MacDiarmid is most imaginatively convincing. It could indeed be argued that the progress of MacDiarmid is from the human to a poetry of landscape and stones and language. It is the aristocratic lonely voice in these poems that convinces. (In fact he seems to me to become astonishingly like Yeats in thought if not in style.) The poems about the masses do not really have much resonance.

If Communism among other things means a concern with people, then MacDiarmid is not a Communist. If Communism among other things means the patience of a Lenin – the patience of stones – and a

kind of ruthlessness then there are these things in the poems. But on
the other hand they are there, as they are in Grassic Gibbon, academically. It is not easy to know how MacDiarmid would have reacted to
the turmoil of a real Communist revolution in his own country and
to the possible murders and killings. I myself find much of what he
says about Lenin distasteful. (This problem of violence is also to be
found in Grassic Gibbon and is to be found, academically, in our own
time in Gunn and MacBeth for instance.) It is fair enough to say that
Lenin had to have a lot of people killed but I do not think that a poet
should speak about this without agony for he should try to see people
not as faceless masses but as individuals. One should try to imagine
what it would mean in the last analysis to oneself. That is why I find
MacDiarmid's poems somewhat unreal and rhetorical. The poems of
those who have actually suffered in these countries are not like this.
And one wonders what happened to Mayakovsky. (Another thought
which might enter one's mind is this: if Scotland had had its Easter
Rising how would this have affected MacDiarmid's poetry? Yeats saw
war close to him and was at times horrified.)

In the later MacDiarmid there is really a great loneliness and cold-
ness. I think his poetry about stones is often magnificent and proud
and it convinces me that it is poetry and not propaganda. It is not a
question of approving or disapproving of this poetry. The poetry
convinces one whether one likes it or not. That is why I often remember a snatch of dialogue between two characters from one of Faulkner's
novels. One of them is praising 'Ode to a Nightingale'. The other
simply remarks that Keats had to write something, didn't he. And I
feel this with the later MacDiarmid that in his latest work he had to
write about something and he wrote about Communism and various
other ideas. This is not at all a question of saying that MacDiarmid
was insincere. It is more profound than that. A man may say that he is
a Communist and in the recesses of his imagination not be so. Milton
was of the devil's party without knowing it. MacDiarmid's later poetry
convinces me when he is at his most aristocratic, a cold eagle, a man
in love with stones. This part of him – the truest part of him at this
stage – knows that he is not like other people, that they have very little
to say to him, that he cannot learn anything from them and that they'll
never learn anything anyway.

Again it is not a question of my approving or disapproving of this –
and I can see quite clearly how he might have arrived at this position –
especially in Scotland – it is merely to say what kind of poetry seems

to me to be successful. Whether for instance Eliot says he is Anglo-Catholic, Royalist and classical seems to me to be irrelevant. It has little to do with his most successful poetry, or even with his truest preoccupations in poetry.

III

If I were therefore to pick MacDiarmid's best books I would pick his earlier ones right up to the *Drunk Man*.

The latter I think is a major work on many levels though Mac-Diarmid finds difficulty with the ending. I am not sure that I completely understand the section about Silence though David Daiches in his introduction to the poem seems quite sure that he understands it. But on balance the image of the thistle and the moonlight does in fact hold the poem together and holds it at the same time in a real physical world. The later poems seem to me not to be able to get hold of a symbol which will be a unifying thread. Here too in this poem a lot of what he says later on is said for the first time and said freshly. I often wonder whether in fact some of *To Circumjack Cencrastus* may not be passages rejected from the previous poem.

In a sense the dialectic seems to work for this poem partly because the symbolism helps it to. The basic groundwork of the poem which in effect is the struggle towards consciousness of a man and of a nation and of humanity is represented lucidly by the thistle and the moonlight. The thistle can be seen to stand for the man distorted by morality and the pressures of existence. The moonlight can be seen to stand for the Platonic idea, complete, unflawed and often deadly.

The fact too that the thistle is the Scottish symbol allows Mac-Diarmid to pass from the personal to the national very easily. It is clear also that to a certain extent he does allow the main character to be different from himself. The protagonist is not wholly himself though he does have a great deal of the knowledge of MacDiarmid. He seems to represent something essentially Scottish. He goes back to Tam o' Shanter, one supposes, and is a human being in whose twists and turns we are interested.

The change in mood and thought (which in others of the poems may seem arbitrary) does not seem so in this poem because the protagonist is after all a drunk man. It is a very gay poem, a very witty poem, the poem of a writer who has not allowed himself to be overwhelmed by the world. One senses in *Cencrastus* a kind of bitterness of which there is little sign in the *Drunk Man*. MacDiarmid in this poem is still able to objectify his insights without rancour. He can be playful in a very funny way, as for instance in the passage about the Chinese at the Burns supper.

The poem does not seem to me to reach any conclusion but it does not seem to matter very much for it is redeemed by so many other qualities, wit, humour, snatches of strange balladic verses, and in general a healthy tone.

Nevertheless in spite of all this and, in spite of the fact that in variety, interest in humanity, glitterings of wit, and sustained rhetoric this poem must undoubtedly be considered major and in spite of the brilliant use to which MacDiarmid puts his symbolism – externalising and internalising the thistle from one moment to another and doing the same with the moonlight (it is perhaps this he learnt from Rilke if he learnt anything) – in spite of the fact that there is a great richness in the poem, one still comes back to the earliest poems of all and one or two lyrics here and there among the later poems.

Essentially MacDiarmid is at his greatest in his lyric poems. Even the *Drunk Man* is itself a collection of lyrics to a great extent and this is proved by the manner in which MacDiarmid himself has presented the poem in his *Collected Poems*, by detached sections. In general he hasn't quite the architectural power necessary for the true long poem and it may be that this is no longer possible anyway.

It is a part of my argument therefore to say that in many of these long poems what he is in effect doing is setting up arguments and then knocking them down with others. Also they lack (these later ones) that which we look for in the greatest poetry, insights into human beings. I believe that it is in the early poems that MacDiarmid is concerned with people and their feelings and that later this disappears even when paradoxically he is claiming to be a Communist. But this is not the whole of my argument. I believe it goes deeper than this.

I believe that what happened to MacDiarmid is as follows. He began as a poet with both a masculine and feminine sensibility and eventually allowed the masculine elements in himself to dominate his work, therefore to a great extent becoming less human than he once was.

For what we find in the early MacDiarmid and miss later is a real tenderness, a real feminine love. It may be strange to say this about MacDiarmid whom one thinks of above all as masculine and a fighter. But I believe that he surrendered or lost a priceless thing when this

K

disappeared from his poetry except now and again. It is for this tenderness and for a kind of hallucinatory quality which owes little to logic or reason that I above all value MacDiarmid.

I should like to say at this point before proceeding that this idea is not new, this idea of the poet being both masculine and feminine at his best. Coleridge remarked on it when writing about Shakespeare. In our own day Robert Graves talks about it. And I believe that it is this insight gained by using both sides of his nature that makes the greatest of all poets. I would maintain that on the basis of the lyrics alone MacDiarmid must be placed very high indeed and I think that in the last analysis when the judgment of literary history has been made that it will be on this side that the scales will come down.

It might also at this point be worth mentioning the distinction Coleridge makes between the Fancy and the Imagination, when one attempts an interpretation of MacDiarmid's lyrics. Some of MacDiarmid's lyrics are fanciful in the Coleridgean sense. Another way of explaining the distinction might be by an analysis of various types of jokes. Everyone knows the kind of joke which has been built up from a single point, very often foliated in order to disguise its point of origin. Most jokes are like this, inexorably labouring to a destination through the usual three stages. However, the jokes of the Goons for instance or the Marx Brothers reveal a new dimension to reality and in this sense are truly imaginative. They seem to take a leap into a new area beyond ordinary experience. The joke itself can be brief and unfoliated but nevertheless its implications with regard to reality are immense.

I would say that an example of the fanciful lyric is the one called 'The Diseased Salmon'.

> I'm gled it's no' my face,
> But a fozie saumon turnin'
> Deid-white i' the blae bracks o' the pool,
> Hoverin' a wee and syne tint again i' the churnin'.
>
> Mony's the face'll turn,
> Like the fozie saumon I see;
> But I hope that mine'll never be ane
> And I can think o' naebody else's I'd like to be.

Here as in the inferior joke the whole point depends on the resemblance between the colour of the salmon and the death colour of a man's face. The rest of the poem is merely a foliage around this. A poem which seems to me to be on the border between the fanciful and the imaginative is the one called 'Wild Roses'.

> Wi' sae mony wild roses
> Dancin' and daffin',
> It looks as tho' a'
> The countryside's laffin'.
>
> But I maun ca' canny
> Gin I'm no' to cumber
> Sic a lichtsome warld
> Wi' my hert's auld lumber.
>
> Hoo I mind noo your face
> When I spiered for a kiss
> 'Ud gae joukin' a' airts
> And colourin' like this!

This poem is more complex than the previous one and the movement of the verse seems to suggest a greater complexity. But it is fanciful, in that the thought can be expressed in intellectual terms and the connections have a logic not far removed from that of the mind. But again this is not wholly true and this is why I said that it is on the border of the purely imaginative. When however we come to 'The Watergaw' we see that we are on a different level altogether.

> Ae weet forenicht i' the yow-trummle
> I saw yon antrin thing,
> A watergaw wi' its chitterin' licht
> Ayont the on-ding;
> An' I thocht o' the last wild look ye gied
> Afore ye deed!
>
> There was nae reek i' the laverock's hoose
> That nicht – an' nane i' mine;
> But I hae thocht o' that foolish licht
> Ever sin' syne;
> An' I think that mebbe at last I ken
> What your look meant then.

Here the whole poem is a continuous trembling analagous to the trembling on the verge of a revelation. All parts of the poem work to the one end. The poem vibrates like the rainbow. The phrase 'yow-trummle' anticipates without actually revealing the rest of the poem.

The second section of the first verse comes as an actual surprise so that one has to return to the beginning again. However no matter how often one goes over this poem one cannot understand by the reason alone how it was created or how the leap from the rainbow to the dying face was made. A kind of shock is achieved which goes beyond logic. MacDiarmid is pointing to something which he himself doesn't understand and we don't either, though at the same time we feel that the image is true and remarkable and is indicating something serious and important. It might be worth examining that single word 'wild' which MacDiarmid uses in the first verse. It seems that no other word would quite do and yet it is not intellectually clear why this should be so. One supposes it to mean 'distracted' in the sense that with the rain falling in front of it it is distracted from itself as someone's mind is often distracted by the downpours of life. But there is more to it than this. There is a kind of hint of the helplessness of the animal in that use of the word 'wild'. It is as if the being were a kind of animal dying and unable to communicate with the human being looking at it and the rain itself becomes the barrier to communication as if one were looking at the animal through a cage. And one might study the use of the word 'foolish'. Is MacDiarmid saying that there is no meaning to existence? Certainly it would be worth comparing with this poem other poems about the rainbow. One might for instance compare with it the closing lines of *The Quaker Graveyard in Nantucket* when one reads of God surviving the rainbow of his will. Again, the strictly fanciful poem by Thomas Campbell on the same subject, might show us by contrast the imaginative power of MacDiarmid's lyric.

The point is that the poem defeats the mind and yet the whole being is satisfied by it. There does seem to be a connection between the face dying and the rainbow beyond the rain. (Does the rain represent the tears of the person looking at the dying face?) The connection does not seem to be a religious one, though the rainbow of course has religious connotations. There was Noah's flood and the rainbow.

Whatever the imagination is, there is no doubt that it is what we require in poetry at the highest level. How it operates is incomprehensible. What it creates is, strictly speaking, incapable of being managed by the mind. This is true on a very slightly lesser level of 'The Bonnie Broukit Bairn'.

In this poem there are combined in a short space many of the elements which make MacDiarmid's poems distinctive – the concern with the universe and images of it, the intellectual wit, the class-distinction if one cares to call it that (the Cinderella theme in the poem). For the child is contrasted with the women in their beautiful dresses. (We might notice the hissing sound of the first two lines which might be there to reproduce the whispering and the gossip.) Then again he may be thinking that Earth is the only planet not called after a god. The daring ending is exactly right with the Scottish word 'clanjamfrie' which the women – Edinburgh women possibly? – might not know. Others of these lyrics which are roughly on this level are 'In the Hedge-Back', 'The Eemis Stane', 'O Wha's the Bride?' (from *A Drunk Man*) and above all 'Empty Vessel'. 'Trompe L'Oeil' is an example of the purely fanciful.

Along with 'The Watergaw' the 'Empty Vessel' seems to me to be on the highest level of the imagination. One points to the use of the word 'swing' – a word which one associates with children – but the mind is again defeated by this most moving poem. I have already said that in these poems there is a tenderness which the later MacDiarmid seems to have lost, surrendering himself instead to the masculine principle of reason. All these poems which I have mentioned illustrate this tenderness in some degree or another, this concern with humanity in an almost feminine way. In another of his poems MacDiarmid remarks how women will look after sick children when people like himself leave them because they are bored, and defeated by sickness. He talks of the patience of women in situations like this. There is a kind of patient looking behind these lyrics emerging later in a hallucinatory light and revealing what one can only call love. These lyrics are imaginatively in love with the universe. Whatever achievements Mac-Diarmid later made nothing comes near to the authority of these lyrics, an authority which rests only on themselves. They demand no proof and ask no questions or, if they do, they do not expect an answer. The poems themselves are answers on the imaginative level. The poems answer by music and language and the answer is love, the love which comes from tenderness and care. I know for instance of no poem like 'The Bonnie Broukit Bairn'. Here there is applied to the universe a parochial language, which seems to make it familiar and loved.

Poets of course will always undervalue poems like these because they are small but they are making a great mistake. The only authority poetry ultimately has is the imagination. If we cannot claim this power and see it now and again in action how can we defend ourselves against science? When the ideas in the poem are detachable they can be contradicted and often are. MacDiarmid can be contradicted when one discusses his *In Memoriam James Joyce*. He cannot be attacked at all on the level of these lyrics. They are the real proof of his genius. Their loss would be irreparable. The loss of much else of his work would not be.

The lyrics cannot be duplicated anywhere else in literature. In no other lyrics do I find their special combination of imaginative power, tenderness, wit, intelligence (but an intelligence which has not been divorced from the feelings). Clearly it would be difficult to sustain this achievement. However, though it is clear that it was necessary for MacDiarmid to move on, this does not prevent us saying that his lyrics are his greatest achievement. I can imagine most of his other work as being in a certain sense unnecessary, that is poetically unnecessary. The lyrics made themselves necessary. They appeared through him. The will cannot make poetry. Neither can intelligence. That is why poetry is so unfair. But then that is also why it is different from a craft.

MacDiarmid's Three Hymns to Lenin

SYDNEY GOODSIR SMITH

All Hugh MacDiarmid's three Hymns to Lenin belong to the 1930s, his most prolific poetical period. The 'First Hymn' was written for Lascelles Abercrombie's *New English Poems* (1930) and was subsequently published in *First Hymn to Lenin and Other Poems* in 1931. The 'Second Hymn' first appeared in T. S. Eliot's quarterly, *The Criterion*, in 1932, which says something for the editorial breadth of mind, and was published privately later in the same year by Valda Trevlyn from Sussex, and publicly in *Second Hymn to Lenin and Other Poems* by Stanley Nott in 1935. The 'Third Hymn', though composed during this period (*c.* 1935) in Shetland, did not see the light of day until 1955 in MacDiarmid's own quarterly, *The Voice of Scotland*, though he had quoted bits of it in his autobiography, *Lucky Poet* (Methuen, 1943). All three Hymns were eventually brought together in *Three Hymns to Lenin*, published by Castle Wynd Printers, Edinburgh, in 1957.

In almost all MacDiarmid's thought and work, two or three interrelated themes have been constant: Scottish Nationalism (which includes anti-Englishism), the literary revival of Scots and Gaelic (which was part of the general Renaissance programme) and Communism. The seeming contradiction between Communism and Nationalism is reconciled by MacDiarmid's belief that the U.S.S.R. encourages minority cultures and languages within the Soviet Union and grants autonomy with the right of secession to the smaller republics (see *Scots Independent*, August 1945). 'The Red Scotland line we advocate is in perfect keeping with the dicta of Marx, Engels, Lenin and Stalin, and with the practice of the Soviet Union in regard to minority elements. We too in Scotland must have an autonomous republic and equal freedom and facilitation for our Scots Gaelic and Scots Vernacular languages. Our minimal demand is to have Scotland on the same footing in all these respects as one of the autonomous republics of the U.S.S.R.' (*Lucky Poet*, p. 145).

Politically, this is the John Maclean line. John Maclean, first Soviet consul appointed by Lenin in Europe (his consulate was in a Glasgow

tenement), stood out for a Scottish Workers' Republic and considered
it would be a mistake for the Scottish Communists to join with their
English brethren in forming the Communist Party of Great Britain.
He believed the English movement would hold the Scots back if they
combined; that Scotland would opt for Communism long before
England would; that, in fact, England never would go Communist but
that Scotland, by achieving this in separation, would pull her English
comrades along behind her to the Promised Land.

In 1922 on Red Clydeside this was a perfectly tenable and even
feasible theory, but Maclean, jailed for sedition four times, was frust-
trated in his aims; his prophecy was realised only too accurately and
he died in 1923 a disappointed man mourned by thousands of rebellious
Glasgow workers. He became one of MacDiarmid's heroes and his
policy is still rooted deeply at the heart of the poet's thought.

> Scotland has had few men whose names
> Matter – or should matter – to intelligent people,
> But of these Maclean, next to Burns, was the greatest
> And it should be of him, with every Scotsman and Scotswoman
> To the end of time, as it was of Lenin in Russia
> When you might talk to a woman who had been
> A young girl in 1917 and find
> That the name of Stalin lit no fires,
> But when you asked her if she had seen Lenin
> Her eyes lighted up and her reply
> Was the Russian word which means
> Both beautiful and red.
> Lenin, she said, was 'krassivy, krassivy'.
> John Maclean too was 'krassivy, krassivy',
> A description no other Scot has ever deserved.

Communism as a force in British politics died the death in Hungary
in 1956, but in the 1920s and 1930s it was very much alive, just as it
was all over Europe during the German occupation; it was, as John
Maclean and Hugh MacDiarmid thought of it, the hope of down-
trodden humanity.

We are not here concerned with whether MacDiarmid was right or
wrong in his beliefs any more than, at this date, we would be concerned with whether W. B. Yeats was in his opposite beliefs. The
opinions and beliefs of a major poet (the case is often different with the
minor ones) can be of interest, eventually, only in so far as they affect

his poetry; we are not going to quarrel about them. You can still be a good Presbyterian and read and enjoy St. John of the Cross – at least, I should hope so. A Christian who cannot appreciate the pagan Parthenon or the glories of a Buddhist shrine is in sad case aesthetically, though his soul may rejoice in freedom from contamination.

Of course, this breadth of outlook, which we take for granted to some extent, is very much easier to indulge when contemplating works of the past in which, to our eyes, the issues that called them to birth have long been overlaid by those of the clamant but equally transitory present. It is sometimes not so easy to separate political from aesthetic views calmly when the subject is bang up in front of your face. We have all heard of the banning of Beethoven and Wagner from British concert halls in World War I and the sudden enormous popularity of Russian music and literature in World War II when Tolstoy's *War and Peace*, unlikely as it must seem today, sat almost permanently at the top of the Best Sellers List. When MacDiarmid and Roy Campbell conducted their public flyting they were not writing as artists altogether – if at all! That the closed mind can be a positive threat to a culture and to the production of works of the spirit (of art, in fact) is evidenced at home by the Reformation, the effects of which we have not yet thrown off after four hundred years, and abroad by the Socialist Realism creed in the U.S.S.R. The first years of the Revolution – the period that initially inspired such idealists as MacDiarmid – produced in Russia a great renaissance of poetry, music and film. Under Stalin and the imposition of political direction of the arts the inspiration dried up and even such world-famous masters as Prokofiev and Shostakovitch were on occasion banned and disciplined. Remember the history of *Lady Macbeth of Mtsensk*.

This is not to say that 'political' or didactic art must be inferior art: it can easily be shown that all ancient art is didactic. The bard educates the tribe by singing of its ancient glories in order to inspire emulation of its heroes in the present and future. Homer is didactic; Dante is didactic; Shakespeare's historical plays are didactic; Barbour and Henryson are didactic; Milton is didactic. All Christian art, indeed all religious art of any period or culture, is didactic. All royal portraiture from the Pharaohs to Queen Victoria, and even beyond, is designed to impress you with the power and glory of the ruler. This is not to say that Michelangelo's tombs of the Medici are bad art because they are directed art. In this century, much of Yeats's poetry is didactic, all Brecht's (call it *engagé* if you must), all Mayakovsky's, practically

all of Attila Jozsef's; so is a great deal of Scottish poetry, Gaelic and
Scots, ancient and modern. MacDiarmid's poetry is didactic, political,
almost all the time, and the gospels he bears witness to are those
seeming irreconcilables, Scottish Nationalism and Communism.

He has obviously been taxed with this evident inconsistency for he
sometimes takes the trouble to answer such criticism. In August 1945
he wrote in the *Scots Independent*:

> I write as a Scottish Communist. These words mean exactly
> what they say. They do not mean Russian Communist. Russia
> stands at a very different stage of development from Scotland, and
> has a very different historical background. My Russian comrades
> can get on with their own affairs. I, on the other hand, am almost
> exclusively concerned with Scotland. The application of Commun-
> ism in any country depends upon the accurate analysis of all the
> elements in its economic, political, cultural and social position
> and potentialities in the light of Dialectical Materialism. I accept
> that method of interpreting history, but I personally do not feel
> qualified to apply it myself to any country but Scotland, the only
> country of which I have the necessary first-hand knowledge and
> into whose problems and potentialities I have made the necessary
> intensive and comprehensive research.

A decade earlier, in 1936, in dealing with John Maclean's Scottish
Republican line, he wrote (as quoted in *Lucky Poet*):

> Scottish separation is part of the process of England's Imperial
> disintegration and is a help towards the ultimate triumph of the
> workers of the world. . . . As against the all-too-simple cry that the
> interests of the workers in Scotland and England are identical, we
> have no hesitation in stressing that far more exact dialectical
> discrimination must be given to the alleged consequences of the
> identity of the interests of Scottish workers and English workers,
> since this in no wise conflicts with the question of Scottish indepen-
> dence nor necessarily involves any incorporating union of the two
> peoples, whose relationships signally illustrate the fact that, as Marx,
> and subsequently Lenin, insisted: 'No nation that enslaves another
> can itself be free.' The freeing of Scotland should be a foremost
> plank in the programme of the English workers themselves – in
> their own no less than in Scotland's interests.

With the bourgeoisification of the British 'masses' and the rise of

Russia's 'imperialistic' pretensions the Workers of the World bit may sound somewhat dated today, but that is the basis of MacDiarmid's political philosophy and certainly the Nationalist part of it needs little change to adapt it to the circumstances of 1962.

If the reader is unimpressed with the poet's reconciliation of these seeming inconsistencies I would suggest that, in any event, the inconsistencies of an artist are essential to his nature – as two such different types of poet, Keats and Whitman, understood very well. Inconsistency may be a characteristic of many artists but it is also a characteristic of all Scots – dare I add all Christians and all Communists? As MacDiarmid is an artist and a Scot, a Communist and – at any rate, by birth – a Christian, how could he possibly avoid inconsistencies? It is his reconciliation of these, his exemplification of the Caledonian Antisyzygy, in fact, that makes him MacDiarmid. In the Lenin poems Communism is naturally the dominant partner – as Scottish Nationalism is in *A Drunk Man* – but even in these, with their declared theme, the other half of the marriage is implicit – either by the use of the Scots language in the First and Second Hymns or in the subject-matter, Glasgow slums, in the Third.

Aesthetically, it can be argued that the adoption of English for the 'Third Hymn' is a mistake, formally speaking. But a poet of this stature does not make such a decision idly. Why then? All his life, and even today when most of his new work appearing is in English, he has advocated for Scottish poets the use of the two ancient languages, Gaelic and Scots. Why has the man who more than anyone else, indeed almost single-handed, promoted, stimulated and contributed to the revival or renaissance of the Scottish tradition ceased to practise what he preaches? Why in the 'Hymns to Lenin' did he use Scots for the 'First' and 'Second' and English for the 'Third'? Politically speaking, the use of the Scots language is part of his Nationalist programme, part of his original aim in the 1920s to revive the whole idea and soul of the nation, using a literary renaissance as the spearhead for an entire political and cultural rebirth. Almost all his early work was in Scots, once he had announced the programme in his monthly, *The Scottish Chapbook*, late in 1922. He continued to write a certain amount of poetry in English, but the proportion, as published, was not high until about 1934 in *Stony Limits*. *Scots Unbound* of 1932, for instance, contained only four short poems in English out of the thirty-odd pages of the longish philosophical and philological flights of 'Depth and the Chthonian Image', 'Tarras' ('This Bolshevik bog! Suits me doon to the grun'!'), the virtuoso piece 'Water Music' and the title poem, which are all in Scots and mostly in a very rich, even dictionary-dredging Scots. It should be noted, however, that the mostly English *Stony Limits*, which dredged the English geological dictionary, did originally contain an important long poem in colloquial Scots, 'Ode to All Rebels', which was rejected by the publishers – for other than linguistic reasons.[1] But the other important long poem in this book, 'Lament for the Great Music', was in English; it is one of his greatest works.

In his next book, *Second Hymn to Lenin and Other Poems* of 1935, the title poem, whose actual composition dates from a year or two before this, is the only one in Scots and it is in a much more dilute Scots than the 'First Hymn' of five years back. Perhaps it is significant that the collection includes, as separate poems, many extracts from the 'Ode to All Rebels', rejected from *Stony Limits*, which in their removal have suffered a sea change and now appear in English versions. One of these is a very short piece which, as printed in the 'Ode', runs:

> Here at the heicht o' passion
> > As lovers dae
> I can only speak brokenly
> > O' trifles tae.
>
> Idiot incoherence
> > I ken fu' weel
> Is the only language
> > That wi' God can deal.

As printed in the *Second Hymn to Lenin and Other Poems*, it reads:

> Here at the height of passion
> > As lovers do
> I can only speak brokenly
> > Of trifles too.
>
> Idiot incoherence
> > I know full well
> Is the only language
> > That with God can deal.

Some people would say there was not much difference here, just one word, 'ken' for 'know', and one bad rhyme, 'well' for 'weel'; the

[1] This poem was subsequently published in its original form in *The Voice of Scotland*, vol. 4, nos. 1 and 2, in 1947, and in book form in the Castle Wynd edition of *Stony Limits and Scots Unbound* in 1955.

rest is merely pronunciation. Maybe. Poetry is not quite so simple as that, but we have no space to delve. One question is, have these poems lost anything in their translation? I would say yes, but there is no doubt they are still effective and moving in their new guise, and the thought, profound or otherwise, is naturally unaffected. But they seem to have lost something of the full charge, their totality, and an immediacy, a vigour – their virr is what I mean – that they have in Scots. Others may not agree, but it seems to me as if a little of the heart has gone and a little of the head come in – as of course it must in the mere act of translating. I must admit I liked them well in English before I knew the Scots originals. This, however, opens up an irrelevant though exciting avenue that I will not explore here, not even turn a single stone upon it, for at the moment there is the other question, why MacDiarmid turned from Scots to English in the course of the 'Three Hymns', why likewise he translated those extracts from 'Ode to All Rebels' between 1934, say, and 1935.

The 'First Hymn' (1930) and, particularly, its accompanying poems are in a fairly rich Scots, the 'Second' (1932) thinner, more city vernacular than country, and in the 'Third' (1935) Scots is dropped altogether in favour of English. In the 'Ode to All Rebels' he is still using a rich but vernacular Scots, which seems to date it before the philological *Scots Unbound* of 1932. But the English translated extracts would seem to date from 1933 or 1934 because one of them, the famous 'O, she was fu' o' lovin' fuss', is printed in the original Scots version in Macmillan's *Selected Poems* of 1934 and in English in *Second Hymn etc.* of 1935.

It is only a guess on my part, but I think possibly his later turning to English was due to a desire to speak to a more international public than he thought he could reach in Scots, and this coincided with his increasing interest, at this time, in international or communist politics. In 1926, with *A Drunk Man*, he had conquered Scotland – the Young Chevalier at Holyroodhouse – but he sought a further throne and adopted the weapon of the enemy to secure it. Having achieved this – advancing beyond Derby – by getting his English poem, 'Cornish Heroic Song', published in *The Criterion*, the ark of the English covenant, which had already published the 'Second Hymn' in Scots, his eagle eye surveys the Atlantic and even the steppes of Muscovy and the plains of China and he becomes increasingly – and, for many, bafflingly – polyglot, at least in the use of quotation.

Whether, in fact, the use of English and other lingos is better than

Scots for this international purpose is not at all certain to my mind,
though superficially it seems obvious enough. Yet Scots has always
been acceptable in America, more so than in England, and, of course,
Burns's Scots has not prevented him from travelling round the world.
It is significant that the first *Collected Poems* of MacDiarmid should
come out under an American imprint.

An interesting aspect of MacDiarmid's composition in the two
languages is that when using Scots he inclines to a strict verse form
and generally uses rhyme; when using English he inclines, not exclusively, to free, rhythmic, declamatory, rhetorical, sometimes
positively prose-like verse. This seems to me to argue that the Scots
language may release in him a vein of poetry as song – though much
of it, as the 'First Hymn', for instance, is its very opposite, that of
downright 'plain speaking' – whereas English prompts him to a
magisterial, lecture-like delivery. Naturally, there are exceptions to
this; I am thinking of the wonderful Shetland landscape, 'Island
Funeral'. With English, also, he seems to require a much larger canvas
and a longer line. Can it be that the Scots language, because richer in
sound-words, is more apt for the succinct, telling, almost proverbial
summing-up of an argument in a common, concrete, workaday phrase,
whereas literary English, being bookish and removed from the common vernacular of the street, has become increasingly abstract and
consequently feebler at the 'nutshell' phrase but more capable of
enlarging on an abstract, rather vague intellectual idea?

Compare in the 'Three Hymns', for instance, the various means
employed for the expression of comparable though not exactly similar
thoughts about the minds of poet and man of action:

From the 'First Hymn to Lenin':

> Descendant o' the unkent Bards wha made
> Sangs peerless through a' post-anonymous days
> I glimpse again in you that mightier poo'er
> Than fashes wi' the laurels and the bays
> But kens that it is shared by ilka man
>   Since time began.

From the 'Second Hymn':

> Your knowledge in your ain sphere
> Was exact and complete
> But your sphere's elementary and sune by
> As a poet maun see't. . . .

> Unremittin', relentless,
> Organised to the last degree,
> Ah, Lenin, politics is bairns' play
> To what this maun be!

From the 'Third Hymn':

On days of revolutionary turning points you literally flourished,
Became clairvoyant, foresaw the movement of classes,
And the probable zig-zags of the revolution
As if on your own palm;
Not only an analytical mind but also
A great contructive, synthesizing mind
Able to build up in thought the new reality
As it must actually come
By force of definite laws eventually. . . .
Such clairvoyance is the result
Of a profound and all-sided knowledge of life
With all its richness of colour, connections and relations
Hence the logic of your speeches . . .
As some great seaman or some poet grasps
The practical meaning, ideal beauty, traditional fascination,
Intellectual importance and emotional chances combined
In any instant in his particular situation,
So here there is a like accumulation of effects
On countless plains of significance at once, . . .

As usual with almost all works of art, the historical context of these poems is important for a just appreciation. When the 'First Hymn' was written, romantic adulation of the Russian Revolution and a kind of parlour Communism was rapidly becoming the intellectual fashion in Left Wing circles; all Nationalism was equated with Nazism and Fascism. With the outbreak of the Spanish Civil War in 1936 and the forming of the International Brigade this had become an othodoxy with very few dissidents. It was dewy-eyed, but it was innocently sincere in the warm bosoms of the younger English liberal bourgeoisie. They were anti-Imperialist and anti-Fascist and when the Imperial British government at last agreed with them and declared war on their Fascist enemy they had theoretically nothing to grumble about, but it didn't seem quite right somehow, especially as their golden boy was sitting on the fence in the Kremlin and concluding a truce with the Fascist beasts. Many became pacifists to avoid the quandary; some went to America. Then Russia became involved, perforce, and everything was all right again. Throughout all this, and ever since, MacDiarmid never budged an inch from his original two-fisted position. If he now seems to be unique and stubborn in sticking to his principles of thirty years ago, when all the rest have changed sides with the tide, we must not on that account conclude that those principles were wrong at the time he wrote those poems.

To the leftish young, before 1939, Russia appeared the great white hope of freedom. One may consider that those hopes have been belied since, as all political ideals are belied in practice – but the poetry that those ideals inspired remains in the books. Wordsworth may have deplored the results of the French Revolution but 'Bliss was it in that dawn to be alive . . . to be young was very heaven' is still expressive of the aspiring dreams of youth and liberty. Art transcends the mutability of politics. Nobody today could applaud the violence of seventeenth-century life on the borders of Scotland and England – but who does not catch his breath at the balladry that society produced? The Greek pantheon was very different from the home life of our beloved Queen, but the horrors of a remorseless heathen deity visited upon Oedipus can still excite the pity of a non-believing welfare-state audience; great art even enables a monster like Macbeth to become positively sympathetic.

I do not suggest the 'Three Hymns to Lenin' are on this level, but the idealism of the first two and the humanitarian loathing of oppression and exploitation voiced in the third are still as viable now as when they were first written in the enthusiastic climate that surrounded Lenin's name in the 1930s – whatever future revelations may show of the true face of their hero. Would you dub Yeats and Pound black fascists and ban them from the libraries?

Lenin and Bolshevism as a theme in MacDiarmid's poetry is of course by no means confined to the 'Three Hymns'. It runs through all his work, especially his work of the 1930s, alongside and together with that of Scottish Nationalism, and it produced some of his very finest poems, as 'The Seamless Garment' from *The First Hymn, etc.*, and the well-known anthology piece, 'The Skeleton of the Future' from *Stony Limits*. During this period his monumental 'Lament for the Great Music', a celebration of the MacCrimmons and other great pipers, expressed his yearning, as a Borderer, for the resurgence and unity of all Scotland through an understanding and absorption of the

Gaelic ethos into the entire soul of the nation. This desire for greater understanding within Scotland then opens out wider to embrace the whole world through Communism and the defeat of the Bankers (Social Credit), and, at length, as at the beginning in certain poems in *Sangschaw*, would comprehend the universe and all within it. From this extraordinary vision, with its faint echoes of Whitman, evolved the huge fragments of the 1930s only now [1962] achieving publication – *In Memoriam James Joyce* (Maclellan, 1955), *The Kind of Poetry I Want* (Duval, 1961) – to which he gave the grand overall title of *Mature Art*, scheduled for publication by the Obelisk Press in Paris but cancelled on the outbreak of war.

This transcendental desire, beyond the ability of man to realise but within the secret potential of every artist's private dream, he has expressed often at great length. He has also expressed the same thing very simply and shortly – and beautifully – in one of the English poems in the *Second Hymn, etc.* which gains in impact, I think, over some of the grander expressions by its element of personality and the immediacy of the last two lines that draw all together with a wonderful compassion:

O ease my spirit increasingly of the load
Of my personal limitations and the riddling differences
Between man and man with a more constant insight
Into the fundamental similarity of all activites.

And quicken me to the gloriously and terribly illuminating
Integration of the physical and the spiritual till I feel how easily
I could put my hand gently on the whole round world
As on my sweetheart's head and draw it to me.

Does it matter whether a breathing of the human spirit such as that was written by an egotistical, pigheaded, atheistical Red or by a holy imperial teetotalistical Roller?

No; political theories and political empires can change the face of the world and affect the ways of life and thought of millions of mankind – but Sappho has outlived many tyrants and Virgil many empires. Who remembers Shelley's politics and who Ozymandias? MacDiarmid's politics are the chiefest inspiration of his poetry – you can like them or lump them, but you cannot have one without the other. If you are passionate in disagreement and unable to thole his opinions for the sake of his art you are unfortunate for you are cutting yourself off from one of the poetic pleasures of our time.

L

The 'First Hymn', as I have said, is downright plain speaking:

> Christ said: 'Save ye become as bairns again.'
> Bairnly eneuch the feck o' us ha' been!
> Your work needs men; and its worst foes are juist
> The traitors wha through a' history ha' gi'en
> The dope that's gar'd the mass o' folk pay heed
>   And bide bairns indeed . . .

rising towards the end to a more exalted but still direct and simple utterance:

> For now in the flower and iron of the truth
> To you we turn; and turn in vain nae mair,
> Ilka fool has folly eneuch for sadness
> But at last we are wise and wi' laughter tear
> The veil of being, and are face to face
>   Wi' the human race.

The 'Third Hymn' is a rhetorical outburst prompted by the poet's indignation at the living hell of Glasgow slums during the great depression of the 1930s:

> Hard test, my master, for another reason.
> The whole of Russia had no Hell like this.
> There is no place in all the white man's world
> So sunk in the unspeakable abyss.
> Only a country whose chief glory is the Kirk,
> A country with our fetish of efficiency and thrift,
> With endless loving sentiment to mask the facts,
> Has such an infernal masterpiece in its gift.
>
> A horror that might sicken your stomach even,
> The peak of the capitalist system and the trough of Hell,
> Fit testimonial to our ultra-pious race,
> A people greedy, lying and unconscionable
> Beyond compare . . .

moving from this, through stages of satire and anger, to his final grand peroration:

> We do not play or keep any mere game's conventions.
> Our concern is human wholeness – the child-like spirit
> Newborn every day – not, indeed, as careless of tradition
> Nor of the lessons of the past: these it must needs inherit.

But as capable of such complete assimilation and surrender,
So all-inclusive, unfenced-off, uncategoried, sensitive and
    tender,
That growth is unconditioned and unwarped – Ah, Lenin,
Life and that more abundantly, thou Fire of Freedom,
Fire-like in your purity and heaven-seeking vehemence,
Yet the adjective must not suggest merely meteoric,
Spectacular – not the flying sparks but the intense
Glowing core of your character, your large and splendid
    stability
Made you the man you are – the live heart of all humanity!

Spirit of Lenin, light on this city now!

Light up this city now!

Admirable as this rhetoric is – and who dares nowadays to be so
unashamedly equal to a grand occasion as MacDiarmid? – it is to the
'Second Hymn' that I keep returning. As a purely personal, indeed
subjective, judgment I should say it is the most successful of the three,
if for no other reason than for its memorable, even proverbial quality
and for the homely and typically Caledonian ambivalence of the poet
towards his master. MacDiarmid may or may not be a political philosopher, but he is a true poet who can remark to the great tyrant, with
an odd mixture of arrogance and humility:

Sae here, twixt poetry and politics,
There's nae doot in the en'.
Poetry includes that and s'ud be
The greatest poo'er amang men.

It's the greatest, *in posse* at least,
That men ha'e discovered yet
Tho' nae doot they're unconscious still
O' ithers faur greater than it.

You confined yoursel' to your work
– A step at a time;
But, as the loon is in the man,
That'll be ta'en up i' the rhyme,

Ta'en up like a pool in the sands
Aince the tide rows in,
When life opens its hert and sings
Withoot scruple or sin.

Your knowledge in your ain sphere
Was exact and complete
But your sphere's elementary and sune by
As a poet maun see't . . .

. . . Freend, foe; past, present, future;
Success, failure; joy, fear;
Life, Death; and a'thing else,
For us are equal here . . .

Ah, Lenin, politics is bairns' play
To what this maun be!

MacDiarmid the Marxist Poet

DAVID CRAIG

When people speak of the 1930s as a time when poets were on the
Left, they are thinking of W. H. Auden, Cecil Day Lewis, Stephen
Spender, Louis MacNeice. Literary reputations are made (or sup-
pressed) so exclusively in London that it is too often forgotten, or
never realised, that while those others left barely one unquestionably
outstanding piece of Marxist writing, there are among Hugh Mac-
Diarmid's poems fully twenty pieces in which his Marxism or Communism found a style, an imagery and rhythm, that drew on the very
fibre of that movement. While MacSpaunday was, or were, embed-
ding the correctly ruthless and scientific imagery (pylons, aerodromes,
rifles) in an incongruous basis of the old Romantic or the new clever-
clever style, or forcing their verse to run with a jaunty popularness
that remained painfully *voulu* because it had at its heart no fellow-
feeling for the people, MacDiarmid rose to a truly Marxist intellectual
content and a truly vernacular speech-idiom.

It is surely in his poetry, and nowhere else, that his Marxism lies.
He has piled up a mass of other writing, the bulk of it polemical, but
one looks in vain amongst it for coherent Communist thinking. His
autobiography *Lucky Poet*, his biographical and literary essays, his
many editorials and introductions cannot be said to amount to a body
of thought that is capable of study. Rather it is a caddis-case of intellectual bits and pieces with a *personality* inside it, and it is the personality that dominates, not any firmly grasped material from wider life.

In the poetry, however, there is a great deal of clear, sound Marxism.
In the fine 'The Seamless Garment' (from *First Hymn to Lenin*, 1931),
he says:

> The mair we mak' natural as breathin', the mair
> Energy for ither things we'll can spare . . .

and in the 'Second Hymn to Lenin' (1932) he says, catching perfectly
the thumping vehemence of the platform speaker:

> Oh, it's nonsense, nonsense, nonsense,
> Nonsense at this time o' day

> That breid-and-butter problems
> S'ud be in ony man's way. . . .

This faith that human experience and culture will expand immensely in an era of abundance and social ownership has been an essential of Communist thinking, from Marx's *Critique of the Gotha Programme* (1875) and Engel's *Socialism: Utopian and Scientific* (1880) to Lenin's *The State and Revolution* (1918), and it appears again, with confidence that it is on the verge of realisation, in the *Programme of the Communist Party of the Soviet Union* adopted by their 22nd Congress in October 1961.

Again, when MacDiarmid says in the 'First Hymn to Lenin' (1931),

> Christ said: 'Save ye become as bairns again.'
> Bairnly eneuch the feck o' us ha' been!
> Your work needs men; and its worst foes are juist
> The traitors wha through a' history ha' gi'en
> The dope that's gar'd the mass o' folk pay heed
> And bide bairns indeed.

he directly recalls Marx's description of religion as 'the *opium* of the people' and Lenin's fine expansion of this, both humanist and thoroughly militant: 'Religion is a sort of spiritual dope in which the slaves of capital drown the image of man, their demand for a life more or less worthy of human beings.'[1] And when MacDiarmid says in the second-last stanza of the 'Hymn',

> . . . at last we are wise and wi' laughter tear
> The veil of being, and are face to face
> Wi' the human race,

he is surely putting into verse one of the deepest thoughts in Marx's *Capital*: 'The religious reflex of the real world can . . . only then finally vanish, when the practical relations of everyday life offer to man none but perfectly intelligible and reasonable relations with regard to his fellowmen and to nature. The life-process of society, which is based on the process of material production, does not strip off its mystical veil until it is treated as production by freely associated men, and is consciously regulated by them in accordance with a settled plan.'[2]

[1] Marx, Introduction to *Contribution to the Critique of Hegel's Philosophy of Right*: Marx and Engels, *On Religion*, Moscow 1957, p. 42; Lenin, 'Socialism and Religion', 1905: Moscow, 1954, p. 6.

[2] *Capital*, I, chap. 1, section 4, 'The Fetishism of Commodities'.

Those passages were written when MacDiarmid had just come to
Communism, in the first onset of the Depression, when the lines of
unemployed men stretched, I am told, from Motherwell to Wishaw.
He had been a socialist of sorts for years. Before he was 20 he had
served on a Fabian Research Committee on Land Problems and Rural
Development, contributing 'valuable memoranda' to the report published in 1913. In the 1930s he was again doing practical work for
the people, organising the cottars of Whalsay in the Shetlands to fight
in the courts against the increased assessments of their houses.[1]
W. R. Aitken's first check-list of MacDiarmid's works, in the section
on books and periodicals announced but never published, consists
mainly, for the years from 1935 to the war, of work specifically on
socialism, and there is also mention in *Lucky Poet* (p. 204) of a promised
biography of John Maclean, evidently in the mid-1930s. MacDiarmid's
work in general, like Lewis Grassic Gibbon's, takes its place as a key
part of the social movement that included the Clydeside Shop Stewards'
Movement, outstanding political leaders such as Keir Hardie, Willie
Gallacher and John Maclean, and the important contribution made by
Red Clydeside to the founding of the Communist Party of Great
Britain in 1920.

It would be misleading to draw a hard-and-fast line at the point
where one supposes his pre-Marxist poetry ends and his Marxist begins.
With one exception there is no expressed awareness of Communism
in his poetry before the 'Hymns to Lenin'. But his very coming to
Scots as the indispensable new medium for writers living and working
in Scotland contained within itself the germ of a progressive trend. In
writing his Scots lyrics in the mid-1920s, MacDiarmid was acting as a
Nationalist, as he was when he helped to found the National Party of
Scotland. In recent years, as the undeveloped countries – India, Ghana,
Kenya, Algeria, Congo, Cuba and many more – have struggled for
their independence from imperialism, we have become familiar with
the truth that nationalism is often a first stage to socialism. Mao
Tse-tung and Chiang Kai Shek could collaborate to defeat the
Japanese, but the Communists had to fight and defeat the Kuomintang
to establish socialism. Castro's rising in Cuba against native and
American economic tyranny found itself, once it had to begin construction, turning into a Marxist-Leninist revolution. Such are the
reasons why MacDiarmid's singling out of Scots, the language of a

[1] W. R. Aitken, 'C. M. Grieve/Hugh MacDiarmid': *The Bibliotheck*, vol, 1, no. 4,
Autumn 1958, p. 3; MacDiarmid, *Lucky Poet* (1943), p. 87.

small, exploited, non-imperialist nation, as the vital medium for Scotland's poetry seems to me, in a potential way, progressive.

This trend in his thinking soon found, with the fertility of genius, its own style. There is a note in MacDiarmid's poetry of 1930–35 that can be heard nowhere else, and it is the very sound of his Marxism finding its voice. It occurs, for example, along with many other *timbres*, in 'Lo! A Child is Born' – a poem long ago picked out by John Speirs as outstanding.[1] It is an allegory in nineteen lines of the birth-pangs of history, and here is its superb close:

. . . Then I thought of the whole world. Who cares for its travail
And seeks to encompass it in like loving-kindness and peace?
There is a monstrous din of the sterile who contribute nothing
To the great end in view, and the future fumbles,
A bad birth, not like the child in that gracious home
Heard in the quietness turning in its mother's womb,
A strategic mind already, seeking the best way
To present himself to life, and at last, resolved,
Springing into history quivering like a fish,
Dropping into the world like a ripe fruit in due time. –
But where is the Past to which Time, smiling through her tears
At her new-born son, can turn crying: 'I love you'?

The peak of intensity is reached in the splendid double simile of fish and fruit. Here feelings are marvellously united: the measured, nearly Bibilical gravity of the repeated participles, 'Springing . . . Dropping', allied to the richness of the images, creates a feeling both springy and solid. The momentum at this point seems both to flow onwards and yet gather itself monumentally. With the unerring touch of genius the poet has evoked sheer vitality in nature and at the same time the experience of dwelling on it with steady intellectual intent.

The lines remind me strongly of Yeats's consummate passage from 'Sailing to Byzantium':

. . . The young
In one another's arms, birds in the trees
– Those dying generations – at their song,
The salmon-falls, the mackerel-crowded seas,
Fish, flesh, or fowl, commend all summer long
Whatever is begotten, born, and dies . . .

Both poets can make us feel how even as they experience nature in its

---

[1] Speirs, *The Scots Literary Tradition* (1940), p. 187.

full teeming power, their analytic intellects permeate their responses.
But Yeats comes, deliberately, to the verge of an almost luxurious
surrender to ripeness. MacDiarmid, characteristically, has less free
flow of Romantic emotion; his impulses are subordinate to his long-
range concerns.

'Lo! A Child' is less clearly socialist than other outstanding poems
of that period; it could be just humanist. But the sense it gives of
someone looking out over the whole of humanity's historic struggle
to develop can be seen to draw directly from his Marxism. 'Strategic
mind' is clue enough: Lenin's concern with strategy – the finding and
co-operating with key trends of progress – has had a special fascination
for MacDiarmid:

> Lenin was like that wi' the workin'-class life.
>
> At hame wi't a'.
>
> His fause movements coudna' been fewer,
>
> The best weaver earth ever saw.
>
> A' he'd to dae wi' moved intact,
>
> Clean, clear and exact.
>
> On days of revolutionary turning points you literally flourished,
>
> Became clairvoyant, foresaw the movement of classes,
>
> And the probable zig-zags of revolution
>
> As if on your palm. . . .

Lenin's mastery has evidently typified for MacDiarmid a kind of
clarity he has desperately wanted since 1930.

At the very start of the 1930s he was writing his most concentrated,
serious, and distinctive poetry, and in it that note I have mentioned
can be heard time and time again. But I think it occurs first in *Penny
Wheep* (1926), in a poem adapted from the German called 'The Dead
Liebknecht'. MacDiarmid had nothing to do with revolutionary
socialism in those days. Yet here he is coming onto his deepest vein
in a poem on the German Communist leader who was murdered along
with Rosa Luxemburg during the suppression of the short-lived
revolution in Germany just after the Great War. The poem ends:

> The factory horns begin to blaw
> Thro' a' the city, blare on blare,
> The lowsin' time o' workers a',
> Like emmits skailin' everywhere.
> And wi' his white teeth shinin' yet
> The corpse lies smilin' underfit.

We bring up with a deep shock at the final image – saved from the merely creepy (the *Cabinet of Dr. Caligari* touch in German art of the 1920s) by its setting in a realistic contemporary environment. Closing on such an image makes us feel a potent force biding unshaken just under the surface of society; and this is the gist of the finest touch from 'John McLean (1879–1923)' (one of the revolutionary poems kept out of *Stony Limits* when Gollancz published it in 1934):

> . . . 'justice' may well do its filthy work
>   Behind walls as filthy as these
> And congratulate itself blindly and never know
> The prisoner takes the light with him as he goes below.

This passage is fine also in the movement of the words in that last line – falling onto the page one by one as though forced out from the poet's depths, enacting the slow steps of the sentenced man. This is also the movement of 'Another Epitaph for an Army of Mercenaries' (from *Second Hymn to Lenin*, 1935), which is surely one of the finest pieces that speak out for socialism's traditional belief in peace:

> It is a God-damned lie to say that these
> Saved, or knew, anything worth any man's pride.
> They were professional murderers and they took
> Their blood money and impious risks and died.
> In spite of all their kind some elements of worth
> With difficulty persist here and there on earth.

Who else has written with quite that dogged toughness, every phrase doing its terse bit to establish an unanswerable logic, and without the least concession to the easy-flowing or the 'beautiful'? We can feel in this verse that grips so hard on experience and measures itself out so sparingly a rare mental stamina, the quality that could sustain, as Yeats did, a complex *argument* down many long lines – but with fewer flourishes than Yeats and greater earnestness:

> Christ's cited no' by chance or juist because
> You mark the greatest turnin'-point since him. . . .
> Certes nae ither, if no' you's dune this.
> It maitters little. What you've dune's the thing,
> No' hoo't compares, corrects, or complements
> The work o' Christ that's taen owre lang to bring
> Sic a successor to keep the reference back
>   Natural to mak'.

This extraordinarily intent, intellectually concentrated vein is the perfect style for his key progressive ideas on culture:

> Gin I canna win through to the man in the street,
>> The wife by the hearth,
> A' the cleverness on earth'll no mak' up
>> For the damnable dearth.
>
> 'Haud on, haud on; what poet's dune that?
>> Is Shakespeare read,
> Or Dante or Milton or Goethe or Burns?'
>> – You heard what I said.[1]

It is also the right style for his core-idea of what he himself has had it in him to give to the progressive struggle:

> And as for me in my fricative work
>> I ken fu' weel
> Sic an integrity's what I maun hae,
>> Indivisible, real,
> Woven owre close for the point o' a pin
>> Onywhere to win in.[2]

Again the words bind together with rare density, in a way that veritably enacts their content ('the seamless garment'). And finally there is the little poem called 'The Skeleton of the Future', subtitled 'At Lenin's Tomb':

> Red granite and black diorite, with the blue
> Of the labradorite crystals gleaming like precious stones
> In the light reflected from the snow; and behind them
> The eternal lightning of Lenin's bones.

Reading this, we realise that no other British poet has *cared* enough for politics to exalt a political leader as high as that – and not through empty rhetoric: 'eternal lightning' is an image full of meaning.

These examples have almost all been militant, revolutionary-socialist. But that is not why they have picked themselves. As poetry what they have in common is that utter intentness, the whole being focussed on its object, all self-regarding feelings burned away by the intensity of concern for a large objective purpose. The most comparable thing I know in British literature is the outstanding cluster of poems by Englishmen of the Civil War period in which we can feel the gallantry of the gentleman steadied and hardened into a new gravity by the dire epoch through which his class was passing – the

---

[1] "Second Hymn to Lenin" [Ed.].   [2] "The Seamless Garment" [Ed.].

poems I mean are Marvell's 'Horatian Ode Upon Cromwell's Return
From Ireland', Shirley's 'The glories of our blood and state', and
Lestrange's 'Loyalty Confin'd'. Like MacDiarmid's poems they
typify what he himself calls, in the 'Second Hymn', 'Disinterestedness,
Oor profoundest word yet'. It is by no means his only Marxist vein:
for example, there is also a fleering radicalism, speaking out with a
verve that recalls Burns flinging at genteel society, in the poem 'Tarras'
(from *Scots Unbound*, 1932):

> This Bolshevik bog! Suits me doon to the grun'!
> For by fike and finnick the world's no' run.

But the intent and utterly serious vein does seem to be the core.

It still crops up occasionally in the 'Third Hymn to Lenin', for
example the fine stanza that opens 'What seaman in the history of the
world before'. This 'Hymn' seems to have been drafted in the middle
or later 1930s. But apart from such fragments, the vein is finished.
And nothing else takes its place. MacDiarmid's work runs out into a
vast graveyard of ideas – the 'Cornish Heroic Song' (1939), *In
Memoriam James Joyce* (1955), *The Kind of Poetry I Want* (1961) –
terrible monuments to his final failure to fulfil a text from Lenin that
he quotes twice in *Lucky Poet*: 'It would be a serious mistake to suppose
that one can become a Communist without *making one's own* the
treasures of human knowledge. . . . Communism becomes an empty
phrase, a mere façade, and the Communist a mere bluffer, if he has not
worked over in his consciousness the whole inheritance of human
knowledge' (italics mine: Speech to the 1922 Comintern Congress).

The examples necessary to back this judgment are in the nature of
the case so colossal that they would use up far more space than they
deserve. Perhaps it will be enough, and fair to the poet, if I quote the
end of 'On a Raised Beach' from *Stony Limits* – written at a time when
creative rhythms were still moving in him (the preceding section,
beginning '. . . if only one of these stones would move', is in fact very
fine and characteristic):

> Diallage of the world's debate, end of the long auxesis,
> Although no ébrillade of Pegasus can here avail,
> I prefer your enchorial characters – the futhorc of the future –
> To the hieroglyphics of all the other forms of Nature.
> Song, your apprentice encrinite, seems to sweep
> The Heavens with a last entrochal movement. . . .

Is further quotation necessary? Do the forced, limping rhythms and musty poetic-diction encourage us even to look up in a dictionary 'auxesis', 'futhorc' and the rest? The Communist poet (he joined the Party the year that volume came out) is breaking down into the sort of chaos that was diagnosed by one of the profoundest English Marxist critics, Christopher Caudwell: 'Only when the bourgeois passes to the anarchistic stage where he negates all bourgeois society and deliberately chooses words with only personal associations, can rhythm vanish, for the poet now dreads even the social bond of having instincts common with other men, and therefore chooses just those words which will have a *cerebral* peculiarity. If he chooses words with too strong an emotional association, this, coupled with the hypnosis of a strong ryhthm, will sink him into the common lair of the human instincts.'[1] Just such a revulsion from instinctual experience – a desperation to get up into the free air of pure intellect – appears in 'Harry Semen' from *Stony Limits* ('A' the sperm that's gane for naething rises up to dam / In sick-white onanism the single seed / Frae which in sheer irrelevance I cam') and in many another poem of that time.

The reasons can hardly have been purely psychological. This most poignant occurrence, the running-out of a wonderful creative flow, must make us look back at the flow itself, and if we consider Mac-Diarmid as a Communist and a Communist poet, some very odd things come to light even in the 'Hymns to Lenin'. In the 'Second Hymn' MacDiarmid confides to Lenin that 'politics is bairns' play' to what poetry must be – a claim difficult to reconcile with responsible Communism. Babette Deutsch in *This Modern Poetry* interprets 'poetry' in the 'Hymn' to mean the whole distinctively human imaginative faculty. Of course, if you stretch terms far enough you can prove anything, and if 'politics' were so treated, it could easily be made to mean the whole human social organisation, in which case to exalt 'poetry' above it, or vice versa, could lead only to the inanest metaphysical speculations. Again, in the finely outspoken lyric from the second 'Hymn', 'Oh, it's nonsense, nonsense, nonsense,' the argument runs into this:

> Sport, love, and parentage,
> Trade, politics, and law
> S'ud be nae mair to us than braith
> We hardly ken we draw.

[1] Caudwell, *Illusion and Reality* (1946 ed.), p. 125.

This simple assertion deserves a simple reply: how *could* love and parentage, vital physical-emotional links between us as human beings, ever dwindle to mere reflexes, in any conceivable stage of mankind's development?

Surely the poet here is no Marxist, no historical materialist. He is using Marxism to license an almost maniacal wish to escape from the necessities of existence as we know it. In the 'Third Hymn', dating probably from a few years later, the self-styled materialist is writing:

> . . . only one or two in every million men today
> Know that thought is reality – and thought alone! . . .

But this is the most arrant idealism – treating the mental processes that depend on material existence as somehow higher than it, more 'real'. It is what the great thinkers in the Marxist-Leninist tradition have specifically fought against time and again.[1] They have fought it because they know that idealism cannot help being accompanied by reactionary tendencies when it comes to concrete social issues. And sure enough we find MacDiarmid writing in 'Reflections in a Scottish Slum', published in the anthology *Honour'd Shade* (1959) just three years after he rejoined the Communist Party:

> . . . It is good that the voice of the indigent,
> Too long stifled, should manage
> To make itself heard.
> But I cannot consent to listen
> To nothing but that voice.

Who asked him to listen to nothing else? The Aunt Sally he is knocking down is the merest figment from the bourgeois bogey-version of socialism ('levelling-down instead of levelling-up', etc, etc). Its occurrence suggests a quake in the foundations of his Communism. He is forgetting what every socialist should have forever in his mind, the words of Gene Debs, fearless pioneer of American trade-unionism: 'While there is a lower class I am of it, while there is a criminal class I am of it, while there is a soul in prison I am not free.'

If we consider MacDiarmid's Communism as a body of opinions, the inconsistencies typical of his thinking are as crippling there as anywhere. Politically he had started as a Fabian, turning Scottish Nationalist in the mid-1920s. Although fellow-feeling with the workers has certainly been strong in him, pure nationalism has been

---

[1] E.g. Engels, *Ludwig Feuerbach and the Outcome of Classical German Philosophy* (1888); Lenin, *Materialism and Empirio-Criticism* (1908).

even stronger. He is for workers' republics. But this turns out to mean a 'Celtic Union of Socialist Soviet Republics' embracing Scotland, Ireland, Wales and Cornwall![1] How could such a fantasy (usually unsupported by any evidence regarding the economic viability or convenience of such a union – or the desire of the peoples for it) ever have been put forward seriously?

The most objective reason for this must be that MacDiarmid was a victim of the confusions that have made unity of the Left so hard to achieve in Britain for generations now. Communists are banned in many cases from participation in labour institutions such as the Trade Union Congress, the Labour Party Conference and trades councils. Nationalism, even when it refuses to commit itself to any class and economic policy for the period after its precious Independence has been won, can still attract political support. Gallacher himself had a struggle before he understood why the Scottish Communists should go in with a British Party rather than remain in puny isolation.

Perhaps the most constructive way of making the point is to put MacDiarmid's work side by side with Bertolt Brecht's, as he too is a poet with that fine 'disinterestedness' permeating the very tones of his verse. He too was a Communist, and a man formed by the Great War and its aftermath. He too can base a spare stating (rather than evoking) poetry on a straight, terse vernacular: this stanza from 'A Worker Reads History' could almost have come from the 'Second Hymn to Lenin':

> Every page a victory,
> At whose expense the victory ball?
> Every ten years a great man,
> Who paid the piper?

Brecht too can make breathtaking transitions from 'low' language to a lofty style from classic literature – very disparate manners fused together by his sense of history and his position as an intellectual aligned with the workers. The passage from MacDiarmid's *A Drunk Man Looks at the Thistle* (1926) that begins in the old ballad way 'O wha's the bride that cairries the bunch / O' thistles blinterin' white' and works up through proverb-like couplets, coarse colloquial asides and gnomic folk-rhymes to the sardonically desperate 'song',

> O Scotland is
> THE barren fig –

[1] See for example *Lucky Poet*, p. 26; *Francis George Scott* (1955), p. 37 – here Ireland for some reason has been dropped.

this passage has many a counterpart in Brecht: the entire *Threepenny Opera*, for example, or (in a condensed way) the extraordinarily poignant 'Nanna's song' from *Round Heads and Pointed Heads* that gets its effect by modulating from jaunty folk-song to flat speech, mocking cliché and traditional refrain:

> And, though you may learn your trade well,
> Learn it at Lechery Fair,
> Bartering lust for small change
> Is a hard thing to do.
> Well, it comes to you.
> But you don't grow younger there.
> (After all you can't stay seventeen forever.)
> Thank God it's all over with quickly,
> All the love and the grief we must bear.
> Where are the tears of yester evening?
> Where are the snows of yester year?

But differences are equally marked. MacDiarmid wanted his poems to be 'spoken in the factories and fields'. Brecht's *were* sung in the Army, on United Front marches, in the workers' theatres. Brecht can bring poetry to the verge of prose – factual, barely rhythmical – but it never sounds like broken-down verse, it does not run out of control into delirious verbosity. 'The Rug-weavers of Kajan-Bulak Honour Lenin', for example,[1] could be 'prose'. But it is so controlled by its intentness on realisable social needs that it becomes a finished, lucid fifty lines such as we fail to find in any section whatsoever of Mac-Diarmid's *colossi*. Brecht could in fact dare to break up the poetic forms because he never lost his creative rhythm – the forms were not crumbling helplessly in his hands.

No doubt temperament plays its part in the difference, but full weight must be given also to the political situations of the two men. Brecht was forced to a deadly point of responsibility and a pitch of urgency by the most savage of all reactionary antagonists – German Fascism. The duties of a Communist poet could hardly have been clearer than in such a society. By contrast it is perhaps small wonder that MacDiarmid's gifts should have been allowed to splairge all over the place in the un-urgent, fumbling, amateurish *milieu* of Scottish Nationalism.

At the time when MacDiarmid's poetry was coming to grief, he

---

[1] All the Brecht examples come from his *Selected Poems*, trans. H. R. Hays (New York, 1959), pp. 109, 87, 135–7.

was obliged to leave the Communist Party because he had pursued narrow nationalist ends incompatible with the main purposes of the workers' movement. But there has also been continuity in his position. In the article he wrote for the *Daily Worker* of March 28, 1957, on 'Why I Rejoined', he used points that he had first made in the 'First Hymn to Lenin' of 1930: 'Even if the figures of the enemies of Communism were accurate, the killings, starvings, frame-ups, unjust judgments and all the rest of it are a mere bagatelle to the utterly mercenary and unjustifiable wars, the ruthless exploitation, the preventable deaths due to slums, and other damnable consequences of the profit motive, which must be laid to the account of the so-called "free nations of the West".'

So his convictions and the creative work that has depended so much on them have gone in and out, now clear, now muddied, often losing themselves, often failing to achieve wholeness. Setting that vein of rare intentness from the early 1930s in the perspective of his life's work, we can see that it was too much an evocation of only the *attitude* of seriousness and militancy. The subject-matter from social experience that should have been dealt with in the light of these attitudes never really appeared. The poems singled out in this essay are like a foretaste of what a masterly progressive poet might achieve – but the substantial doing of it never materialises. Yet even to have evoked the idea of such a poetry, to have brought it to the verge of realisation, is an achievement outstanding and unique (for obvious reasons) in the literature of the English-speaking world.

Hugh MacDiarmid and Gaelic Literature

DOUGLAS SEALY

For what mess of pottage, what Southern filth,
What lack of intricacy, fineness, impossible achievement,
Have we bartered this birthright, for what hurdy-gurdy
Exchanged this incomparable instrument?

An insistence on the study and restoration of Gaelic has always been one of the planks in MacDiarmid's platform. A knowledge of Gaelic was not only desirable but also necessary for the complete exploration of Scotland and for the understanding of its history. Scots, MacDiarmid has claimed, included English and even went beyond it; but Gaelic, so far from including English might almost be said to ignore it, and the elements of the Scottish psyche which are expressed in it are therefore the least likely to be contaminated by what MacDiarmid has called 'the wandering abscess of the English influence'.

Although Gaelic is not English, it might be wiser to regard it as contributory to the Scottish psyche rather than as the essence of it, for as T. F. O'Rahilly wrote in *Irish Dialects Past and Present* (1932), 'To the Gaelic-speaking Scotsman of the past Ireland was the mother-country, whose culture and whose traditions belonged no less to himself than to his kinsmen in Ireland'. Scottish Gaelic did not become independent till the middle of the eighteenth century and it was greatly influenced by the numerous Norse settlers, as can readily be seen in many place-names.

There were other reasons for MacDiarmid's interest in Gaelic. He was attracted by the recognised position of the poet in Gaelic society and by the fact that he had to undergo a stringent training in the details of his craft. A poet was a poet and a carpenter was a carpenter; there were no part-time poets, Sunday painters or do-it-yourself kits; there were only professionals. And MacDiarmid is fond of quoting from Henri Hubert's *Les Celtes*: 'Celtic literature was essentially a poetic literature. . . . We must not think of Celtic poetry as lyrical outpourings, but as elaborately ingenious exercises on the part of rather pedantic literary men. Yet Celtic literature was popular as no other was.' The first two statements are correct but the implications of 'popular as no other was' are completely misleading. To quote O'Rahilly again: 'Down to the seventeenth century our Irish writers, in so far as their writings have survived, belonged exclusively to the upper classes. . . . The poets of the schools rigidly retained to the last not only an archaic diction but also an old pronunciation. . . . In more than one Irish tale a king, before whom a poet has recited verses, is made to exclaim: "An excellent poem, only I do not understand a word of it." ' In a story about the seventh-century king Guaire we read of a poet reciting a poem in poetical jargon and then explaining it to the king before receiving his reward. And David Greene in *Seven Centuries of Irish Learning* (ed. Ó Cuív) writes on these poets or professional panegyrists: 'Their weakness was that they were, by the very nature of their calling, the paid propagandists of the existing order of things . . . When that order vanished, they vanished with it. They had no interest in the common people. . . . They made the Irish language a better literary medium than it had ever been before, while at the same time denying it all possibility of intellectual development.' There were occasional poems and poets of great talent, but the picture drawn by David Greene gives a correct overall impression. After the collapse of the Gaelic aristocracy the syllabic verse of the schools gave way to the accentual verse of the people, which had arisen from some of the older Irish metres under the influence of the French song metres of the Anglo-Norman settlers, and reached the peak of its technical development six senturies later with the poets of the Munster school, whose work has been ably championed and described by Daniel Corkery in *The Hidden Ireland*.

This book is another source book for MacDiarmid's ideas of Gaelic literature – 'he tells,' writes MacDiarmid, 'how men labouring in the fields all day entered again at night into full possession of the high Bardic tradition and rejoiced in complex literary allusiveness and intricate rules of versification.' In other words they were a literary élite and Corkery does not forget to tell us that there were other anonymous poets, living side by side with them, who wrote a very different kind of verse with simpler metres and a more frank and passionate message, and who neglected the tales of Troy or of Deirdre for themes of local relevance, where love and death and sorrow gained no added lustre from references to the past. It is this anonymous poetry that is one of the glories of our literature. So much of the more sophisticated poetry is spoilt by an excess of ornament, by long strings of alliterative adjectives, matter being so often subordinated to form, that while one can admire this poetry as a literary *tour de force* one must withhold the highest praise. This poetry loses everything when it is translated, not so the Amhráin na nDaoine or Songs of the People, as the anonymous songs are called.

> Do you remember going to Mass that day?
> A thin needle would not have gone between us.
> Now this year a man with a horse could go
> Or a ship in sail on a day of violence and storm.

The force of that is apparent even in prose translation.

It is by force and simplicity that many of the poems in Robert Conquest's collection of verse from the Soviet bloc, *Back to Life*, make their point. The Polish poet, Adam Wazyk, says of his own 'Poem for Adults'.

> This is a naked poem
> before it is clothed
> with vexations, colours and the smells of this earth.

The aim is to shed all irrelevance, all merely decorative detail. If there is ever to be again a popular poetry it will have to be like this, a 'naked' poetry. Irish songs are full of this nakedness, so are the Spanish Cantes Flamencos:

> The two of us in a little room
> If you were to give me poison
> I would take poison

and in Willard R. Trask's collection *The Unwritten Song: Poetry of the Primitive and Traditional Peoples of the World* one finds this nakedness continually, just as one finds it in the anonymous or obscurely authored Scottish Gaelic songs of the sixteenth, seventeenth and eighteenth centuries. Sorley MacLean in *Scottish Art and Letters*, *3* (1947) compares them with the Border Ballads and says that 'in the Gaelic anonyms there is far more of the variety of life realised on a high level, and though there is often in them the same bare concentration, there is often a rich texture of imagery, and always the Gaelic music and finish which prevents them from being so unequal as the Ballads'. Although MacDiarmid would probably not care to write such poetry himself, as he has never retreated from the attitude expressed in 1926: 'The highest art at any time can only be appreciated by an infinitesimal minority of the people – if by any' (*Selected Essays*, p. 44), it seems to be something of this nature that he had in mind when he referred to 'a "bareness and coolness of expression" as in the Sagas, or the hardness of the ancient Gaelic classics – the literature of men conscious of their own reality as well as that of outer reality, because fully conscious of the society which makes them what they are' (*Islands of Scotland*, p. 27). It is certainly what Norman MacCaig means when he speaks of his own 'attempt to achieve the simple and direct, but highly charged statements which seem to me the greatest achievement of Gaelic, as of other poetry'. Could we take as a further example the words of Vergil?

> Venit summa dies et ineluctabile tempus
> Dardaniae. Fuimus Troes. Fuit Ilium et ingens
> Gloria Teucrorum.

Nevertheless, it is not so much these anonymous authors that MacDiarmid admires but the two great names of the eighteenth century, Alexander MacDonald and Duncan MacInyre, for he has translated, with the assistance of Sorley MacLean, the major poem of each and written a poem to each of these poets as well. His translation of MacDonald's 'Birlinn of Clanranald' is vigorous and probably gives as good an impression of the original as English could. The original describes, in Douglas Young's words, 'the voyage of a chief's galley across the Minch as if it were going from Heaven to Hell and back' and it does so with resource and energy, though to my mind eighteenth-century Scottish Gaelic poetry suffers from the same defects as eighteenth-century Irish poetry, though to a lesser extent; the Scottish Gaelic poems are much more alive and popular in the sense alluded to above. I suspect that what MacDiarmid admires is more the man than the poetry, for as he says in *In Memoriam James Joyce*:

> . . . the authors I love best are they
> Who have lived, knocked about in the world,
> Had a thousand adventures of every sort,
> And penetrated every kind of milieu,
> Feeling, watching, taking stock the whole time;
> Men for whom writing was first and above all
> A pleasure, men who, when they sat down to write,
> Had merely to let their pens run freely,
> So great was the pressure of memory
> And the weight of the thousand living images
> That dwelt with them.

MacDonald is said to have entered the pulpit of the Parish Church of Islandfinnan on a certain Sunday in 1745 to utter propaganda for the Jacobite cause, at one point removing his coat and displaying underneath it a tartan plaid, while he recited the couplet:

> Sìos an clò dubh,
> Suas am breacan!

He fought as a Captain in the Prince's Army and after the battle of Culloden took refuge with his wife in the wilds of Glencoe, where he remained till the passing of the Indemnity Act. MacDiarmid's exhilarating poem to MacDonald, 'To Alasdair Mac Mhaighstir Alasdair', ignores MacDonald's personal history and instead uses MacDonald and his poetry as a pretext for a description of all that a poet should be. MacDonald joins the other figures in the MacDiarmid pantheon, Lenin, Doughty, F. G. Scott, Korzybski, to name a few, and is seen as an apotheosis of MacDiarmid himself:

> Jaupin the stars, or thrawin lang strings
>   O' duileasg owre the sun
> Till like a jeelyfish it swings
>   In deeps rewon,
> And in your brain as in God's ain
>   A'thing's ane again.

The translation of MacIntyre's 'Praise of Ben Dorain' is less successful. MacDiarmid doesn't attempt to represent the original metric scheme and frequently uses far more words than necessary. It is interesting to compare MacDiarmid's version with some others.

> I
>
> I the band am admiring
>   Defiling in order,
> And with noise retiring
>   Up the Strone's rocky border;
> 'Twixt Craobh-ainnis they tarry
> And the mouth of Strong Corrie
> A fed and horned quarry
>   That buy not their portion . . .
>
> (trans. George Calder, 1912)

2

Graceful to see to me was a group
Lined up in the order of march to troop
Down by the Sron rock south through the loop
'Twixt Craobh na h-ainnis moor and the scoop
Of Corrie-dhaingean; no goog* on that herd,   * unfledged bird
And none with a staring hide covered,
That for bite and sup never begged or chaffered
Nor yet lacked though to that they'd not stoop.
That was the fine line to be watching oop
The seen parts of a path between noop and noop.

(trans. MacDiarmid, 1940)

3

That troupe was beloved
assembling in order –
ascending, bright hooved,
each cliff that's in nature.

Between the Poor Pastures
and the Corrie of Fastness –
not buying repast there
but eating it freely.

(trans. Iain Crichton Smith, *Akros*, 1969)

A prose rendering might run as follows: 'I thought the band was beautiful as it advanced in order, noisily ascending the rock of Srone; between the moorland of Craobh na h-ainnis and the mouth of Coire-daingean, it was a well-fed high-headed herd that doesn't buy its portion.' It is impossible to convey in English the music and elegance of the original, and MacDiarmid's translation is at its best when he forgets his original and writes:

Volatile, vigilant there
One with the horizon she goes
Where horizons horizons disclose,
Or lies like a star hidden away
By the broad light of day.
Earth has nothing to match her.

This is more reminiscent of the early MacDiarmid of 'A Herd of Does' than of MacIntyre. Although MacIntyre's poetry is perhaps finer than MacDonald's – Sorley MacLean says MacDonald 'realises dynamic

nature with a vigour immediacy and exactness which would appear to
me unrivalled if I could forget the delicacy which MacIntyre adds and
which make the latter's poetry the very greatest of eighteenth-century
Gaelic Nature poetry' – MacDiarmid is less in sympathy with the
gentle simple deerstalker. 'How difficult to make out such a genius as
yours,' he says in his poem to MacIntyre, which displays a learning
that would have bewildered the unlettered Highlandman, but he does
pay real tribute at the end of the poem in a moving passage describing
deer browsing on twigs above the watchers:

> . . . only in *your* poetry can we feel we stand
> Some snowy November evening under the birch-trees
> By a tributary burn that flows
> Into the remote and lovely Dundonnell river
> And receive the most intimate, most initiating experience. . . .

MacDiarmid's translations from Gaelic are competent but not in the
same class as his translations from twentieth-century continental poets.
His method is to work over translations by other hands ('creative
transcription' to use the words of K. S. Sorabji) and it is interesting to
note in this context that a passage in the very fine translation from
Rilke to be found in *To Circumjack Cencrastus* is given a lift by the use
of the Gaelic word *caoin* (Anglicé 'keen').

> Surely the keening women should have keened
> In truth – women who weep for pay and whine
> The whole night through if they are paid enough,
> When there's no other sound.

> Ob man nicht dennoch hätte Klagefrauen
> auftreiben müssen? Weiber, welche weinen
> für Geld, und die man so bezahlen kann,
> dass sie die Nacht durch heulen, wenn es still wird.

No English word could have translated Klage as well as the Gaelic has
done.

MacDiarmid, busy with poetry and politics, not to mention the task
of survival, cannot have had much time to spare for the study of
Gaelic and had to rely to a large extent on the writings of others in his
efforts to keep the Gaelic tradition before Scotland's eye. For instance
the requirements he postulates for Gaelic poetry:

Cruadal (hardihood), gaisge (valour) and that sentiment
For which English has no name, but which
In Greek is αἰδώς and in Gaelic nàire . . .

are quoted verbatim from W. J. Watson's Bardachd Ghaidhlig and the
passages dealing with Gaelic literature in *To Circumjack Cencrastus*
are based on a reading of Aodh De Blácam's *Gaelic Literature Surveyed*.
This is an excellent book but definitely propagandist, and it would
not be wise to accept all its literary estimates, but this is what Mac-
Diarmid has done and in an otherwise fine passage where the Gaelic
poets are likened to peaks rising from the mist:

> The great poets of Gaelic Ireland
> Soared up frae the rags and tatters
> O' the muckle grey mist o' Englishry –

he then proceeds to list the poets – 'Raifteri, Ó Rathaille, Ó Súillea-
bháin, Feiriter, Haicéad and Céitinn.' Whatever about the others,
Raifteri was no peak, at best he was a pleasant enough foothill.
MacDiarmid was on safer ground when he merely borrowed or adapted
quotations from the Irish poets, out of De Blácam's book, as in *To
Circumjack Cencrastus*, and also in 'Lament for the Great Music' in
Stony Limits, where there are at least a dozen citations from *Gaelic
Literature Surveyed*. The Great Music is of course the classical music
of the Great Highland Bagpipe, dating from around 1600, an extraordinary and unique survival of a sophisticated art from the mediaeval
Gaelic world, with its own scale or scales, its own concept of melody
as an intricate pattern of conventional motifs, its own rhythms and a
mysterious appeal which no amount of theorizing or analysis has been
able to explain away. The art of pìobaireachd lies on the very edge of
improvisation and must still be handed down from piper to piper, for
the written scores are unable to convey the subtleties of timing that
make the pìobaireachd live. Its affinities would seem to be with the
East rather than the West and there is a possibility that it may have
taken over the classical music of the Gaelic harp. Here indeed was a
link between Gaeldom and the modern world and MacDiarmid has
made good use of it in the Lament.

In his efforts to discover the lost history underlying the present state
of Scotland MacDiarmid has frequently mentioned Waddell's *Edda* and
The Chronicles of Eri edited by L. Albert, with an essay establishing
their historical veracity. Among the proofs of the authenticity of the

Chronicles offered us we are shown a portrait of the author, Roger O'Connor, a sturdy rubicund gentleman, and asked could the owner of such an honest face be guilty of fraud! MacDiarmid cannot have seen the original edition of the Chronicles, published in 1822 which contains a facsimile of a page from the 'original manuscript in the Phoenician dialect of the Scythian language'. This page shows some gibberish of a vaguely Irish character, written in Irish script, and could only have been concocted by O'Connor. Albert tells us that there are similarities between O'Connor's history and the old Irish manuscripts that describe the wanderings of the Gael before they reached Ireland, the 'faked and distorted versions of the Leinster or Tara records' as Albert calls them. But these old Irish manuscripts are as much a fabrication as the Chronicles, and are finally based on the Old Testament. (See R. A. S. MacAlister's *Lebor Gabála Érenn*, Vol. 1.) As M. A. O'Brien writes in *Early Irish Society*, ed. Myles Dillon, 1954; 'Some time after 431 Irish learned men became acquainted with world history from scriptural and classical sources. They must have been amazed at the silence of these works about their own country, and so, fired, no doubt, by an abundant patriotism they set about reconstructing the pre-Christian history of Ireland.' MacDiarmid was not the only one to be taken in by Roger O'Connor and L. Albert for in 1940, four years after Albert's edition, a book appeared about the Chronicles by R. Perry, a British Israelite, who found in the Chronicles support for the wildest of theories. Reviewing Perry's book in *Irish Historical Studies* MacAlister described the Chronicles, accurately, as 'actually an amalgam of bombastic paraphrases of Irish annalistic matter, irreverent parodies of Biblical excerpts, 'etymologies' (which have to be seen to be believed) and wildly irresponsible inventions resembling those in the closely analagous book of Mormon . . .' If the Chronicles had inspired MacDiarmid to write some poems all might have been well, but 'The Fingers of Baal Contract in the Communist Salute', to be found in the little pamphlet *Poems of the East West Synthesis* is among the contenders for the place of MacDiarmid's worst verse.

The British Edda, by L. A. Waddell, author of many books including *The Phoenician Origin of the Britons*, is a translation from the Icelandic of the Elder Edda which purports to show, by real or imagined resemblances between proper names, and by illustrations taken from ancient Sumerian seals, that the gods of Scandinavian mythology were originally human beings who lived in the Euphrates basin around 3380–3350 B.C. and that Adam, Thor, Dardanos first king of

Troy, Midas, St. George, the Indian god Indara, King Arthur and others were originally the same man. The whole concept seems on a par with proving by cryptograms that Queen Victoria wrote 'In Memoriam', and as for the Sumerian seals they could be used to illustrate many different kinds of books – here is the text accompanying the seal on page 82: 'We then find in the Edda that Eve as Freyia or "The Friend"is installed at home with Adam-Thor as Queen of the Goths, and holding receptions in a garden saloon [sic] in which we gain a glimpse of her happy, gracious, social life.' However *The British Edda* supplied MacDiarmid with one poem 'The Pot Hat or The Ballad of the Holy Grail', which is an adaptation of Scene XXIII: compare MacDiarmid's

> It sat at the feet of the witches
> Mair lurid than the nails on the toes
> O' yon nether maimers squat in their mess
> When he dirled it frae under their nose.

with Waddell's

> This titbit of Gull, Ullar (Cain) loos'd
> In the teeth of the three tied witches,
> Those nether maimers amid their mess,
> And he dirled out the beaker (afore) their nose.

It also supplied the title of the poem 'Larking Dallier' and a metaphor in 'Vestigia Nulla Retrorsum' – 'the sink of swords'.

These books have little to do with Gaelic Literature, but MacDiarmid is not a scholar, he is a poet; he intuits first and reasons afterwards. He imaginatively grasps the need for a renaissance of Gaelic and in order to present a case the world is then ransacked for supporting materials, not all chosen with equal care. It is important when one is reading MacDiarmid to separate what is of value from the merely silly, so let us return to the 'Lament for the Great Music', which MacDiarmid calls a key poem in his concern with Scottish Gaelic and his effort to bring out an underlying unity of the Scots and Gaelic elements of Scotland. He writes,

> . . . I know the root I am gripping in the darkness here
> Is the unstruck note that gives all the others scope,
> That deepest root from which even Freedom can unfold.

The important thing here is to notice that MacDiarmid is not seeking primarily or at all for a linguistic change. 'Freedom' means a Scotland

> 'where the supreme values
> Which the people recognise are states of mind,
> Their ruling passion the attainment of higher consciousness.

The Celts, as he tells us in 'Credo for a Celtic Poet' (*Agenda*, Winter 1967) 'never fell into that cardinal blunder of mistaking means for ends' and for MacDiarmid language itself, whether Gaelic, English, or Scots is only a means towards some end which he has adumbrated variously in political terms as Red Scotland and Pan Celticism, though these in turn are means towards 'higher consciousness'. MacDiarmid's earliest poems in *Northern Numbers* and *Annals of the Five Senses* showed nothing particularly Scottish, but since then his work has been so inextricably interwoven with the Scottish Scene that any dereliction of his country cannot but affect his verse. Ibsen felt bitter about Norway's betrayal of the Danes in 1864 and it is lines from Ibsen's *Brand*, written in 1865, that MacDiarmid goes on to quote in the 'Lament'.

> I too who have never become eingebürgert elsewhere
> Feel changed in Scotland, grown strange to myself,
> And waken to its realities as baffled Samson woke
> Shorn and tethered. 'My native land should be to me
> As a root to a tree. If a man's labour fills no want there
> His deeds are doomed and his music mute.'

This is not chauvinism. It is the faith of Joan of Arc, who would not look behind to see if anyone was following her. MacDiarmid is the piper who pipes himself and the troops 'through battle and into daith'; he is not the cook or the engineer or the ambulance driver. Despite the elegiac note of the 'Lament' his work does not look back, it looks forward, though in full consciousness of the past and all its traditions: he has brought science and technology into his poetry as an ingredient and not just as an exotic decoration. So his message for the Gaels is that they must bring their language up to date, they must catch up with 'machineries o' expression like the English, French or German'. It is a measure of the distance yet to go that when MacDiarmid wishes to make an important quotation he does not turn to Gaelic.

In Memoriam James Joyce, that cento of passages from other authors, contains less than a dozen references to Gaelic literature (mostly only a word or two, whereas there is a page on Racine, and there are five pages on Karl Kraus, borrowed from the *Times Literary Supplement*. It is plain that whatever sources MacDiarmid had at hand did not refer to Gaelic literature, and that his own background could not furnish the gap. In his poem 'A Golden Wine in the Gaidhealtacht' he admits, by implication, his ignorance of Gaelic:

> In Scotland, in the Gaidhealtacht there's a golden wine
> Still to be found in a few houses here and there
> Where the secret of its making has been kept for centuries
> *– Nor would it avail to steal the secret, since it cannot be*
>   *made elsewhere.*

The long poem 'Island Funeral' does not refer to Gaelic language or literature at all. Ostensibly about the Hebrides, 'our Gaelic islands', it is an amalgam of a description of the Aran islands in Ireland (limestone rock, currachs, black shawls, crimson skirts, rawhide shoes), a description of certain isolated communities and their carpentry, and a critique of a cornet player in a jazzband. These disparate elements have been worked together to make a poem which is in effect an extension of the 'lament'. We are to understand that there has been at times in the past a 'Gaelic dynamic' which if it could be revived would lead to the MacDiarmid Utopia.

References to this 'Gaelic dynamic' run through MacDiarmid's work, but it is hard to build up a picture of exactly what he means. He quotes a review of Bringmann's *Geshichte Irlands* (1939): 'Gaeldom was moving towards – and but for the English would have realised – a real people's state', and also 'Irish must and will become once more the living language of Ireland'. It is likely that Bringmann had been influenced by a reading of the historians of the early 1900s. So was James Connolly, who believed that in Ancient Ireland there was communal ownership of land and equality and democracy, and that therefore the Gaelic Revival and Socialism should go hand in hand. These ideas are briefly touched upon in Connolly's *Labour in Irish History*, which he opens by praising Mrs. Stopford Green's *The Making of Ireland and its Undoing* (1908). Mrs. Green does say, on page 107: 'The propertied classes (i.e. the English) evidently feared the Irish land system as expressing what might be called the Socialism of the time. We may see their instinctive antipathy in the crude accounts they give of Irish customs. "They of the wild Irish as unreasonable beasts lived without any knowledge of God or good

manners, in common of their goods, cattle, women, children, and
every other thing. . . ." ' This hardly proves that the ancient Irish
were Socialists, but Connolly, and Bringmann, and MacDiarmid, were
too ready to believe, on too little evidence, what they wanted to believe.
It is also necessary to point out that the connotations of the German
'Volksstaat' and the English 'people's state' are not the same. In the
second edition of Bringmann's history (1953) he has dropped the
reference to Gaeldom moving towards a people's state. This curious
book moves from 300 B.C. to A.D. 1921 in 37 pages and the remaining
98 pages are devoted to the period from 1921 to 1952, and the hero
of the book is not the 'Volk' but De Valera, 'ihr Führer'.

MacDiarmid refers us to a book called *The Gaelic Commonwealth*
by Father William Ferris (Dublin, 1923). Ferris regards the Catholic
Church as the model for the Commonwealth. 'The statecraft of the
Gaelic Commonwealth and of the Catholic Church, by their strong
points of resemblance, mutually support each other in a most extraordinary manner. The sole difference between them is that in the
Catholic Church all power comes from the Pope, as Vicar of Christ,
whereas in the Gaelic State all power comes from the people. The
religious power coming from above and the secular power coming
from below dovetail into each other, as it were, and together produce
the nearest approach to Utopia ever likely to be realised on this earth.'
Ferris will have nothing to do with parliamentary rule, regards
Socialism as 'this delirium and dotage of democracy', and wants a
High King. Though Ferris wishes to abolish Rent, Wages, Usury and
all forms of exploitation, his Commonwealth is hardly what Mac-
Diarmid had in mind when he wrote, 'Only in Gaeldom can there be
the necessary counter idea to the Russian idea. The dictatorship of the
proletariat is confronted by the Gaelic Commonwealth with its aristocratic culture, the high place it gave to its scholars and poets', etc.

Recent historians have painted a less rosy and more plausible
picture of Irish society in early times. Ancient Irish society was,
according to D. A. Binchy (*Early Irish Society*, ed. Myles Dillon, 1954)
'tribal, rural, hierarchical . . . and the family, not the individual was
the unit,' and in the grades of society 'the real distinction was between
those of gentle birth, those whose family tree was preserved among the
genealogies, and the commoner or churl'. The poets, men of art, men
whose skill gave them a status beyond that due to their birth, belonged
to a caste intercalated between the two grades, and 'in that aristocratic
and rural society it was quite possible, owing to the system of patron-

age, to produce great literature and great art'. That society was 'a complete contrast to the unitary, urbanised, egalitarian and individualist society of our time', and 'the inequality of man . . . had been erected into a legal principle. . . . Most men were free – the number of slaves seems to have been comparatively small – but they were certainly not equal.'

MacDiarmid's acquaintance with Gaelic Literature and History is superficial, his readiness to believe in the bizarre surprising. Does this matter? He himself thinks not for he writes in his essay, 'The Caledonian Antisyzygy and the Gaelic Idea': 'It does not matter a rap whether the whole conception of this Gaelic Idea is as far-fetched as Dostoevsky's Russian Idea . . . The point is that Dostoevsky's was a great creative idea – a dynamic myth – and in no way devalued by the difference of the actual happenings in Russia from any Dostoevsky dreamed or desired. . . . It would not matter so far as positing it is concerned whether there had never been any Gaelic language or literature, not to mention clans and tartans, at all. It is an intellectual conception . . . It calls us to a redefinition and extension of our national principle of freedom on the plane of world affairs, and in an abandonment alike of our monstrous neglect and ignorance of Gaelic and of the barren conservatism and loss of the creative spirit on the part of those professedly Gaelic and concerned with its maintenance and development.'

The 'Gaelic Idea' is as much an aberration as Yeats' 'A Vision', or Graves' 'White Goddess', the defects of their ideas inextricably associated with their qualities as authors. The spirits gave Yeats metaphors for his poetry and perhaps the ancestors of the Clann Diarmaid have had an incalculable effect on Christopher Murray Grieve. MacDiarmid has shown the way, the onus is on the reader to read the classical Gaelic poets and for that the Gaelic language is a *sine qua non*. The old living patterns of the Gael are 'curjute and devauld' and disappeared with the social structures that gave birth to them. Only by retaining the Gaelic language – since every language of its own nature determines what can be said in it, can we be sure of cultivating the soil from which alone a Gaelic 'dynamic' or 'idea' could spring, without necessarily knowing or foreseeing what shape it might take. The men of the Irish Revival knew this and made their slogans 'Tír gan teanga, tír gan anam' (A country without its own language is a country without a soul) and 'Beatha teanga í a labhairt' (A language lives when it is spoken). Saunders Lewis in Wales has said that the Welsh tongue is more important than even the independence of his country. Only by speaking and reading Gaelic can we discover the truth of MacDiarmid's contentions.

> Today the spiritual values of Gaelic civilization have not dissolved.
> They have, however, shifted. They no longer form one
> With the flesh of human substance. We can still
> Attain to every one of the subtlest goods in Gaelic culture,
> But only mentally, analytically, or rationally. We must return
> To the ancient classical Gaelic poets. For in them
> The inestimable treasure is wholly in contact
> With the immense surface of the unconscious. That is how
> They can be of service to us now – that is how
> They were never more important than they are today . . .

> Le moment semble venu d'une résurrection de l'humain.

It is quite possible that the above impressive passage originally referred to something else and that MacDiarmid borrowed the passage and substituted the word Gaelic for whatever term was in the original, thus doing something 'similar to what is done when a green light on a railway replaces a red light, or vice versa, in a given lamp.' For as early as *Annals of the Fives Senses* (1923) he wrote that 'these perhaps strange fish of mine are discernible almost entirely through "a strong solution of books" – and not only of books but of magazines and newspaper articles and even of speeches', thus anticipating Thomas Mann who wrote in *The Genesis of a Novel* of 'my own growing inclination, which I discovered was not mine alone, to look upon all life as a cultural product taking the form of mythic cliché, and to prefer quotation to independent invention'. At different times in the past there have been men who possessed the qualities admired by MacDiarmid, and in the future such men would be found again, indeed if all went well, far more men of such a kind would exist. The men of genius we now have are the inheritors, the preservers and the carriers on of the proud tradition. The Gaelic world, and its pipe music in particular, were eminently suitable symbols for the process of the things of value in the past being transmitted to futurity. Both seemed to have had their day, yet the Great Music stubbornly remains, and Gaelic speaking Scotland has thrown up at least five poets of the highest excellence and greatest interest. Here indeed is an inestimable treasure, here is *The Kind of Poetry I Want*.

> A poetry – since I was born a Scottish Gael
> Of earth's subtlest speech . . .

Thirty years ago from Raasay and Kintyre and from the Desert War in Africa where they both fought came the voices of Sorley MacLean and George Campbell Hay, and their poetry was better than any English poetry written during the war. More recently, from Lewis, has come the poetry of Derick Thomson, Domhnall MacAulay and Iain Crichton Smith, the latter best known for his poems in English. Sorley MacLean and Crichton Smith have addressed poems to MacDiarmid, and MacDiarmid has undoubtedly been an inspiration to writers in Gaelic, as he has been to writers in Scots and writers in English. MacDiarmid's propaganda for the Gaelic dynamic has been justified in the work of these men, and the Gaelic Literature of the future will be in his debt.

N

Lament for the Great Music

TOM SCOTT

MacDiarmid published this poem of some 600 lines in *Stony Limits* (1934). It is in the lingua franca, not Scots, and together with the title poem of homage to that great epic poet C. M. Doughty, is his highest achievement in Sudron at least up to that time. His conception of the Scottish literary revival was then undergoing a sea-change from a purely national revival of Scots, in which he had already published three volumes which were the best work in Scots since the eighteenth century, to a pan-Celtic vision rooted in Gaelic. The problem of a Gaelic poet is different from that of a Scots poet: the Scots poet writes in both Scots and English and/or an amalgam of the two, whereas the Gaelic poet must choose between Gaelic and a translator's English or Scots. This shift to a pan-Celtic European vision influenced Grieve's return to a form of the Sudron tongue, which he has chiefly (but by no means entirely) used ever since with varying degrees of success and failure, but rarely with the tact and assured mastery of his poems in Scots. He has little native Gaelic to use.

The term 'Great Music' is a translation of the Gaelic *Ceol Mor* as applied to the pibroch music of the MacCrimmons, those traditional pipers to the clan MacLeod of Skye. They flourished in the late seventeenth and eighteenth century, creating in the pibroch one of the greatest achievements of all music, comparable to the preludes and fugues of Bach, and the most original contribution Scotland has made to European art of any sort. The mood of the poem is of heroic elegy, not only for the lost glory of the pibroch, but the high Celtic culture of which it was the culminating (apparently) expression – itself a mighty lament for a race oppressed and threatened with total extinction. The pibroch is of sonata or concerto length, of great classical dignity and simplicity of theme, yet moving through its succeeding variations to an almost incredible intricacy and complexity – and the mood of heroic elegy is its own most characteristic one. No other music known to me can match it for dignity and noble pathos, and it is astonishing that a Celto-Teutonic people (and all the British are more or less that, the Celtic strain dominant here, the Teutonic there) should be so unaware of the musical treasure created in these islands and held here by a few in trust for the human race.

MacDiarmid in his lament for a lament is here discovering the deepest historic roots of his own psyche, and is inspired by the majesty and pathos of the fate of aristocratic Gaeldom to a classical verse which has never been equalled, let alone surpassed, since Milton, in these islands. This is evident even in the quiet opening lines:

> Fold of value in the world west from Greece
> Over whom it has been our duty to keep guard
> Have we slept on our watch; have death and dishonour
> Reached you through our neglect and left you in lasting sleep?

Here already he has struck the theme he has been searching for in certain previous works, the theme which will allow him to explore the Celtic roots of Scotland. This theme became dominant in *To Circumjack Cencrastus* (1930), where he speaks of a European Fourfold Idea pillaring up European culture – the Teutonic Idea of the North, the Classical Idea of the Mediterranean South, the Russian Idea of the East, and the Celtic Idea of the West. In that poem he found no 'objective correlative' for his intuitive apprehension of the Celtic Idea, but here, in the *Ceol Mor*, he strikes it. It is significant, not only for Scotland but for Europe, that when he finds it, the mood is elegiac.

The *Ceol Mor* is at once reality and symbol, as the Thistle was to him. As I see it, the movement of European poetry leads up to the allegorical form dominant in the Middle Ages; and when that breaks up, takes the twin lines of realism and symbolism; and in the twentieth century (beginning earlier, probably with Goethe), the realist and symbolist lines re-integrate into a new polysemous art in which, instead of the abstract theology (or theory) of allegory proper, reality itself in the historical and scientific senses, becomes the adequate 'symbol' or allegorical term of a new vision. I call this new art, to which all modern art is moving. 'Polysemous Veritism', to distinguish it from Dante's 'Polysemous Allegory'. I have no scope here to develop this view, but MacDiarmid's work, like that of Pound, Joyce and many others, is a major contribution. Through the reality-symbol of the *Ceol Mor* he breaks through into the real Celtic world as Yeats never did. The ancient world comes alive to him, and this is at once manifested in the intensity of his rhythms – urgent, vibrant, strong, of classical nobility and dignity, like the Great Music itself. The heroic ghosts of the Celtic world rise to meet him, shadowy though they still are, and with them the Celtic Church, the Nynian-Columban root of Scottish Christianity, and the awareness of that extraordinary culture, compounded of heroism and an almost tender delicacy of feeling, which the Teutonic has never yet caught up with. Shakespeare comes near it, being himself the greatest product of the Celto-Teutonic blend (The Tempest is an almost purely Celtic poem, with Prospero an Arch-Druid) yet born.

As always when the Muse is ardently responsive, MacDiarmid plunges deep into thought, argument, discussion, proliferation of *aperçus* and concepts, rugging at problems others have scarcely thought of: he is on chatting terms with the perennial mysteries, the eternal questions. In fact, he is a natural theologian (i.e. a student of reality), and it is because of this that he has poured intense scorn on an orthodox religion that has lost all its inspiration (or murdered it) and is no longer anything but empty, alienated form, far-strayed from its own Christ.

But his chief concern, as always, is with Scotland, and it is to Scotland he returns again and again:

> These things will pass. 'The world will come to an end
> But love and music will last for ever.'
> Sumeria is buried in the desert sands,
> Atlantis in the ocean waves – happier these
> Than Scotland, for all is gone, no travesty
> Of their ancient glory lives
> On the lips of degenerate sons as here.
> This is what is hard to bear; the decivilised have every grace
> As the antecendents of their vulgarities . . .
>
> We who are strong think only in terms
> Of classes and masses, in terms of mankind.
> We have no use for the great music.
> All we need is a few good-going tunes.

The passion of utterance here is unmistakable, and is the one element missing, at this pitch of intensity, in most of the other poems in this volume (*Stony Limits*).

He can hear the great pibroch of the MacCrimmons in his ear as he writes, and the fire burns in him:

> The bagpipes commit to the winds of Heaven
> The deepest emotions of the Scotsman's heart
> In joy and sorrow, in war and peace.

He speaks of two of the greatest pibrochs, *The Lament for the Children* and *I gave a kiss to the King's hand*, marvelling at what he considers the triviality of the occasion that gave rise to the magnificence of the latter: and he tells a story of the quality of these pipers. The pipers of Lord Louis Gordon refused to play for him because, after the battle of Inverurie in 1745, Gordon held the great piper Duncan Ban MacCrimmon prisoner of war. What other army, then or since, has had such men? These 'barbarian' Gaels knew, as MacDiarmid puts it,

> That Kings and Generals are only shadows of time
> But time has no dominion over genius.

Their tribute of silence to a piper of genius is one of the most striking cultural gestures I have ever heard of. What indeed was the whole misconceived Rising of 1745, the right rebellion in the wrong cause of the obsolete Stewarts, what was war itself, compared to the genius of Duncan Ban? These men knew the meaning of reverence for art.

The poet goes on to muse on the impermanence of temporal things:

> Yet the waves will not wash the feet
> Of MacLeod's Maidens for ever, and all modern Science
> May vanish from human memory as the great days
> Of Assyria and Egypt and Rome . . .

> The State has its roots in time. It will culminate in time.
> Greater things than this will fall . . .

Even the great *a priori* principles may not be as eternal as they seem – who can guarantee that two and two may not make five in some other planet? They too may be wearable as the Skye rocks (MacLeod's Maidens) mentioned above. His musing leads on, as always, to language and he meditates on the 'language where language ends', saying it reminds him of a sunset he once saw in a highland place 'When the tide-forsaken river was a winding ribbon of ebony' and a great light suddenly lit up the foreground . . . and he had the sense of a man returning from foreign scenes to the place of his birth.

So his thought runs on, typically seeming to range away from the central theme, like a setter chasing up many cross-scents, yet still coming back always to the main one. For him this is not only the great music, the *Ceol Mor*, but the Celtic root it stems from: and he asks whether the apparent decay of Celtic civilisation is not just a

shedding of dead leaves to prepare for a coming spring. To this root
he grips in the darkness, and in a swift appraisal of his own situation
as the one great Scottish poet in two centuries, he speaks of his
bafflement at the lack of comprehension in his own countrymen, which
estranges him from them and from himself:

> And waken to its (Scotland's) realities as baffled Samson woke
> Shorn and tethered. My native land should be to me
> As a root to a tree. If a man's labour fills no want there
> His deeds are doomed and his music mute.
> This Scotland is not Scotland . . .

There is the crux – the Scotland of to-day is no longer Scotland, but
a philistine travesty of itself. It is Scotshire, a county in the north of
England, an ex-country, an Esau land that has sold its birthright for a
mess of English pottage. The Scotland of today would be a foreign
land to the MacCrimmons. He, as poet, presents the Scottish people
with their own image, the thing they have become, and he calls them
back, like a true bard, to their own heritage. But so lost they are that
they do not recognise it, or him. This is the measure of how deep the
rot has gone since 1707.

At this point the note of elegy, the lament for the great music,
modulates into an elegy for the whole of Scotland, the 'broken image
of the lost kingdom' (it is Edwin Muir's phrase) that every Scot carries
deep in his soul. But it is not only the lost kingdom that concerns
MacDiarmid – he knows there is no way back to outmoded states –
but with the lost freedom to create new forms of society and art. The
great Scottish Idea, the one that Scotland gave to the world out of the
agony of the Wars of Independence, is Freedom – the 'nobill thing' of
Barbour's famous outburst in *The Brus*. This is the *sine qua non* of
existence, whether of nations or persons, and the tragic irony of
Scotland is that she, who gave birth to the idea of national independence and integrity out of the abstract ruling-class gangsterdom which
was feudalism, owing allegiance to no country and no people but itself,
should almost alone of European nations have betrayed and lost this
freedom to live and change. Truly, such a Scotland is not Scotland:
it is only a corpse breeding and spreading corruption.

He goes on to brood on what the MacCrimmons would think of our
modern cities 'swollen huge with thoughts not thought, that should
have been thought', and with songs unsung, with

Tears unshed for ever and deeds undone beyond achievement now?
These denationalised Scots have killed the soul
Which is universally human; they are men without souls;
All the more heavily the judgement falls upon them
Since it is a universal law of life they have sinned against.

There, surely, is the answer to the particular kind of 'trahison des clercs' found in those Anglo-Scots intellectuals who bleat of false antithesis, 'internationalism, not nationalism' – as if it were possible to have the one without the other. They sin against the universal law of life which invests life in individuals, not conglomerations – yes, even in the ant-hill. In the place of living, separate identities having mostly their differences in common, these ghouls would reduce all to a horrible 'international', characterless, abstract fog, a devitalised non-entity. That phoney distortion of Marxism was given the lie long since and utterly by Tito. But their 'international' equals 'English', and behind the pseudo-internationalism of the Anglo-Scots lurks the face of the Auld Enemy – English imperialism.

His thought runs on round these 'eternal embers' of Scottish culture, and he says he feels he knows the pibroch music best when

Away here I hold a glass of water between me and the sun
And can only tell the one from the other by the lint-white quiver,
The trembling life of the water . . .

That remarkable image of a real observation (compare Dunbar's description of the water in the fourth stanza of *The Goldyn Targe*) is typical 'polysemous veritism' – the image being the exact symbol, the real cohering with the apparent in vibrant meaning. This image of light is, at one level, the Great Music itself (and the greater music of reality beyond it); but radiating out from the actuality and reference, he sees the whole spirit of man as sunlike:

Our spirit is of a being indestructible . . .
It is like the sun which seems to set to our earthly eyes
But in reality shines on unceasingly . . .

Thus – and it is typical of the man – in the very moment of deepest lamentation, instead of regret, he re-affirms the indestructibleness of the spirit, and the mood of elegy gives way to heroic affirmation.

In this mood he meditates on the source of this mighty spirit, and

decides 'it is not lawful' to probe its sources (an unusual law-abiding-
ness in him), as if it were a thing subject to space and time. We must
wait and watch for it to reveal itself to us, as the eye

> Waits patiently for the rising sun. The mind creates only to destroy;
> Amid the desolation language rises, and towers
> Above the ruins . . .

And in the same way the music rises, its relations with itself rather
than anything external. He reflects on the nature of pibroch and its
relations to other musical forms; and the stupid neglect of pibroch
leads back to himself:

> I am as lonely and unfrequented as your music is.
> I have had to get rid of my friends . . .
> If one's capital consists in a calling
> And a mission in life one cannot afford to keep friends.
> I could not stand undivided and true amongst them.

This is an extraordinary passage, and only those who know the weight
of sheer negation the unusual individual has to try to bear up under,
will understand it. 'Hell is other people' for the man of vision. Only
those who conform are welcome in a group: the non-conformist,
the man who bears the burden of the mystery, can only be smothered
by its smug defensiveness. His solitude is a tragic and heroic fate which
must be borne for the ultimate good of the race. Thus a Rilke is quite
right in saying that a poet must love his loneliness and celebrate it with
harmonious lamentations – and MacDiarmid was one of the earliest
paraphrasers of Rilke.

The happiest of such solitaries are those who are 'companioned
by a future', foreseeing the struggle of a nation into consciousness
of its existence, and who sing out of that consciousness, animated and
restrained by a mystical sense of the high destiny of a people. Such are
not swallowed up by the petty cares of individual being. But is
MacDiarmid one such? He thinks not:

> But I am companioned by an irrecoverable past,
> By a mystical sense of such a destiny foregone . . .
> Time out of mind . . . Oh, Alba, my son, my son!

The adaptation of David's incomparable cry over Absalom is startling
and revealing. Alba, the ancient Scotland, is seen by this twentieth
century poet as an Absalom son for whom he would gladly die. What

kind of poet can utter such a cry? The answer is as direct as genius – a bard, a *fili*, a poet in the great Celtic tradition too long dormant and decayed, but at last showing signs of stirring among the scunnersome poeticules of our benighted age. Here MacDiarmid speaks with the eternal voice of the bard of his people, to whom all time is but a thought rooted in the mind of eternity. This is the voice of the keeper of the nation's conscience and traditions, the guardian of the welfare of the race. This is not the voice of C. M. Grieve speaking, but the timeless voice of Scottish poetry itself speaking immortally through him.

Yet even in this moment of realising his national identity, he looks beyond his own nation, out of his own nation, to the fraternal nations around him: for when one has found and is sure of one's own identity, both personal and national, the gaze no longer looks inward to the lost self but outward to the other selves. Thus in finding his national identity, the poet finds, as part of that identity, the between-nations, the socialist inter-national, and affirms both as aspects of each other. For through national sovereignty alone a people can come to full maturity and international responsibility. This is what our Anglo-Scots intellectuals, their bright heads darkened by their benighted souls, can never understand. Through self-realisation one comes to realise others:

> Not to one country or race, but to humanity,
> Not to this age but to all time,
> As your pibrochs that reached to Eternity . . .

The poem goes on for pages after that, but there, at its highest illumination, I must leave it. It is a great poem, one of his best, and the best heroic elegy written by a Scot in the lingua franca.

Poetry and Knowledge
in MacDiarmid's Later Work

EDWIN MORGAN

In the Preface to the *Lyrical Ballads*, Wordsworth makes some striking comments on poetry and science which are quite often quoted but very seldom believed. After claiming that poetry is the 'impassioned expression which is in the countenance of all Science' (a phrase referred to approvingly by Hugh MacDiarmid), he goes on in no less confident vein:

> If the labours of Men of science should ever create any material revolution, direct or indirect, in our condition, and in the impressions which we habitually receive, the Poet will sleep then no more than at present; he will be ready to follow the steps of the Man of science, not only in those general indirect effects, but he will be at his side, carrying sensation into the midst of the objects of the science itself. The remotest discoveries of the Chemist, the Botanist, or Mineralogist, will be as proper objects of the Poet's art as any upon which it can be employed, if the time should ever come when these things shall be familiar to us, and the relations under which they are contemplated by the followers of these respective sciences shall be manifestly and palpably material to us as enjoying and suffering beings.

Wordsworth envisages not simply the acceptance by poetry of facts or things or attitudes which science may unavoidably set within man's future environment (once they have become an intimate part of that environment), but also a more positive co-operation by which poets will be 'carrying sensation into the midst of the objects of the science itself' – in other words, helping to further the process of assimilation instead of passively hoping that schools, television programmes, 'popular science', and the passage of time will float the new material some day into the trembling ambit of the sensitive but unknowledgeable muse.

A good deal of MacDiarmid's poetry, from the *Stony Limits* volume of 1934 onwards through *A Kist of Whistles* (1947), *in Memoriam James Joyce* (1955), and *The Kind of Poetry I Want* (1961), has been a practical exploration of both aspects of Wordsworth's ideal. His search, as he says in *In Memoriam James Joyce*, is for

> The point where science and art can meet,
> For there are two kinds of knowledge,
> Knowing about things and knowing things,
> Scientific data and aesthetic realisation,
> And I seek their perfect fusion in my work.

Some would deny that there is any such meeting-point, or argue that there may have been once but could not be today, or fall back on the belief that to press for such a fusion would be inevitably to dilute both science and art. One does not have to evoke the theory of 'two cultures' to feel that there is something unduly inhibiting about such views. A poetry of knowledge may be difficult to produce, but its challenge is present in our time, and its absence ought to tantalise and stimulate. It should not be necessary to apologise for such attempts as are being made within the arts to show man inhabiting a world of which science and technology are a formidable part. It should not be necessary but it seems to be; because we are apt to forget how unhelpfully and unhealthily antiscientific the dominant literary atmosphere has been. This is where the later work of Hugh MacDiarmid would have value even if only the value of a corrective to the onesidedness of (for example) Yeats and Lawrence. Such a corrective is surely to be welcomed, and studied carefully and without prejudice. Only those to whom 'a poem is a poem and I am not interested in anything else' can turn unconcerned from the spectacle of a man writing with the quixotic aim of seeing poetry, or one kind of poetry, accepted as

> A protest, invaluable to science itself,
> Against the exclusion of value
> From the essence of matter of fact.

MacDiarmid himself would readily admit that success in writing such poetry, and success in recommending it to others, can only be achieved gradually, and to some extent luckily. The 'lucky poet' is here the poet who chances his reputation by courting heavy odds. When a hard thing is beginning to be done, failures have to be accepted, but one moves ahead. The appeal to the future, either as a period when better poetry of the same kind will be written or as a

period more likely to understand the value of the first stumbling
efforts, is sometimes made in these poems of MacDiarmid's, and
although it is not in itself the strongest of arguments it is an essential
part of the evolutionary credo implicit in the poetry. *In Memoriam
James Joyce*, as I have described elsewhere,[1] is concerned with the
fragmentation of human cultures and the desirability of bringing
together (as the 'imaginary museum' of modern photographic repro-
duction has done for painting and sculpture) the knowledge, achievement, and beauty left isolated and sterile in unfamiliar languages and
literatures. The interests and faculties required to assimilate this material
will grow, though slowly, until the ideal situation heaves in sight with

> Omnilateral aristology obligatory on everybody.

Appeal to the future, however, does not banish the haunting problem
of communication, even for MacDiarmid, as is clear from a passage
like the following, where he says he has

> spent many of my happiest busman's holidays
> In books like Leonard Bloomfield's *Language*,
> Happy as most men are with mountains and forests
> Among phonemes, tagmemes, taxemes,
> Relation-axis constructions,
> The phrasal sandhi-type and zero-anaphora.
> (What? Complaint that I should sing
> Of philological, literary and musical matters
>
> Rather than of daffodils and nightingales,
> Mountains, seas, stars and like properties . . .)

That comment shows him still on the defensive, which is hardly
surprising when we consider the inaptness of the word 'sing' as applied
to the preceding lines. This does not mean, however, that it is impossible to write poetry about phonemes and taxemes; only that in order
to do so, one must replace a bare catalogue of terms by a more per-
suasive, sophisticated proof that these things can be related to us all as
(in Wordsworth's phrase) 'enjoying and suffering beings'. In relying
so much as he does on the catalogue, on mere mention of the thing
itself, MacDiarmid is doing no more than initial spadework; he
sacrifices 'poetry' for the sake of an advance in the art of poetry which

---

[1] 'Jujitsu for the Educated', *Twentieth Century*, September 1956.

he believes to be feasible, though others may carry it further than he can. The kind of poetry he wants is 'a learned poetry', and also 'a poetry which fully understands / That the era of technology is a necessary fact'. He is willing to accept the extremer implications of this, as in the short poem 'The Changeful World'.

> Earth has gone through many changes.
> Why should it now cease changing?
> Would a world all machines be as strange as
> That in which the saurians went ranging?

But this science-fiction mood is not so typical as his concentration on present knowledge (and theory) and his attempts to relate this to human experience and to his own aesthetics. In all his 'poems of know-ledge', therefore, the method of analogy is widely used, sometimes with carefully worked out parallels, sometimes with an oblique hint thrown off to the agile reader. Although this method, which has be-come MacDiarmid's trademark, can quickly be ridiculed or parodied, it has at its best produced a very remarkable blending of fact and imagination. In *In Memoriam James Joyce* itself, there is the fine passage on the importance to the work of art of what is *not* present, led up to by the introduction of the haemolytic streptococcus which is 'in the sore throat preceding rheumatic fever' but at the height of the fever is gone, like the mysterious 'silence supervening at poetry's height' or an awesome pause in music. In many of the shorter poems there are striking illustrations of the same mastery of unexpected analogy: in *Stony Limits*, the elegy on Charles Doughty, where the growth of the poem that he wishes he could write to praise Doughty is described in terms of crystal growth in rocks and then, by a daring shift of perspective, in terms of the great rayed craters of the moon; in 'Dytiscus', with the mocking comparison between the water-beetle and man striving to breathe a 'diviner' air than that of his muddy environment; in 'Cornish Heroic Song for Valda Trevlyn', the buccal cavity of the white whale with its 'heavy oily blood-rich tongue which is the killer [whale]'s especial delight', and the analogy drawn between the Celtic genius and the 'hideous khaki Empire' of the English; the parturient, self-flyping guinea worm of 'To a Friend and Fellow-Poet' [Ruth Pitter], with its extraordinary description of a desperate yet delicate fecundity applied to the process of poetic creation; the extraction of mercury from cinnabar in 'Crystals Like

Blood', where iron piledrivers are crumbling the ore and a conveyor draws it up into a huge grey-white kiln –

> So I remember how mercury is got
> When I contrast my living memory of you
> And your dear body rotting here in the clay
> – And feel once again released in me
> The bright torrents of felicity, naturalness, and faith
> My treadmill memory draws from you yet.

Surely the main thing to be said about this poetry is not 'the details are not always accurate' or 'the process has not always been fully understood by the poet' or 'in any case these are only analogies or extended similes which are being used by the poet for normal aesthetic purposes'. To an expert in some particular discipline (e.g. linguistics in *In Memoriam James Joyce*,[1] geology in *Stony Limits*[2]) MacDiarmid is bound to reveal some inadequacies which betray the lack of an intimate familiarity with the subject. Such inadequacies seem, however, fewer or less damaging than one might suppose. Further investigation of the scientific background of these poems may qualify this statement, but it looks at present as if Wordsworth was right in assuming that the poet could still use his natural insight and mental tact in penetrating regions of knowledge as well as the more obvious regions of feeling. As for the objection that these analogies are no more than a refurbishing of heroic simile, it must be remembered that something more than illustration is at stake. The poem 'To a Friend and Fellow-Poet' is equally 'about' the guinea worm and the poetic process; if it shows the poetic process in a new light, it also throws poetic light on an extremely interesting bit of zoology.

The Kind of Poetry I Want affords the best vantage-point for considering the whole problem. A fair amount of technical material is

[1] The poem speaks about 'Vogule, / The smallest of the Baltic-Finnish language group, / Spoken by only 5000 people'; but there is no 'Baltic-Finnish language group', and even if there was, Vogul (which is wrongly spelt) could hardly belong to it, since it is spoken in Siberia, thousands of miles from the Baltic area; it is spoken by more than 5000 people, and even if it was spoken by only 5000 it would not be the smallest of the group MacDiarmid is referring to (under the wrong name). Vogul is a Ugrian (or Finno-Ugrian) tongue, belonging to the Uralian linguistic stock, and there are at least two smaller languages, Livonian and Vodian, in the group.

[2] To a geologist, 'crossing shear planes' are not 'extruded' as the poem says they are; and 'ultra-basic xenoliths that make men look like midges' (presuming that this refers to size rather than durability) would be exceedingly unlikely since most xenoliths are even smaller than man-size.

scattered throughout, but very often in reference to easily assimilable activities and pursuits – fishing, piping, dance, film, music – and the originality consists mainly in the precision with which things like 'a 3-inch anti-kink minnow, brown and gold' are mentioned. Most of these references are analogical: the activities described are models, in their richly ordered complexity and grace, for the sort of poetry MacDiarmid would like to see. At the same time – and this is what is distinctive – the analogies are intended to be themselves examples (not always successful, naturally) of such a poetry in its early stages of development. I say 'early stages of development' because it is more a 'poem of knowledge' than a 'poem of science': it opens out into various sciences, but is concerned to present the reader with thresholds and vistas rather than with entry and possession. It distinguishes its own aim, nevertheless, pointing clearly in a direction taken by few:

> The poetry of one who practises his art
> Not like a man who works that he may live
> But as one who is bent on doing nothing but work,
> Confident that he who lives does not work,
> That one must die to life in order to be
> Utterly a creator – refusing to sanction
> The irresponsible lyricism in which sense impressions
> Are employed to substitute ecstasy for information . . .

What in fact happens in *The Kind of Poetry I Want* – and it is a measure of the poem's great interest –is that a balance is struck between 'sense impressions' and 'information' which makes it possible for much of the information to be seen not in a textbook context but in a life context, and this, though not the poem's primary intention, helps the reader to edge his way in towards the more intellectual passion at the centre. The kind of poetry MacDiarmid wants to see is glimpsed through glasses of varying fineness and power. It is likened to the dancing of Fred Astaire (complex but apparently easy); to bagpipe music (involving skilled improvisation); to fishing (observation, choice, grace of action); to bending a piece of wire back and forward to breaking-point (an experiment with an aim – finding out how words, like atoms, behave); to the mixture of races in Spain and the mixture of cultures in India (a wide range and fusion of individual enriching factors); to the eleven-year cycle supposed by some to govern sunspots, Nile flood levels, wheat prices, tree-rings, measles epidemics, Bank of England discount rates, and many other phenomena (a Jamesian 'figure in the carpet', perhaps, though the analogy is not made syntactically clear); to living flesh suddenly touched in a mineral world (shock of the unexpected); to a busy, sparkling operating theatre 'in which the poet exists only as a nurse during an operation' (devotion of contributing to a larger, complex whole – no doubt the 'operation' of apathectomy on all mankind); to a documentary film about sheep-dogs in which physical setting and elementary natural movement are more important than the story being told (information better than ecstasy – though the information itself is a sort of ecstasy); to the ironic baa of a wild goat chased by man onto crags where he can't be followed (posing questions rather than giving easy answers); and to hedge-laying (craftsmanlike but abstruse).

From these analogies, two main and apparently contradictory models for poetry emerge. On the one hand MacDiarmid wants a poetry of great complexity, coupled with great order, 'organised to the last degree', a product of the 'crystallising will', subtle yet proportioned 'masterpieces of intricate lucidity' on the highest level, and on the lowest at least 'artful tessellations'. Where this conception is leading is seen in the admiring reference to Coleridge's 'coadunation' and 'multeity in unity', and in the autobiographical passage describing the changes in a man's life – and in all life – from less to more organic. Like the humble but exemplary lancelet which almost crossed the gulf from invertebrate to vertebrate and pointed the way as a prototype for others –

> If I have evolved myself out of something
> Like an amphioxus, it is clear
> I have become *better* by the change,
> I have risen in the organic scale,
> I have become more organic.

The poem as organism, as a complex structure ordered with such finesse that the code has swallowed the key, is of course a familiar model in recent aesthetic theory, but it would be surprising if Mac-Diarmid accepted it as it has usually been propounded, since he does not himself write, or apparently very much enjoy, poetry conceived on such principles. He does not, however, go the whole way with organism despite his praise of 'the more organic'. The important difference is that he demands lucidity (whereas in organismic theory ambiguity is welcome), and tries to ensure it by his insistence on reference to 'fact and science' rather than to (say) myth and mythmaking: that is, poetry should emulate the expository power of a T. H. Huxley or a J. P. Joule in making the abstruse stand out 'in cut-gem clearness'.

But as a far greater qualification of this model of poetry, other analogies lead MacDiarmid away from 'organising', though not necessarily from 'the organic'. We have his belief in poetry that is 'never afraid to leap', poetry improvising like expert pipe-music, poetry going up like fireworks, poetry with unforeseen Beethovenian modulations into remote keys, poetry that is 'wilder than a heifer / You have to milk into a gourd', the 'poetry of one like a wild goat on a rock'. We have the notable passage where he asks for a poetry

> With something about it that is plasmic,
> Resilient, and in a way alarming – to make cry
> 'I touched something – and it was *alive*.'
> There is no such shock in touching what
> Has never lived; the mineral world is vast.
> It is mighty, rigid, and brittle. But the hand
> That touches vital matter – though the man were blind –
> Infallibly recognises the feel of life, and recoils in excitement.

Yet this, and in the same sentence, is the poetry he describes as 'full of *cynghanedd*, and hair-trigger relationships'. Of a marriage between Wallace Stevens and Allen Ginsberg one might well say: No go. There is indeed a contradiction here, and it reflects a central contradiction in MacDiarmid's nature which shows elsewhere in the 'metaphysical materialism' of his philosophy. But although MacDiarmid makes it difficult for the reader to envisage in the abstract a poetry which is 'organised to the last degree' and yet 'the poetry of one like a wild goat on a rock', it is important to see that this is not a complete contradiction; nor is *The Kind of Poetry I Want* devoid of hints as to how we must bring the ideas together. Just as some extremely intricate Celtic interlace may gain, not lose, by being slightly asymmetrical; or as film-makers have found (or re-learned, after the great painters), how a carefully played scene will gain, not lose, power by having in the background something irrelevant which shows ordinary 'non-art' life going about its business: so, in poetry, Virgil writes a short line, Shakespeare sketches Parolles, Milton 'by occasion foretells the ruine of our corrupted Clergy'. And so too, although *The Kind of Poetry I Want* like most of MacDiarmid's long poems is loosely rather than closely organised, it shows in some passages how improvisation can still help to prove theme, and how 'irrelevance' can become relevant.

The wild goat, following its instincts in jumping from crag to crag, may be tracing patterns which science cannot yet describe. Is the passage on Mary Webb a 'digression'?

> A poetry abstruse as hedge-laying
> And full as the countryside in which
> I have watched the practice of that great old art,
> – Full of the stumbling boom of bees,
> Cuckoos contradicting nightingales all through a summer day,
> Twilight deepening with a savage orange light,
> Pheasants travelling on fast, dark wings,
> – Or like a village garden I know well
> Where the pear-trees bloom with a bravery of buds,
> The cydonia blossoms gloriously against its wall,
> And roses abound through April, May, and June,
> – And always with a surprising self-sufficiency
> Like that of almost any descriptive passage of Mary Webb's
> – The fact that she was not wholly herself in all she wrote
> Creating a sort of finality and completeness
> In each part of any given whole,
> The integrity of her experience revealing itself in many ways,
> In the fulfilment of rare powers of observation,
> In the kind of inward perception which recognised
> 'The story of any flower' is 'not one of stillness,
> But of faint gradations of movement that we cannot see',
> The outer magic and the inward mystery imaginatively reconciled,
> Her deep kinship, her intuitive sympathy with leaf and flower
> Extending without a break into the human kingdom,
> And flowering there in an exquisite appreciation
> Of the humours of single characters,
> And a rare power to make them live and speak
> In their own right and idiom.

Now Mary Webb's novels are not abstruse; but consider the modulations of the lead-in, if it is a lead-in. The abstruse art of hedge-laying quickly passes into the thick, complicated, rich-looking texture of the hedge itself, the rich living world and natural habitat of the hedgerow, the richness being a link between the 'abstruse' art and the 'full' countryside which is the next comparison; poetry should be full, as fouthy in its language as the English countryside is in sounds and colours or a village garden in flowers. Then comes the oblique move to

'a surprising self-sufficiency', a phrase which, added to the abstruseness
and fullness, reminds us of the 'intricate lucidity' mentioned earlier
in the poem but which hardly prepares us for the sudden illustration
from 'almost any descriptive passage of Mary Webb's'. She has
floated in, perhaps, on the wings of the pheasants, but very soon we
become absorbed in what the poem says about her art, and probably
we forget any analogy to poetry. If we stop at this point, we may ask
ourselves whether the passage is not simply a pleasant interpolated
tribute to someone who was a personal friend of the author's. When
we read on, we see that it is, and it isn't. The quoted passage is followed
by another thirty-odd lines which meditate generalisingly on the value
of such a writer, who with her 'practical working knowledge' can
'capture the elusive spirit of a countryside':

> literary graces concealing
> No poverty of context, lack of virility, emptiness of thought,
> But, held in perfect control,
> Contributing the substance of poetry
> To subjects 'with quietness on them like a veil',
> A manifold of fast-vanishing speech,
> Customs and delights.

The only thing that links Mary Webb and MacDiarmid's aims for
poetry is the idea of a rare, intimate knowledge being used for artistic
purposes. Our first reaction when we see her name is that few writers
could be more different, and we wonder how MacDiarmid could
possibly enlist her among his Zouave acrobats and *cynghanedd*. She
is brought upon the scene without premeditation, but having been
brought, she justifies the suddenness, and we find ourselves looking
at the main ideas of the poem from a new angle.

What MacDiarmid seems to be adumbrating in *The Kind of Poetry
I Want* – it is nowhere made sharp and definite – is a poetry which is
highly organised in parts, but not prescriptively with regard to the
whole. It is not so much an organism as a colony, a living and in one
sense formless association of organisms which share a common
experience. Shape and architectonics are not so important as the quick
movements of the thought – the feelers in the water, moved partly by
the surrounding currents and partly by their own volition and partly in
response to the movement of neighbour tentacles – while a succession
of images, illustrations, and analogies is presented to it. As zoologists
may argue whether a colony is an organism, critics may hesitate to

say that the kind of *poetry* MacDiarmid wants is a kind of *poem*. A movement towards a more 'open' conception of the poem than has prevailed in the modern period is however gaining ground, and I see no reason why we should deny ourselves, for love of architectonics, the ingredient and emergent pleasures of a poetry in evolution.

> The ingredients resemble the things
> For which a woman with child longs.
> Like the juice of the oyster,
> The aroma of the wild strawberry,
> The most subtle and diversified elements
> Are here intermingled to form
> A higher organism.

The longings are perhaps not 'sensible', perhaps not 'compatible'; and yet they are a part of the great process of creation, they take their place in the effort to bring something new into the world. That is the value of Hugh MacDiarmid's later poetry.

Hugh MacDiarmid:
Visionnaire du Langage

MICHEL HABART

Il y a trente ans que Hugh MacDiarmid, en publiant *Un homme ivre regarde le chardon*,[1] annonçait la renaissance littéraire écossaise en même temps qu'il lui donnait son plus beau poème. Le déclin pitoyable de la poésie écossaise – des grands jours de la poésie courtoise de Dunbar et Henryson aux exercices de style pour école du dimanche où elle avait fini par sombrer – faisait de ce réveil un événement surprenant.

Une première renaissance, illustrée au XVIIIe siècle par Allan Ramsay et Robert Burns, n'avait été qu'une brève illusion. En marge de l'évolution culturelle, vouée au 'pastoral', l'heritage qu'elle laissait était condamné à la stérilité. Et les écrivains écossais qui succédèrent, comme Walter Scott (en dépit de sa contribution aux *Border Ballads*), John Davidson, Robert Louis Stevenson, James Thomson (nom si injustement négligé), furent d'abord des poètes anglais.

C'est ainsi que *Sangschaw* et *Penny Wheep*, les premiers recueils de Hugh MacDiarmid écrits en *Lallans*, furent, pour la culture écossaise, un exemple salutaire et décisif. Une poésie véritablement moderne dans son langage et son inspiration pouvait-elle donc s'exprimer dans un dialecte traditionnel?

En réalité, c'était, pour la littérature écossaise, le problème capital du langage maternel en poésie qui de nouveau se posait. Puisque le *Lallans* était sans aucun doute mieux adapté aux exigences du tempérament écossais, étail-il sage et légitime d'y renoncer pour l'usage exclusif de l'anglais littéraire, dans le seul but de donner à l'œuvre une audience élargie? Il est certain que l'anglais littéraire ne répond pas entièrement à la gamme émotionnelle des peuples celtiques. Il suffit de voir avec quelle ferveur (mêlée de défi), l'Ecossais, une fois en pays anglais, cultive son accent d'origine, ce précieux vestige du dialecte natal, pour comprendre ce que celui-ci représente pour les complexes de l'exil. Plus qu'aucun autre, le poète souffre de ne pouvoir user du langage de son enfance, le seul qui lui donne accès aux zones subconscientes où

[1] *A Drunk Man looks at the Thistle.*

se forme le substrat affectif de sa personnalité, le seul qui puisse vraiment se porter garant de l'expression authentique de ses sentiments. C'est par les associations émotionnelles du langage maternel que le poète reste en communication avec les symbolismes collectif et infantile dont se nourrit son inspiration profonde. Pour Hugh MacDiarmid, l'abandon du Lallans se justifiait d'autant moins que ce dialecte est relativement accessible au lecteur anglais et que l'effort qu'il demande ne dépasse pas après tout celui qu'exige, dans sa propre langue, tout modernisme poétique.

Jusqu'à quel point d'ailleurs, l'usage des dialectes n'est-il pas en mesure d'enrichir, en la renouvelant, la langue littéraire commune d'une nation? Jusqu'à quel point ne l'aiderait-il pas à résister aux nivellements journalistique, universitaire ou administratif qui peu à peu dégradent un langage vivant en cette prose de mandarins qui est le mal chronique de la culture occidentale? 'Je pense', écrivait T. S. Eliot à Hugh MacDiarmid, 'que la poésie *Scots* est d'une influence fertilisante pour la poésie anglaise et qu'il est de l'intérêt de celle-ci que cette poésie fleurisse.'

Un usage mal compris du dialecte peut, il est vrai, encourager l'écrivain à limiter ses horizons et s'enliser dans le régionalisme. Hugh MacDiarmid a su en éviter l'écueil. Les thèmes qu'il traite sont d'une telle envergure que toute accusation de provincialisme semblerait absurde. Certains critiques se sont évidemment empressés de voir en lui le Burns du xxe siècle. La comparaison est injuste. L'amour de la femme, celui du whisky, une nationalisme obstiné, une coriace anglophobie, leur sont peut-être des traits communs. Ils ne touchent guère à l'essence de leur création. Le slogan de Hugh MacDiarmid: 'Non pas Burns, mais Dunbar', définissait son ambition. Son œuvre s'en est montrée digne. En dépit d'une certaine rhétorique 'coin de feu' qui, par instants, alourdit le poème, *Un homme ivre regarde le chardon* reste le chef-d'œuvre de la poésie écossaise moderne. En fait, Hugh Mac-Diarmid se compare plus justement à Rilke dont il fut le premier à traduire le *Requiem für eine Freundin*, et son poème *Vestigia Nulla Retrorsum* est un magnifique hommage au poète allemand.

*   *   *

Plus encore que les précédentes, la nouvelle œuvre de Hugh MacDiarmid – *In Memoriam James Joyce* – écrite peu de temps avant la guerre, apporte de nouveaux et importants éléments aux problèmes de la création poétique.

C'est une suite de méditations en prose scandée (en *chopped-up prose*, dira un critique mal disposé), coupée de passages lyriques d'une surprenante beauté, sur les rapports des premiers langages et de la pensée, sur l'universalité de l'œuvre d'art, et surtout sur les problèmes des relations linguistiques, qui, pour le poète, prennent une importance capitale dans un monde qui s'achemine rapidement vers l'unité. C'est en hommage aux fabuleuses explorations d'*Ulysse* et surtout de *Finnegans' Wake* dans les immenses et nouvelles possibilités offertes au langage que l'œuvre (dont le second titre est *A Vision of World Language*) est dédiée à la mémoire de Joyce.

Le poème apporte avec lui un formidable appareil de mots puisés à travers le monde, des Iles Shetland à la Chine, 'une sorte de jiu-jitsu pour l'homme cultivé', nous dit l'auteur.

S'il demande un effort de participation soutenu, cet effort trouve sa récompense. L'œuvre, en effet, réalise ce tour de force de donner au discours poétique une tension intellectuelle qui, l'animant du rythme intérieur de la pensée, soulève le lecteur au-dessus d'obstacles qui, sans cet élan, lui paraîtraient infranchissables.

Ce style a la force nerveuse de celui d'Ezra Pound ou de Wyndham Lewis. Comment d'ailleurs ne pas penser aux *Cantos* et aussi à ce chef-d'œuvre ignoré, l'*Anathemata* de David Jones? On n'en reste pas moins surpris de voir que, dans son poème, l'auteur renonce à un dialecte auquel il doit tant pour l'anglais littéraire, si du moins je puis qualifier d'anglais littéraire un langage poétique qui apporte tant d'éléments nouveaux. Trahison? Désaveu? Aveu d'impuissance? Ou seulement la crainte d'imposer au lecteur anglais un fardeau supplémentaire? Dans sa préface, Hugh MacDiarmid, prévenant nos réserves, compare, non sans mélancolie, sa destinée poétique à celle de Hofmannsthal, qui, après la crise retracée dans la fameuse *Lettre de Lord Chandos*, devint, pour certains de ses amis, une sorte de renégat, pire, un faux Messie. C'est une crise de même nature, nous dit-il, qui a transformé sa méthode poétique. Non pas seulement une crise de style. Mais une crise affective, imaginative, d'une telle ampleur que pour lui les possibilités du langage et de la connaissance en furent bouleversées. Le problème particulier du dialecte, du même coup, passait au second plan.

Dans *In Memoriam*, le discours poétique – car il s'agit bien ici de discours – veut faire de chacune de ses phrases une phase déterminante de l'expérience humaine, cherchant à créer un champ d'idées multiples que seule l'épaisseur du langage poétique est capable d'engendrer.

Comment ne pas se référer là encore, aux *Cantos* d'Ezra Pound?

Pourtant la différence est capitale. Alors que l'esthétique des *Cantos* est essentiellement impressionniste, le discours d'*In Memoriam* est conduit de la façon la plus rigoureuse. Pour le poète, l'humanité est maintenant lancée dans une évolution intellectuelle destinée à faire de l'homme un être totalement différent, et aucune œuvre d'art – sauf peut-être celle de Joyce – n'a tenté de réaliser et d'exprimer cette transition dans les limites d'une seule vie. Nos langages et nos littératures ne sont pas à la mesure de cette mission. Il s'agit donc de leur donner une densité nouvelle, et ceci à l'échelle planétaire. Sans les efforts des quelques rares écrivains plus ou moins conscients de cette nécessité, comme Pound, Eliot ou Joyce, la littérature anglaise se serait irrémédiablement assoupie dans cette platitude, ce conformisme suburbain, qui est sa tentation majeure. C'est bien cet universalisme 'agissant' de la culture que Goethe annonçait lorsqu'il parlait de littérature universelle, et non une admiration platonique des quelques grands chefs-d'œuvre du passé. Une nouvelle tension est établie entre l'homme et l'univers. Elle peut, elle doit renouveler le langage du poète et ses rapports avec le monde. Cette conscience planétaire, dont on trouve déjà l'écho dans l'Iliade, la Divine Comédie, Don Quichotte, et surtout dans la littérature sanscrite, deviendra l'élément essentiel de l'expression littéraire, tout comme la nation était l'élément essentiel d'une littérature 'nationale'. Rendre présents à l'homme la multiplicité des âmes et l'abîme du temps, tel est ce que le poète appelle la 'nouvelle ambiance', ambiance dont *In Memoriam* est profondément imprégné

> Toutes les mélodies déjà entendues ou jamais proférées
> Résonnent ensemble de toutes leurs notes, pour nous soulever,
> Nous embrasser, nous emporter – mélodies d'amour et de passion,
> De printemps et d'hiver, de mélancolie et d'abandon.
> Esprits de millions d'êtres
> Sur des millions de siècles
> Vision de la Forme Universelle (Visva-Rupa-Darsanam)
> Devant laquelle Arjuna se prosternait, tout crispé de terreur.[1]

Les sciences linguistiques jouent dans cette tentative un rôle déterminant. Aussi bien n'est-ce pas de Glasgow que nous est venu, avec *The Principles of Semantics* de Stephen Ullman, l'ouvrage fondamental de la sémantique moderne? Le poème exalte les travaux

---

[1] *In Memoriam James Joyce*, p. 15.

de Rudolf Carnap, de Gardiner et Jespersen. Dans cette perspective totale, les différences formelles qui séparent la poésie de la prose, perdent leur sens. Hugh MacDiarmid fait sienne la thèse du grand poète juif Chaim Bialik sur 'la folie de différencier prose et poésie'. Il fait sienne aussi l'ambition de retrouver, en dehors de toute prosodie formelle, le rythme intérieur de la pensée, ce rythme qui court '*comme un fil rouge et brûlant*' tout au long du Deutéronome par exemple, réussissant à faire d'un simple report de chroniques et de lois un très grand livre poétique. C'est bien ce même fil rouge et brûlant que nous retrouvons à travers *In Memoriam*.

Voilà ce que signifie l'exploration des dictionnaires,
Tout les abîmes et les sommets de la pensée,
Tout les risques, toutes les épreuves de l'esprit,
Entre les débris des littératures passées
Et la matière première des littératures à venir.
Mais *tout* le langage? Un éblouissement de lampe-à-arc.
Plus d'illusions, ni de refuges pittoresques,
Ni d'ornières toutes prêtes où assoupir
Nos complaisances. Chaque instant est exigence
Reprise nouvelle de nos forces.
Plus de guenilles à partager
Avec ces aveugles aux cerveaux satisfaits
Qui cultivent, raillait Disraeli,
'Les âneries de leurs prédécesseurs',

*   *   *

Dont les âmes vivant dans une torpeur sacrée,
Prosternées devant des autels refroidis et des dieux trépassés

*   *   *

Tout le langage!
Et non pas distiller, à la Valéry, des mots comme 'pur'
Dans le goutte à goutte d'une minutie de chimiste,
Et non pas trouver l'essence du poème
Dans le maniement correct de l'e muet!
– Je pense ici à l'inconséquence de Chaucer
Avec sa prononciation de l'e final –
(Bien qu'il y ait *tout* la différence du monde
Entre whisky et whiskey, bien sûr!)[1]

[1] *Ibid.*, p. 90.

Il est aisé de reprocher aux complications de cette sorte de kaléido-
scope culturel (qui prend par moments l'allure fâcheuse d'un réper-
toire), leur excès de didactisme, voire leur pédantisme. Pourtant une
poésie résolument moderne – à moins de rester en marge et de se
limiter, comme dirait William Empson, à 'quelque version de pastoral'
– doit consentir à la complexité croissante des cultures et de la société,
complexité favorisée par l'isolement du créateur dans un monde qui,
cessant d'êtrel ocal, organique, hiérarchisé, ne peut plus lui fournir le
cadre tout fait de traditions, de langage et de symbolique où venait
s'ajuster sa sensibilité:

> Un langage qui serve nos ambitions,
> Merveilleuse lucidité, légère et ardente lumière,
>
> *   *   *
>
> Flexible comme une jeune baguette de coudrier,
> Sûre comme une aile de mouette,
> Claire comme une eau de montagne,
> Profonde comme des yeux de femme en présence de l'amour,
> Exprimant la complexe vision de toute chose en une,
> Laissant passer toutes impressions, toute expérience,
>   toutes doctrines,
> Pour n'en retenir que le grain,
> En assumant l'innombrable promesse
> Qu'il porte en son germe.[1]

Si cette complexité poétique, qui en France date de Baudelaire, a
pris un départ plus tardif en Angleterre (1910–20), le danger qu'elle
représente pour l'unité de l'inspiration, n'en est apparu que plus
soudain et plus urgent, en même temps que se découvrait le seul
remède qui permit au poète de conjurer cette dispersion: une récon-
ciliation de la culture et de la Société. C'est en effet dans un cadre
culturel élargi que le poète anglais essaie d'échapper à cette dichotomie
de l'art et de la vie, fatale à la civilisation comme à la poésie. Eliot,
Pound, Empson, sont les meilleurs exemples de cette poésie érudite où
l'obscurité (ou plutôt l'opacité) ne vient pas de l'usage d'un matériau
subconscient, mais de l'extraordinaire diversité des allusions culturelles.

C'est dans ce développement qu'il faut situer, pour les comprendre
des œuvres comme l'*In Memoriam* de Hugh MacDiarmid ou l'*Anathemata* de David Jones.

*   *   *

[1] *Ibid.* pp 88–9.

Embrasser, dans leurs diversités, l'ensemble des cultures pour les unir sur le plan cosmique, tel est bien le dessein d'*In Memoriam*. 'Mais cette unification, écrit le poète, ne peut s'achever que dans une société où la communauté d'action atteindra son expression maximum.' On s'en doute, cette société ne peut être que la société marxiste, puisque les contradictions de la société libérale sont décidément sans espoir. Que n'a-t-on dit du marxisme de Hugh MacDiarmid, dont l'œuvre apparaît à certains comme une provocation politique?

Ses 'Hymnes à Lénine' (dont le second fut publié par T. S. Eliot dans sa revue *Le Criterion*), ses poèmes activistes comme 'Fascistes, vous avez tué mes Camarades', ses appels révolutionnaires, forment une part importante de son œuvre poétique. C'est en cherchant à incarner ses idées politiques qu'il trouve, semble-t-il, ses accents les plus fermes et les plus émouvants, et il est singulièrement à l'aise dans ce mélange inattendu que constituent l'intensité intellectuelle d'un esprit moderne, et la féerie mystique de la ballade traditionnelle. On comprend que le poète se soit fait le traducteur enthousiaste d'Alexandre Blok.

Vu d'un peu plus près, ce marxisme, il faut bien le dire, n'a pas l'air très cohérent, et parait tenir beaucoup plus d'une sorte d'anarchisme philosophique, où surgissent des références aussi imprévues que Vladimir Soloviev, Keyserling, John Cowper Powys et même Gurdjieff, que d'un matérialisme dialectique orthodoxe. En tous cas, ce marxiste réalise cet étrange paradoxe d'être en même temps le seul grand poète mystique que l'Ecosse ait produit.

Tout aussi imprévue et paradoxale est la haine maniaque que le poète n'a cessé de nourrir contre l'Angleterre et qu'il déploie de nouveau dans *In Memoriam*, en dépit de son repentir vers la langue anglaise. Quel que soit le bien fondé des thèses nationalistes, il est difficile d'affirmer que la littérature écossaise représente une littérature autonome. En fait, elle dépend étroitement de l'histoire littéraire anglaise, dont elle reste un chapitre mineur. Même dans sa période la plus glorieuse, la poésie *Scots* tenait de très près à ses modèles anglais. Et à la question 'Qu'est-ce qu'un poème écossais?', les plus chauvins des Ecossais seraient bien embarrassés de donner une définition précise qui ne risquât d'en exclure leurs glories les plus sûres. Si le reniement total du dialecte natal est pour l'Ecossais une mutilation, l'anglophobie aveugle en est une autre.

Comment, d'ailleurs, Hugh MacDiarmid pourra-t-il bien empêcher qu'*In Memoriam James Joyce* ne devienne un grand poème … anglais?

Toute l'exécration qu'il voue à l'anglo-saxon ne peut rien contre cette ironie. Dylan Thomas évoque quelque part 'toutes les statues que l'Ecosse élèvera un jour à Hugh MacDiarmid', mais que celui-ci prenne garde plutôt que l'Angleterre, dans un accès d'humour, n'ait l'outrecuidance de lui élever à son tour un mémorial. Car devant quel méfait d'annexion reculerait cette 'race intensément vulgaire, et à l'esprit infantile'?

Hugh MacDiarmid: The Later Poetry

G. S. FRASER

I. THE NOTION OF THE DISCURSIVE POEM

This essay is a kind of appendage to Iain Crichton Smith's *The Golden Lyric* (Akros Publications, 1967), which was at once a wonderful appreciation of Hugh MacDiarmid's early poems, and a wonderful polemic against his later development. I am going to consider the longer, the later, what might be called the discursive poems. I want to consider first of all, in a way that I think MacDiarmid might approve of, the whole notion of a poem as *either* an imitation of a mode of discourse *or* a mode of discourse in itself.

Prose is written in sentences and paragraphs. Poetry is, by and large (there would be exceptions in some imagist and some surrealist poems), written in sentences and paragraphs, but it is also written in *lines*, which establish, even in free verse poems like Pound's *Cantos* or MacDiarmid's *In Memoriam James Joyce*, a greater expectation of regularity than prose tends to. Prose and verse both have inescapably rhythm; rhythm or prosody is a quality emerging from the fairly limited phonetics and vocabulary of all languages, from the necessity of our repeating either phrases or patterns of phrase. In verse, we draw attention to it; in prose, we try, usually, to distract attention from it towards a development and elaboration of something that we might call meaning, argument, or sense. In prose, we are trying to *say* something – in great philosophical prose, like Wittgenstein's, say, to *say* something at the very moment we are for the first time *thinking* it.

Poetry is not the most convenient or direct mode for either human saying or human thinking. The profoundest limiting remark about poetry as a mode that I ever heard was made by a post-office girl on a day-release course at Kingsway College, London. I had been reading some poems by Yeats and Eliot and others. 'Poetry,' this girl said, 'seems to be a very *round-about* way of saying things.' It is very difficult to say things; if we set before ourselves the barriers of rhyme and regular rhythm we make the saying more difficult. T. S. Eliot once remarked in a correspondence in *The Times Literary Supplement* on

Shakespeare's adaptations of North's Plutarch in *Coriolanus*, *Anthony and Cleopatra* and elsewhere, that we can find many examples of prose, with slight alterations, being turned into great verse (Yeats's verse setting of Pater's famous Mona Lisa passage at the beginning of *The Oxford Book of Modern Verse* might be another example); but that even very great verse, transcribed as prose, will not be even good prose. Milton's *Paradise Lost* is a very great poem; but a French translation into prose, however, in fact, scholarly and precise, would tend to be boring, since it would lose the special quality, the pacing and pausing of the verse paragraph, the modulation of feeling and tone, that makes the poem great.

The poem, as such, makes sense but its greatness is in how the limitation and narrowness of its rhythmical form, and yet the varieties of tone it achieves *within* that limitation and narrowness, controls our response of feeling more precisely than prose can ever control it. Poetry can perhaps never *convince* us of anything, other than its own internal coherence, and the validity of our final mood of response to it, if we have attended to it with enough patience and impersonal alertness. But MacDiarmid, in his later poetry, Crichton Smith insists, uses poetry as if it were prose (or even as if it were an inferior type of prose, polemical political rhetoric) primarily to *convince* us. To make us agree with him, about a variety of topics about which he holds strong and passionate, but also sometimes limited and cantankerous, views. MacDiarmid's later poetry, for Crichton Smith, is what Keats called 'poetry with a palpable design on us'. It tries to bully us, often, into taking up attitudes which it is not proper we should take up unless, in prose, or in unspoken thought, we had argued out the question for ourselves. It is demanding and peremptory, Crichton Smith thinks, in an essentially unpoetic way. *Style*, as in Dante or Milton, can properly be demanding and peremptory; *ideas* cannot. The poetry of the doggedly argumentative mood is a poetry demanding a doggedly argumentative answer, which the greatest poetry does not demand.

I agree with Crichton Smith that MacDiarmid's later poetry is extraordinarily uneven, and also that the unevenness comes partly from a demand for submission, for practical assent, upon the part of the reader, that is not a properly poetic demand. But I think one can make a much better case for much of MacDiarmid's later poetry, if one thinks of the argument in the poems as being directed not against a reader who is being bullied but against MacDiarmid himself. I shall try to illustrate this point by quotations and analyses. The element of

greatness in MacDiarmid's later poetry lies in an inwardness, an un-
ending inner struggle, in a strenuously lonely man, whose loneliness
can, for the reader, be an emblem of his own. The true poet (and this
applies to a poet as utterly in contrast with MacDiarmid as Yeats) is
less an individual person, with a definite role in society, than an attempt
at least at the universal role in a particular historical period. He is less
like a man than like a country or even a great society; we witness
within him the drama of a kind of civil war. The rhetoric of Mac-
Diarmid's best poetry is not the argument with others but the argument
with oneself.

The 'ideas', which to Crichton Smith seem so peremptory and
cantankerous (so much the ideas of an aggressively self-educated man)
are in the end elements in a total composition: like Yeats's 'images'.
The pose of wanting to change the reader and the world radically and
immediately is part of a properly poetic strategy; the building up of a
persona, which is something like Hobbes's Leviathan, or the giant
figures in Blake, a kind of composite emblematic Man. MacDiarmid is
a poet of the 'egotistical Sublime': one who tries to include everything
(including long passages lifted from other writers) in himself, rather
than, like Yeats, to lose himself in everything. But I want, before
labouring this point, to consider the nature of the discursive peom.

2. POETRY AS IMITATION OF DISCOURSE: POETRY AS DISCOURSE, NAKEDLY

'Poetry' – to repeat that phrase – 'is a round-about way of saying
things.' And a widely acceptable definition of the discursive poem
might be that it is an imitation of some human mode of discourse
rather than, nakedly, discourse in itself. There are, of course, great
English (I cannot, off hand, think of very many very great Scottish,
but some of Burns's verse epistles are very good 'think-poems' as
well as first-rate social-conversational pieces. He thinks in fits and
starts.) discursive poems, very near the tone and mode of good plain
prose. In one of these, *Religio Laici*, Dryden says:

> And this unpolished, rugged verse I chose,
> As fittest for discourse, and nearest prose.

But the real *thinking* has been done in prose, or silently, before the
composition of the verse starts. As Pope says, in another great discursive poem:

> True wit is nature to advantage dressed,
> What oft was thought, but ne'er so well expressed.

The primary thinking that has gone into such traditional discursive poems as *Religio Laici* or *An Essay on Criticism* is not thinking about the subject matter (about that the author has made up his mind already) but the mode of poetical presentation. Dryden had a powerful mind and the arguments for and against a merely natural theology have rarely been more concisely and cogently expressed than in *Religio Laici*: but what the poem convinces us of is not of the necessity of joining the Church of England but of its plain eloquence. Pope had a much less powerful mind though a much more various and alert sensibility than Dryden. But, again, *An Essay on Criticism*, beautifully summarising and exemplifying what in prose were already becoming stale commonplaces of neo-classical criticism, would not alter a single one of our critical attitudes (as Dr. Johnson's critical prose might, perhaps). It convinces us, in its sparkle and variety and assuredness, of Pope's youthful genius.

After these, in a later period, the greatest discursive poem in the English language is, I suppose, Wordsworth's *Prelude*, and here the case is slightly different. This is genuinely inward, the exploration of the growth of a poet's mind; there is a sense, quite often, of fumbling and groping: the mind is a much more original and profound mind than Dryden's or Pope's, it is innovating a whole new period of subjective sensibility, of emphasis not on the poetic product but on the poetic process. Yet this Rousseauistic autobiography is, after all, written in the epic blank verse and often in the diction of Milton. The poet's mind has become a 'heroic' subject, in the traditional sense. I think that MacDiarmid's mind has become a heroic subject for him, in that sense; but also, of course, he is a polemical, a satirical, one might say an opinionated poet, as Pope and Dryden were, and as Wordsworth was not. And he differs from them all in not having a set mould, even the set mould of Wordsworth's loose and flexible autobiographical Miltonism, into which to feed an at least partly preformed discourse. He is attempting, one might say, not to write a poetic imitation of discourse, but to discourse *in poetry* freshly and nakedly. How far, and in what ways, does he succeed? Let us look at some examples.

3. SOME PASSAGES FROM 'ON A RAISED BEACH'

Duncan Glen, in his preface to a beautifully printed recent edition of 'On A Raised Beach' refers with regret to the fact that this poem, which was first published in *Stony Limits and other poems* in 1934, has received little critical attention (except from James Burns Singer, in a fine article in *Encounter*) and was cut to a few lines in MacDiarmid's *Collected Poems* of 1962. Burns Singer, with his own special tumbling-over eagerness of language, referred to *Stony Limits* as the first book which established 'those types of versification (that lack of versification) and the concatenation of antagonistic ideas which are (MacDiarmid's) most original and far-reaching contribution to English – as opposed to Scottish – poetry. Here', Singer went on, 'we find those lines larded with learned allusions, interpenetrated by a terrifying stoicism, rich with surface mines of the blackest hatred, categorical polysyllabic, aphoristic lines following one another in ungrammatical abundance. It is a very beautiful, noble, and well-balanced book.' Duncan Glen adds, in his own introduction, that it would be hard to find a better-balanced description of 'On A Raised Beach', taken in isolation.

The first few lines illustrate MacDiarmid's vocabulary at, for the ordinary reader, its most obstinately impenetrable. Fortunately, most of the words are in the two volumes of *The Shorter Oxford Dictionary*, which I happen to have handy (I wonder if he had?):

> All is lithogenesis – or lochia,
> Carpolite fruit of the forbidden tree,
> Stones blacker than any in the Caaba,
> Cream-coloured caen-stone, chatoyant pieces,
> Celadon and corbeau, bistre and beige,
> Glaucous, hoar, enfouldered, cyathiform,
> Making mere faculae of the sun and moon,
> I study your glout, and gloss, but have
> No cadrans to adjust you with, and turn again
> From optik to haptik and like a blind man run
> My fingers over you, arris by arris, burr by burr . . .

It took me about quarter of an hour with the *Petit Larousse* and the *Shorter Oxford English Dictionary* to gloss this, and even yet I am in doubt about *haptik*, which clearly by context refers to touch as opposed to sight but may or may not have something to do with the

P

Scots verb *hap* (preterite *hapt*), to wrap up someone warmly as in a quilt. A prose translation might be:

Everything is born from stones – or is a dead and messy after-birth. Fossil fruit of the forbidden, stones blacker than the sacred stone of Mecca, cream-coloured as the light yellow building stone of Normandy, glittering pieces, green like Chinese jade (or Chinese celadon porcelain) and crow-coloured, dark brown and bown, greeny-grey, frosty, cup-shaped, making mere bright spots the sun and the moon, I study your sulking, and making my commentary, but have no quadrant[1] (clock-face) to adjust you with, and turning from seeing to feeling, and like a blind man run my fingers over you, sharp cutting edge by cutting edge, hard boss in the freestone by hard boss. . . . The translation clearly lacks a certain quality, of sheer miscellaneous pebbly puzzlingness, that the original has. The words as much as the stones are for MacDiarmid poetic objects, and it is interesting also that in the first three lines there would be indirect reminiscences of the book of Genesis Eden, and Mecca, in the fourth line a reference to Normandy (medieval cathedrals?) in the fifth line French colour words and a word for Chinese porcelain, later on a word suggesting Latin poetry ('glaucous')[2] and two archiac words, one from Spenser, 'enfouldered' and 'glout', as well as the scientific word 'faculae'.

The stone beach, indifferent and hostile to man, yet suggests the whole range, or a wide part of it, of human religion, geography, culture. If the word 'hapt' is implied in 'haptik' there is a pathos in stroking tenderly with one's hands what can never respond. The stones, in this long poem, are rather like the notion of 'reality' in Wallace Stevens's poems – something which is a 'vacuum' and with which man was no *noeud vital*, but which the imagination must confront all the same, since it cannot live on the imaginary.

I think MacDiarmid is probably old enough to have read as a boy Hugh Miller's *Old Red Sandstone*, which combined the elements of popular geology with natural theology. At heart, MacDiarmid is still a kind of natural theologian. The broken stones are the most ancient and enduring part of the earth we can get at. They will outlast us. They are not to be glanced at and forgotten, but are endlessly 'open' to the curiosity of the scientist or the poet who can see them as things not

1 There is *cardoon*, French *chardon*, a kind of semi-artichoke, or edible thistle, irrelevant here. Also metathesis.
2 Glaucaus is also a technical term in botany, but I think the Latin poetic context is more to the point here.

of any obvious use to him, not in any sense flattering him, but as sacredly what they are. They can help the human soul by offering it an image of endurance:

> Deep conviction or preference can seldom
> Find direct terms in which to express itself.
> Today on this shingle shelf
> I understand this pensive reluctance so well,
> This not discommendable obstinacy,
> These contrivances of an inexpressive critical feeling,
> These stones with their resolve that Creation shall not be
> Injured by iconoclasts and quacks. Nothing has stirred
> Since I lay down this morning an eternity ago
> But one bird. The widest open door is the least liable to intrusion,
> Ubiquitous as the sunlight, unfrequented as the sun.
> The inward gates of a bird are always open.
> It does not know how to shut them.
> That is the secret of its song,
> But whether any man's are ajar is doubtful.
> I look at these stones and know little about them,
> But I know their gates are open too . . .

As compared with the first passage, what we notice here is deliberate plainness and ineloquence, an unornate reflective quality. It is not so plain as it seems; the word 'Creation', as often in MacDiarmid, suggests that a religious feeling outwardly denied is being sustained somewhere at the back of the mind. The 'openness' of the bird and the stones as compared to the 'shutness' of man – man at the most 'ajar'! – is not an easy concept, and indeed it takes the whole long poem properly to develop it. (Incidentally, Singer seems to me wrong about 'the lack of versification': look for four main sense stresses, as in *Piers Plowman*, forget about stress-syllable metre, and you will scan most of these lines easily enough. There is no doubt about how to read them aloud.)

There are touches in this poem that suggest to me certain elements in the English romantic tradition:

> These stones will reach us long before we reach them.
> Cold, undistracted, eternal and sublime.
> They will stem all the torrents of vicissitude forever
> With a more than Roman peace.
> Death is a physical horror to me no more.

Compare (and, as the examiners say, contrast) Wordsworth:

> No motion has she now, no force.
> She neither hears nor sees.
> Rolled round in earth's diurnal course
> With rocks and stones and trees.

My friend John Hayward once told me that in a reading life-time of,
I suppose, between fifty and sixty years he had read all English poetry,
I suppose he ment that bulk of the best of English poetry, twice over
and hoped to read it three times over before he died. I shall never equal
or begin to compare with his taste or scholarship, but one privilege of a
teacher is to go over the few perfect and the many strong and moving
poems in our language many times with students who are sometimes
receptive. Both these passages are very strong; but the Wordsworth is
perfect; the MacDiarmid is struggling and mannerist, with a touch not
only of romantic feeling, but of the kind of abruptness and surprise
one associates with Jacobean drama. One is showing no disrespect for
the later MacDiarmid in saying that the poetry which, so to say,
'belongs to one's peace' is something other.

The old struggler compels admiration all the same:

> We must reconcile ourselves to the stones,
> Not the stones to us.
> Here a man must shed the encumbrances that muffle
> Contact with elemental things, the subtleties
> That seem inseparable from a humane life, and go apart
> Into a simple and sterner, more beautiful and more oppressive
>   world,
> Austerely intoxicating; the first draught is overpowering;
> Few survive it. It fills me with a sense of perfect form,
> The end seen from the beginning, as in a song.

He goes on (and perhaps goes on too long, making explicit what he
has already implied?):

> It is no song that conveys the feeling
> That there is no reason why it should ever stop,
> But the kindred form I am conscious of here
> Is the beginning and end of the world,
> The unsearchable masterpiece, the music of the spheres,
> Alpha and Omega, the Omnific Word.

He goes on to see in the crystalline world an example, though an almost impossible example, for mankind:

> These stones have the silence of supreme creative power,
> The direct and undisturbed way of working
> Which alone leads to greatness.
> What experience has any man crystallised,
> What weight of conviction accumulated,
> What depth of life suddenly seen entire
> In some nigh supernatural moment
> And made a symbol and lived up to
> With such resolution, such Spartan impassivity?

Well! (one half thinks of answering): the philosophy of Spinoza, the late sculptures of Michelangelo, Milton's *Samson Agonistes*, Mycenae. . . . Human culture, rich in many things, is not lacking in examples, if one's taste runs that way, of the austere sublime. But he goes on again and he reminds me again of the self-tormenting, rich, slightly forced self-communings (in the letters and in the *Reminiscences*, particularly) of Carlyle. Carlylean, a very late type of Scottish Calvinist, seeking a God as hard and testing and as cold as rock: anti-Goethean, ungenerous to the huge rich variety of what human life has been (and has achieved), MacDiarmid *is*: Hebraic, not Hellenic, a man seeking his peace among the mountains and the rocks.

He goes on:

> It is a frenzied and chaotic age . . .

(when was it not, and what else, if humankind retains any energy, would we ever expect it to be?) . . .

> It is a frenzied and chaotic age,
> Like a growth of weeds on the site of a demolished building.
> How shall we set ourselves against it,
> Imperturbable, inscrutable, in the world and yet not in it,
> Silent under the torments it inflicts upon us,
>> With a constant centre,
> With a single inspiration, foundations firm and invariable;
>> By what immense exercise of will,
> Inconceivable discipline, courage, and endurance,
>> Self-purification and anti-humanity,
>>> Be ourselves without interruption,
>>>> Adamantine and inexorable?

This again is the voice of the prophet in the desert. If I were to allow myself to fall into the temptation of argument, I would say: many new buildings have been built in this century (mathematical logic, modular architecture, philosophy and science of language, art as analysis and reconstruction of forms): we need (and humanity would not have survived without) a multiplicity, not a singlness, of inspiration: courage and endurance (think of the wars, revolutions, and famines of this century and of all centuries!) are remarkably common: self-purification does not imply 'anti-humanity' but an insight into the human stuff we are all made of . . . and so on, the Erasmian view against the Lutheran or Calvinist view.

But how irrelevant these debating-society points are against the properly poetic eloquence: MacDiarmid as a brittle but determined version of Samson Agonistes: struggling not merely to submit to, but to *be*, some modern equivalent of the fierce Old Testament God of the *Book of Judges*. This is the poetry of the Elect:

Great work cannot be combined with surrender to the crowd.

It is a deeper struggle than that, that of the man who does not 'surrender to the crowd' but seeks to save its soul: of a man obsessed with the image of the stone rolling away from the tomb, and yet obsessed also with the idea that the meaning of life is acceptance of the fact of death. As E. M. Forster says in *Howords End*: 'Death destroys a man. The idea of death saves him.' Something like that is said towards the end of 'On A Raised Beach'.

> Detached intellectuals, not one stone will move,
> Not the least of them, not a fraction of an inch. It is not
>   The reality of life that is hard to know.
> It is the nearest of all and easiest to grasp,
> But you must participate in it to proclaim it.
> – I lift a stone; it is the meaning of life I clasp
> Which is death, for that is the meaning of death;
> How else does any man yet participate
>   In the life of a stone,
> How else can any man yet become
> Sufficiently at one with creation, sufficiently alone,
> Till as the stone that covers him he lies dumb
> And the stone at the mouth of his grave is not overthrown?

I would take this as one of the least successful passages. It is an orthodox Marxist sentiment that 'detached intellectuals' should not be detached, because in detachment they can see nothing truly, we must participate to understand. What I am questioning is not that (here) but the adequacy of the image. Why should anybody, even 'poetically', want to raise any of the stones on this raised beach? Nature has made them and Man often shows his best respect for nature by leaving her alone. The reproach seems inept. But then we see that lifting a stone is a symbolic Samsonic gesture; this dead weight we are straining to lift is the meaning of life, is – Heidegger rather than Marx! – death. (I think a good Marxian like a good Crocean idealist would not make too much fuss about death; I die, yes, but there will be other poets and critics; the kind of function I approve of goes on; or say the whole human race comes to an end some day: that is a long way off and meanwhile there are plenty of ways in which we can usefully occupy our time. These sentiments are flat, but they express also a common-sense view of things, which can conduce to useful and sane behaviour. More profoundly, is it not nobler to live eternally, as the artist and the thinker do, in time – for thought and art *are* timeless! – rather than to worry too much that one's own life in time must have an end?).

The point of that last passage is that MacDiarmid though a Marxist is not a humanist, indeed he could be described as an anti-humanist. He is preoccupied with death in what is essentially a religious way. It worries me a little, I must confess, that he uses the stones as symbols of death. Some of them of course are fossils. But many of them must be originally of crystalline formation, with their own principles of inner shaping, but not animate. It worries me also – and I mean from a poetic not an argumentative point of view – that MacDiarmid wants us to feel a self-reproach about the stones on the beach. We have done them no harm; could have done them no good. So the feeling seems artificial and strained.

One should note, however, that the central symbolism of this poem, at this point, is Christian, or anti-Christian: there will be no rolling away of the stone from the mouth of the tomb, no resurrection. But this becomes a lament:

> – Each of these stones on this raised beach,
>   Every stone in the world,
> Covers infinite death, beyond the reach
> Of the dead it hides; and cannot be hurled
> Aside yet to let any of them come forth, as love
>   Once made a stone move

> (Though I do not depend on that
>   My case to prove).
> So let us beware of death; the stones will have
> Their revenge; we have lost all approach to them,
> But soon we shall become as those we have betrayed,
> And they will seal us as fast in our graves
> As our indifference and ignorance seals them; . . .

Again, here, the feeling seems strained, for, to repeat, I cannot see what the stones want their revenge for, or what our ignorance and indifference is. Both geology and crystallography are in a thriving condition and, if one is looking for sculpture that respects the essential nature of stone, there is the work of Brancusi, say, and Barbara Hepworth and Henry Moore. To be very Scotch, what is MacDiarmid 'girning' about here? But it is true, I suppose, as the French poet Francis Ponge has said, that language, even poetic language, generalises and that no poet has ever described the unicity, the uniqueness, of some one particular pebble. This may be the sort of betrayal and ignorance that MacDiarmid has in mind, and it makes more poetic sense.

> But let us not be afraid to die.
> No heavier and colder and quieter then,
> No more motionless, do stones lie
>   In death than in life to all men.
> It is no more difficult in death than here
> – Though slow as the stones the powers develop
> To rise from the grave – to get a life worth having;
> And in death – unlike life – we lose nothing that is truly ours.

I feel a fine eloquence here and there is no trouble about grammar – Jimmy Singer was as confidently wrong in saying that the grammar is bad as in saying that there is a 'lack of versification' – but I am puzzled because I can only make sense of this passage in relation to something like the Christian doctrine of the General Resurrection, and I suppose, at least, that as a Marxist MacDiarmid repudiates this doctrine, and from what I know of world religions it is silly to talk of 'something like' the Christian doctrine of the Resurrection. It is a unique doctrine, other world religions believe in a purely spiritual immortality or in absorption in a single cosmic spirit or in reincarnation, but none in the resurrection. Is MacDiarmid saying, like D. H. Lawrence in 'Bavarian Gentians', that out of Hades, the dead winter soil, new life, the life of the released Persephone, grows? I do not think so: there are only barren rocks in this poem, no humus, however thin. He means, I think, some personal doctrine of his own, whose feeling he conveys very power-fully, but whose intellectual nature baffles me. And this is one of the flaws in a powerful poem.

The very last short passage of the poem, like the very first, sends one hurrying to one's dictionaries. Perhaps, once I have deciphered it, it will throw some light on the whole structure?

> Diallage of the world's debate, end of the long auxesis,
> Although no ébrillade of Pegasus can here avail,
> I prefer your enchorial characters – the futhorc of the future –
> To the hieroglyphics of all the other forms of Nature.
> Song, your apprentice encrinite, seems to sweep
> The Heavens with a last entrochal movement;
> And, with the same word that began it, closes
> Earth's vast epanadiplosis.

Ébrillade must be a fairly rare French word, since my *Petit Larousse Illustré* does not have it; but let us guess that it is connected with *briller*, that the *e* is the Latin *ex* or *e*, and that it means something like 'a shining out from', perhaps because of the *ade* termination (like par*ade*, caval*cade*) a kind of processional movement or cavorting of Pegasus that makes him shine out from the sky. 'Enchorial' is used of the popular or demotic as distinct from the priestly or hieratic or hieroglyphic way of writing the ancient Egyptian pictogram-charac-ters. 'Futhorc' – named from the first six letters, f, u, th, o or a, r, k, is the Runic alphabet, connected especially with ancient Scandinavia, but also the word Runic is applied to an interlacing type of ancient Celtic ornament. Runes were the kind of mysterious poems appropri-ately written in the Runic alphabet. The word *futhorc* can also be spelt *futhork* or *futhark*.

'Encrinite' is a fossil crinoid and a crinoid (the root meaning is 'lily-shaped') is an echinoderm, and an echinoderm is a sea-creature of the sea-urchin, sea-cucumber sort, its skin typically covered with spines; what is particular to the crinoid is that it has a calyx-like body, stalked and rooted. An entrochal movement is a wheel-like movement, but the adjective is particularly applied to the wheel-like plates of which certain crinoids are composed. 'Epanadiplosis' is not in either *The Shorter Oxford Dictionary* or, in its French equivalent, in *Le Petit Larousse*. I feel I may have come across it in books, like George Puttenham's, on Renaissance terms of rhetoric, and it could appropri-

ately apply to a piece of writing, like *Finnegans Wake*, which begins in
the middle of a sentence and ends at the beginning of the sentence so
ideally you read circularly on for ever (you could go back now to
the beginning of the 'Raised Beach'.) This guess that *epanadiplosis* is a
rhetorical term of art is plausible because *auxesis* is one, also, meaning
amplificatio or hyperbole.

With all these clues, could we attempt a prose translation of the
final passage? I think that MacDiarmid is no longer addressing the
reader but the stones (like Keats addressing the Urn): he is saying:
'Clock that measures the pettiness of the human struggle, conclusion
of the long hyperbole of man's activity, though no brilliancy of poetic
activity (no shaking of Pegasus's shining hooves in the sky) can avail
me in this desolate rocky place, I prefer your demotic characters – the
marks on the stones that will be the runes of the future – to the
hieroglyphics of all other forms of Nature (including Man). Song,
like the little fossil crinoid which has been your apprentice, seems to
sweep the heavens with his plate-like wheels; and, with the same word
that began it, Earth's circuitous rhetorical statement comes to an end.'

Perhaps here, as in Keats's 'To Autumn' the poetic attempt to
escape from transience to the permanent ends in finding permanence
in the very regularity of the transient, finds something like the music
of the spheres. And a deeply troubled spirit finds escape from the 'fury
and the mire of human veins' not like Yeats in monuments of man's
intellect but in that aspect of the earth, the geological, which is at once
the most obstinate, the most intractable, the slowest to change, and
the furthest from ordinary human sympathies (poets identify themselves easily enough with birds, flowers, moving clouds, bright stars,
the changing moon: MacDiarmid finds his final consolation in an
image of rocky sullenness and stillness, which alone can quiet, for the
time being, his rage at human folly and failure).

4. SOME GENERAL REMARKS ON THE CHARACTER OF MACDIARMID'S LATER POETRY

I have not expounded or in a detailed sense criticised this poem; I
have done a little sight-reading and dictionary-construing: but the
poem has raised certain general thoughts in my mind, which apply,
I think, not only to this but to very much of MacDiarmid's later
poetry, his poetry of self-communing, of naked discourse.

Wölflinn, in his great pioneer book, *The Renaissance and the*

Baroque, has much to say about the new characteristics of the Baroque as compared with the Renaissance: 'the massiveness, the enormous weight, the lack of formal discipline and thorough-going articulation, the increased animation, the restlessness, the violent agitation . . .' He speaks of Michelangelo's influence on the Baroque, and notes, for instance, that unlike a true Renaissance artist, it was not in Michelangelo's nature to express harmony or happiness: 'Michelangelo's men and women appear to be the unresisting victims of an inner compulsion, not harmoniously and uniformly, but fitfully, so that some are expressive to the utmost while others are almost totally lifeless and inert . . . Vitality is unevenly distributed . . . some parts are superhuman in their strength, others all weight.'

It seems to me that on looking over the passages I have quoted from 'On A Raised Beach' and still more on looking through one of the much longer later poems like *In Memoriam James Joyce,* one has an impression not dissimilar to that which Wölflinn describes: 'enormous weight and massiveness', a distinct lack of 'formal discipline and thorough-going articulation' – though they can be scanned, these long poems are not in any particular metre, and though they are argumentative, they have not, quite unlike *Religio Laici* or *An Essay on Criticism,* or even the *Prelude,* a ground-plan of structure, a reason in themselves why, and where, they should begin and end – and on the other hand there is, in the more striking passages, 'the animation, the restlessness, the violent agitation' of which Wölflinn speaks. In writing these long poems, MacDiarmid too appears to be the 'unresisting victim of an inner compulsion, so that some [passages] are expressive to the utmost while others are totally lifeless and inert . . . Vitality is unevenly distributed . . . some parts are superhuman in their strength, others are all weight.'

Even more relevantly, Wölflinn describes how in poetry too in the Baroque age 'the light and easy grace of the Renaissance gave way to seriousness, dignity, the gay playfulness to pompous rustling splendour.' He contrasts the lightness, quickness, and airiness of Ariosto's *Orlando Furioso* (1516) whose opening lines in Sir John Harington's translation are

> Of dames, of knights, of armes, of loves delight,
> Of courtesie, of high attempts I speake,
> Then when the Moores transported all their might
> On Affrick seas the Force of France to breake,

with the opening lines of Tasso's *Gerusalemme Liberata*, which, since
the translation by Hoole is abominably flat and prosaic, I will endeavour
to render myself:

> Those pious arms, and the Chief, I sing
> Who the great sepulchre of Christ set free;
> Much he with heart and much with hand did sway,
> And much he suffered in the glorious quest;
> And in vain Hell opposed him, and in vain
> Took arms the mingled Asian and Libyan throngs;
> Since Heaven was on his side . . .

Wölflinn notes 'the lofty adjectives, the resounding line endings, the
measured repetitions ("much . . .", "much . . .", "in vain", "and in
vain"): the weighty sentence construction, and the generally slower
rhythm." But he notes also that the grandeur is not only in the
expression; the verbal images become larger, and perhaps vaguer.
Boiardo, in the early Renaissance, says: 'To Angelica shines the morning star, the lily in the garden, the rose.' This succession of quick
distinct images does not suit Berni who is making a Baroque *rifacci-
miento* of Boiardo: instead, we get: 'To Angelica shines the bright star
in the east, yes, to be true, it is the sun.' The move from the Renaissance
to the Baroque is a move from a love of details and particulars for their
own sakes (such as we get, for instance, in MacDiarmid's *A Drunk
Man Looks at the Thistle*) to something more monotonous but by
intention at least grander:

'Now, however, we step further back and survey the general effect;
we do not require grandeur in the individual part, but only a general
impression; there is *less perception and more atmosphere* . . . The
baroque has no sense of the significance of individual forms, only for
the more muted effect of the whole. The individual, defined and plastic
form has ceased to matter; compositions are in the mass effects of light
and shade and the most indefinite of all elements have become the real
means of expression.'

The expression 'The Scottish Renaissance' was not a mere slogan.

The best of MacDiarmid's early poems, whether lyrical, satirical,
comical, or a mixture of all three things, have the qualities that
Wölflinn assigns to Renaissance poetry (as, indeed, have the poems of
the Scottish poets who can be considered as his predecessors, Dunbar,
Robert Fergusson, Burns): a sense of the variety of things, a quickness
and gaiety, an untroubled acceptance of life within its limitations, what

we call humanism. MacDiarmid was the leader of the Scottish Renaissance. In his later work, he is anti-humanistic: he seeks transcendence, he tortures himself and strains: he can no longer represent, nor does he desire, the rhythms, the harmonies, the humours of ordinary human happiness. He has a sense of oppressive weight incumbent on him, he sometimes collapses under this inertly, he sometimes struggles against it with titanic energy. Like Michelangelo, he has a certain *terribilità*. There is much less perception, detailed perception, in his late poems, but a much more unified and grandiose atmosphere. He has moved from the humanistic to the religious; he takes on, deliberately, more burdens than he can well bear. He does nothing than can be done easily and gracefully. He is the lone representative of a Scottish (or, as Jimmy Singer suggested, of an English) new Baroque. The repetitions, the vagueness, the grandeurs, the movement and stress and the impatience with the limitations of the human condition itself are all there.

The late poems oppress us or impress us or bore us, sometimes, these abrupt alternations of the strenuous and the inert, but they do not offer us, anyway, any more than Michelangelo does, the ordinary kind of artistic pleasure. They are struggling beyond the limits of art. They are not what I turn to, when I am turning to poetry for pleasure. But let us admire the lonely effort that has gone into them, and let us admire the strong old man, stonily intransigent, implacable, struggling always for transcendence.

A Hugh MacDiarmid Bibliography

W. R. AITKEN

The bibliography of Hugh MacDiarmid is complicated enough, even if one limits the record to the books, pamphlets, and separate publications for which he has been responsible, leaving aside the complexities of his many contributions to books, periodicals, and the press. The poet himself is well aware of these complications; in a recent letter to the present writer he admits: 'I know I am a bibliographer's nightmare.'

The complications of MacDiarmid's bibliography have two main causes: firstly, his use of a number of pseudonyms, possibly not all yet revealed, and secondly, the activities of a number of his friends and admirers in sponsoring limited and other special editions, sometimes as broadsheets or pamphlets printing only one or two poems. These privately printed, limited editions of single poems, or of a few related poems, are mainly the work of K. D. Duval, publisher and joint-editor of the seventieth-birthday *Festschrift* (1962), or of Colin Hamilton, his partner, or of Duncan Glen, who has told the story of his concern with the printing of MacDiarmid's poetry in his essay, *A Small Press and Hugh MacDiarmid* (1970). They must not be dismissed as though they were irresponsibly conceived bibliographical curiosities, produced in deliberately limited editions more for the glory of the printer and publisher than for the poet. It is, for example, very doubtful if the poems contained in *A Lap of Honour* (1967), the first of the collections designed to supplement the *Collected Poems* of 1962, and perhaps the best-planned recent volume of his poetry, would be known but for Duncan Glen's succession of pamphlets, privately printed between 1964 and 1967. Hugh MacDiarmid acknowledges that 'Duncan Glen . . . has done a great deal . . . to recover many poems I'd lost sight of and forgotten I'd written'.

Some of C. M. Grieve's pseudonyms are revealed and discussed in a pamphlet Duncan Glen wrote and published in 1964, *The Literary Masks of Hugh MacDiarmid*. Hugh MacDiarmid made his first appearance in the first number of the literary review, *The Scottish Chapbook*, which Grieve founded in August 1922, and edited and published from his home in Montrose. His first work was a semi-dramatic study, 'Nisbet, an interlude in post-war Glasgow'. The first poem of Hugh MacDiarmid's to be published in *The Scottish Chabpook*, 'The Watergaw', appeared in the third issue, for October 1922 (it had been printed previously in *The Dunfermline Press* for 30 September 1922), and in the same issue Grieve's editorial 'Causerie' drew attention to the new contributor:

> The work of Mr. Hugh M'Diarmid . . . is peculiarly interesting because he is, I think, the first Scottish writer who has addressed himself to the question of the extendability (without psychological violence) of the vernacular to embrace the whole range of modern culture – or, in other words, tried to make up the leeway of the language.

So, like 'Arthur Leslie' thirty years later, Grieve had to explain what MacDiarmid was trying to do.

The relationship between Grieve and MacDiarmid, as between James Leslie Mitchell and Lewis Grassic Gibbon, is difficult to define. Originally it seemed that Grieve wrote in prose while his 'distant cousin' MacDiarmid was the poet, but MacDiarmid later turned to prose and is now the acknowledged author of several volumes of essays and the like and Grieve is silent. Perhaps a clue is to be found in the inscription which that perceptive critic and early admirer, Denis Saurat, wrote in a copy of his *Histoire des Religions*:

> To C. M. Grieve, who will criticize
> and MacDiarmid, who will approve
> Très amicalement,
> D. Saurat.

It is also difficult to ascertain when and how it came to be known that C. M. Grieve and Hugh MacDiarmid were one and the same, but it is certainly true that in the late 1920s and even early 1930s their identity was still unknown to quite a number of people interested in Scottish literature. By 1934, however, when Eric Linklater portrayed Hugh MacDiarmid as Hugh Skene in *Magnus Merriman*, it was generally known that the two were one.

The bibliography which follows does not attempt to record the material about MacDiarmid and his work. One point can be made briefly here, however. Nine years ago there was still no book-length biographical or critical study dealing solely with MacDiarmid's life and work. The first to appear was the seventieth-birthday *Festschrift* edited by

K. D. Duval and Sydney Goodsir Smith (1962); it was followed by Kenneth Buthlay's study in the 'Writers and Critics' series (1964) and by Duncan Glen's historical and critical survey, *Hugh MacDiarmid (Christopher Murray Grieve) and the Scottish Renaissance*, published in the same year. MacDiarmid himself has written: 'It was in 1962, however, that the real break-through came.'

Periodical articles and reviews continue to appear, and there have been a number of essays, and studies, in books or pamphlets, and special MacDiarmid issues of such periodicals as *Agenda* (1967–68) and *Akros* (1970). The second part of the two-part MacDiarmid issue of *Akros* contained a notable contribution from J. K. Annand that puts the record straight regarding certain facts of the poet's early career.

This bibliography can be, of course, only an interim statement, the record of an already prolific writer who is still actively planning further publications with a greater expectation that they will in fact be published than at any time in his long literary career. Hugh MacDiarmid's importance is at last recognised.

A BOOKS

1   *Northern Numbers, being representative selections from certain living Scottish poets*. Edinburgh and London: T. N. Foulis, 1920.
    The foreword is signed with the initials C. M. G.
    Issued in two bindings, cloth and paper, and also bound with the second series in one volume.

2   *Northern Numbers, being representative selections from certain living Scottish poets*. Edited by C. M. Grieve. Second series. Edinburgh and London: T. N. Foulis, 1921.
    Issued in two bindings, cloth and paper, and also bound together with the first series in one volume.

3   *Northern Numbers, being representative selections from certain living Scottish poets*. Edited by C. M. Grieve. Third series. Montrose: C.M. Grieve, 1922.

4   (a) *Annals of the Five Senses*, by C. M. Grieve. Montrose: C. M. Grieve, 1923.
    (b) —— Edinburgh: Porpoise Press, 1930.
    A reissue with a new imprint.

5   *Sangschaw*, by Hugh M'Diarmid. Edinburgh and London: Blackwood, 1925.

6   *Penny Wheep*, by Hugh M'Diarmid. Edinburgh and London: Black-wood, 1926.

7   (a) *A Drunk Man Looks at the Thistle*, by Hugh M'Diarmid. Edin-burgh and London: Blackwood, 1926.

(b) —— With an introduction by David Daiches. New edition. Glasgow: Caledonian Press, 1953.

This edition omits the Author's Note of the original edition but prints an 'Author's note to second edition' (p. vii–xi) as well as the Introduction by David Daiches (p. xiii–xx).

(c) —— Third edition. Edinburgh: Castle Wynd Printers, 1956. Issued in two bindings, cloth and paper.

This edition gives the Author's Note and the entire text as in the first edition and prints as appendixes the Author's Note (Appendix A, p. 97–101) and the Introduction by Dr. David Daiches (Appendix B, p. 103–10) which prefaced the second edition, published in 1953.

(d) —— Fourth edition. Edinburgh: The 200 Burns Club, 1962. Published on the occasion of the poet's seventieth birthday.

(e) —— Illustrated with eight woodcuts by Frans Masereel. Falkland: Kulgin Duval & Colin H. Hamilton, 1969.

160 copies printed in Dante type by Giovanni Mardersteig on the hand-press of the Officina Bodoni in Verona.

All copies numbered, ten not for sale with roman numerals, and all signed by the author, the illustrator and the printer.

Although dated November 1969, the book was not published until summer 1970.

(f) —— Edited by John C. Weston. Amherst, Mass.: The University of Massachusetts Press, 1971.

In this edition the spelling of MacDiarmid's Scots is standardised by the editor in accordance with the poet's statement in his letter pub-lished in *The Scotsman* on 28th September 1968 and reprinted in *Lines Review*, no. 27, November 1968, p. 33.

8   *Robert Burns*, 1759–1796. [Edited by] C. M. Grieve. London: Benn, [1926]. *The Augustan Books of Poetry*.

9   *Contemporary Scottish Studies*, by C. M. Grieve. First series. London: Leonard Parsons, 1926.

These critical studies originally appeared in the *Scottish Educational Journal* (commencing in May 1925) and are reprinted 'practically in their original form'. A promised second series was never published.

10   *Albyn, or Scotland and the Future*, by C. M. Grieve. London: Kegan Paul, Trench, Trubner, 1927. *To-day and To-morrow Series*.

11   *The Lucky Bag*, by Hugh M'Diarmid. Edinburgh: Porpoise Press, 1927. *Porpoise Press Broadsheet*, 3rd series, no. 5.

12   *The Present Position of Scottish Music*, by C. M. Grieve. Montrose: C. M. Grieve, 1927.

Reprinted from the *Border Standard*, 20th and 27th November and 4th December 1927. Among the other books by MacDiarmid listed in *Second Hymn to Lenin* (1935) this pamphlet is cited as *The Present Condition of Scottish Music*, but 'position' not 'condition' is the word in the title.

13   *The Present Condition of Scottish Arts and Affairs*. [Anon.]
Issued by the Committee of the Scottish Centre of the P.E.N. Club. Dalbeattie: *The Stewartry Observer*, [1928].

14   *The Scottish National Association of April Fools*, by Gillechriosd Mac A'Ghreidhir. Reprinted from the *Pictish Review*, 1 (6), April 1928. Aberdeen: The University Press, 1928.

15   *Scotland in* 1980, by C. M. Grieve. Montrose: C. M. Grieve, 1929. Reprinted from the *Scots Independent*, 3 (8), June 1929.

16   *The Handmaid of the Lord*, by Ramon Maria de Tenreiro. London: Secker, 1930.
This anonymous translation is first listed among MacDiarmid's works in *Second Hymn to Lenin* (1935).

17   *To Circumjack Cencrastus, or The Curly Snake*, by Hugh M'Diarmid. Edinburgh and London: Blackwood, 1930.

18   *Living Scottish Poets*. Edited by C. M. Grieve. London: Benn, 1931. *The Augustan Books of Poetry*.

19   *O wha's been here afore me, lass*. With drawing by Frederick Carter. [London: E. Lahr, 1931.] *Blue Moon Poem for Christmas* 1931.
There was also a special edition of 100 numbered copies signed by the author.
This poem had appeared previously in *A Drunk Man Looks at the Thistle* (1926).

20   *First Hymn to Lenin and other poems*, by Hugh McDiarmid. London: Unicorn Press, 1931.
A limited edition of 450 numbered copies and a special large paper edition of 50 copies numbered and signed by the poet. There is an introductory essay by 'AE' (George William Russell) and a portrait frontispiece from a crayon drawing, also by 'AE'.
The 'First Hymn' originally appeared in *New English Poems*, edited by Lascelles Abercrombie (London: Gollancz 1931).
It was reprinted in *Three Hymns to Lenin* (1957).

21   *Warning Democracy*, by C. H. Douglas. London: C. M. Grieve, 1931.

22   *Tarras*. Edinburgh: *The Free Man*, 1932.
Limited edition of 20 copies with frontispiece 'Macdiarmid and the Horse Punchkin' from an oil-painting by William Johnstone.
'Tarras' originally appeared in the *Free Man*, 25th June 1932, and was reprinted in *Scots Unbound* (1932).

23   *Second Hymn to Lenin*. Thakeham: Valda Trevlyn, [1932].
Limited edition of 100 copies.

There is a cover drawing of the poet by Flora Macdonald and a portrait frontispiece by William Johnstone.

An Author's Note states: 'Like the contents of my volume, "First Hymn to Lenin and other Poems" (Unicorn Press, Ltd., 1931), this poem is a short separable item in my long poem "Clann Albainn" [*sic*] now in course of preparation.' In the event *Clann Albann* never appeared; but see notes on the 'complete scheme' in the *Modern Scot*, 2 (2), July 1931, p. 107, and 'Clann Albann: an explanation' in the *Scots Observer*, 12th August 1933.

The 'Second Hymn' originally appeared in *The Criterion* (vol. 11, no. 45, July 1932, p. 593–8). It was reprinted in *Second Hymn to Lenin and other poems* (1935) and *Three Hymns to Lenin* (1957).

24 *Scots Unbound and other poems*. Stirling: Eneas Mackay, 1932.

Edition limited to 350 signed copies.

There is a portrait frontispiece of the poet's head in bronze by William Lamb.

An Author's Note states: 'The poems in this volume, like those in my *First Hymn to Lenin and Other Poems* (Unicorn Press, 1931) and *Second Hymn to Lenin* (Valda Trevlyn, Thakeham, 1932), are separable items from the first volume of my long poem, "Clann Albann," now in preparation.'

The title poem, 'Scots Unbound', was reprinted in *Stony Limits and Scots Unbound* (1956).

25 *Five Bits of Miller*. Now for the first time set up and printed from the manuscript. London: The Author, 1934.

Edition limited to 40 numbered copies signed by the author.

Reprinted in *The Uncanny Scot* (1968).

26 (a) *Scottish Scene, or The Intelligent Man's Guide to Albyn*, [by] Lewis Grassic Gibbon and Hugh MacDiarmid. London: Jarrolds, 1934.

A cheap edition was issued by the same publisher in 1937.

(b) —— London and Melbourne: Hutchinson, for the National Book Association, n.d.

This reset edition was also issued by Readers Union, by arrangement with Hutchinson.

27 *Stony Limits and other poems*. London: Gollancz, 1934.

Reprinted, with the restoration of certain excluded poems and with the title poem of *Scots Unbound* (1932), as *Stony Limits and Scots Unbound and other poems* (1956).

28 *At the Sign of the Thistle: a collection o, essays*. London: Stanley Nott, [1934].

29 *Selected Poems*. London: Macmillan, 1934. *Macmillan's Contemporary Poets*.

A selection, by the poet himself, from *Sangschaw*, *Penny Wheep*, *A Drunk Man Looks at the Thistle*, *Scots Unbound* and *Stony Limits*.

30   *The Birlinn of Clanranald* [*Birlinn Chlann-Raghnaill*], by Alexander
     MacDonald: translated from the Scots Gaelic of Alasdair Mac-
     Mhaighstir Alasdair. St Andrews: The Abbey Book Shop, 1935.
       Limited to 100 numbered copies signed by the translator. Reprinted
       from the *Modern Scot*, 5 (4), January 1935, p. 230–47.

31   *Second Hymn to Lenin and other poems.* London: Stanley Nott, 1935.
     The dust-wrapper carries a drawing of the poet by William John-
     stone.
       The 'Second Hymn' had been published previously in a limited
       edition in 1932. It was reprinted in *Three Hymns to Lenin* (1957).

32   *Charles Doughty and the Need for Heroic Poetry.* [St. Andrews: *The
     Modern Scot*, 1936.]
       A reprint of an article published in the *Modern Scot*, 6 (4), January
       1936, p. 308–18. It is reprinted in *Selected Essays* (1969).

33   *Scottish Eccentrics.* London: Routledge, 1936.

34   *Scotland, and the Question of a Popular Front against Fascism and War.*
     Whalsay: The Hugh MacDiarmid Book Club, [1938].

35   *Dìreadh.* [Dunfermline: *The Voice of Scotland*, 1938.]
     Edition limited to 20 copies.
       A reprint of a long poem published in *The Voice of Scotland*,
       1 (3), December 1938, pp. 13–21. 'One of the shorter separable
       lyrics interspersed in an immensely-long as-yet-unpublished poem,
       Cornish Heroic Song for Valda Trevlyn.'

36   (a) *The Islands of Scotland: Hebrides, Orkneys, and Shetlands.* London:
     Batsford, 1939.
     (b) —— New York: Scribners, 1939.

37   *Speaking for Scotland.* London: The Lumphen Press, 1939. *Broadsheet
     no. 3*, edited by Paul Potts.

38   (a) *The Golden Treasury of Scottish Poetry.* Selected and edited by
     Hugh MacDiarmid. London: Macmillan, 1940.
     (b) —— London: Macmillan, 1946. *Golden Treasury Series.*

39   *Cornish Heroic Song for Valda Trevlyn.* Glasgow: Caledonian Press,
     [1943].
       This 'opening section of an extremely long unpublished poem' was
       first published in the final issue of *The Criterion* (vol. 18, no. 71,
       January 1939, p. 195–203), where the poem is dated 1936. It was
       reprinted in *A Kist of Whistles* (1947).

40   *Lucky Poet: a self-study in literature and political ideas, being the auto-
     biography of Hugh MacDiarmid* (*Christopher Murray Grieve*). London:
     Methuen, 1943.
       There is a frontispiece portrait from a photograph by Helen B.
       Cruickshank.

41   *Selected Poems of Hugh MacDiarmid.* Edited by R. Crombie Saunders.
     Glasgow: Maclellan, 1944. *Poetry Scotland Series*, no. 6.

There is a portrait frontispiece from a photograph.

With the approval of the poet the editor of this selection made 'certain orthographical changes' in the 'texts of the poems in Scots'.

42 *Speaking for Scotland: selected poems of Hugh MacDiarmid*. Baltimore: Contemporary Poetry, 1946. *Distinguished Poets Series*, vol. 3.

This first American edition has an introduction by Compton Mackenzie and a portrait frontispiece from a portrait of the poet by Barker Fairley.

The selection, by the poet himself, is almost the same as the *Selected Poems* published by Macmillan in 1934, with the addition of three poems 'not previously published in book form'.

There is a glossary followed by notes on the pronunciation of Scottish words, a few general notes, and 'literal renderings into English' of five of the poems.

43 *Poems of the East-West Synthesis*. Glasgow: Caledonian Press, 1946.

Reprinted from *The Voice of Scotland*, 2 (3) March and 2 (4) June 1946.

44 *A Kist of Whistles: new poems*. Glasgow: Maclellan, [1947]. *Poetry Scotland Series*, no. 10.

The title is one that MacDiarmid first used in 1922 when a series of poems began to appear in the *Scottish Chapbook* under the heading 'From "A Kist of Whistles"'.

45 *William Soutar: Collected Poems*. Edited with an introductory essay by Hugh MacDiarmid. London: Andrew Dakers, 1948.

The introduction (pp. 9–21) is dated May 1944. It is reprinted in *Selected Essays* (1969).

46 *Robert Burns: Poems*. Selected and introduced by Hugh MacDiarmid. London: Grey Walls Press, 1949. *Crown Classics*.

47 *Cunninghame Graham: a centenary study*. With a foreword by R. E. Muirhead. Glasgow: Caledonian Press, [1952].

48 *The Politics and Poetry of Hugh MacDiarmid*, by Arthur Leslie. Reprinted from *The National Weekly*. Glasgow: Caledonian Press, [1952].

This pseudonymous essay is reprinted in *Selected Essays* (1969), where it is acknowledged to be 'MacDiarmid on MacDiarmid'.

49 *Selections from the Poems of William Dunbar*. Edited with introduction by Hugh MacDiarmid. Edinburgh: Oliver & Boyd, for the Saltire Society, 1952. *The Saltire Classics*.

50 (a) *Selected Poems of Hugh MacDiarmid*. Edited by Oliver Brown. Glasgow: Maclellan, for the Scottish Secretariat, 1954.

Issued in three bindings: paper, cloth and a de luxe edition.

(b) *Poems of Hugh MacDiarmid*. Selected by Oliver Brown. Glasgow: for the Scottish Secretariat, 1955.

Issued in three bindings: paper, cloth and a de luxe edition. A reissue of the above with a different title and imprint.

51 *Francis George Scott: an essay on the occasion of his seventy-fifth birth-day, 25th January 1955.* Edinburgh: M. Macdonald, 1955.

52 *In Memoriam James Joyce: from A Vision of World Language.* With decorations by John Duncan Fergusson. Glasgow: Maclellan, on behalf of the subscribers, 1955.

> Issued in two bindings: a limited edition on special paper, signed by author and artist, and the ordinary cloth edition. A second impression (Glasgow: Maclellan, 1956) corrects a few misprints.

53 *Selected Poems of William Dunbar.* Edited and introduced by Hugh MacDiarmid. Glasgow: Maclellan, 1955.

> A selection of Dunbar's poems by Hugh MacDiarmid was announced to appear in the Crown Classics series of the Grey Walls Press, but the firm went out of business before it was published. This, however, would appear to be the very book: it is printed by the firm who printed MacDiarmid's *Robert Burns* in the same series (see no. 46), and the title-page with Maclellan's imprint is an obvious cancel.

54 *Stony Limits and Scots Unbound and other poems.* Edinburgh: Castle Wynd Printers, 1956.

> Issued in two bindings, cloth and paper.
>
> Reprints, with the restoration of certain excluded poems, *Stony Limits and other poems* (1934) and the title poem, 'Scots Unbound', from *Scots Unbound and other poems* (1932).

55 *Three Hymns to Lenin.* Edinburgh: Castle Wynd Printers, 1957.

> For the 'First Hymn to Lenin' see no. 20 above, and for the 'Second Hymn' see nos. 23 and 31. The 'Third Hymn' was first published in its entirety in *The Voice of Scotland*, 6 (1), April 1955, p. 12–20, although part had been printed in the poet's autobiography, *Lucky Poet* (1943).

56 *The Battle Continues.* Edinburgh: Castle Wynd Printers, 1957.

57 *Burns Today and Tomorrow.* Edinburgh: Castle Wynd Printers, 1959.

> As well as the ordinary edition there was a special limited edition of 25 copies, signed by the author.

58 *The Kind of Poetry I Want.* Edinburgh: K. D. Duval, 1961.

> Printed by Giovanni Mardersteig on the hand-press of the Officina Bodoni in Verona. Edition limited to 300 numbered copies, signed by the poet.
>
> Parts of this poem first appeared in *Lucky Poet* (1943).

59 *David Hume, Scotland's Greatest Son: a transcript of the lecture given at Edinburgh University, April 1961.* Edinburgh: The Paperback, Booksellers, [1962].

> There was also an edition on special paper and limited to 50 numbered copies, signed by the author.

60 *The Man of (almost) Independent Mind.* Edinburgh: Giles Gordon, 1962. Cover title: *Hugh Macdiarmid on Hume.*

61 *Bracken Hills in Autumn.* Edinburgh: Colin H. Hamilton, 1962.
   25 numbered copies, signed by the author and the printer.
   A long-lost poem, written in the early '30s. It is reprinted in the
   Penguin *Selected Poems* (1970).

62 (a) *Collected Poems of Hugh MacDiarmid.* New York: The Macmillan
   Company, 1962.
   There is a portrait frontispiece from a photograph by Douglas
   MacAskill.
   (b) *Collected Poems of Hugh MacDiarmid (C. M. Grieve).* Edinburgh
   and London: Oliver & Boyd, 1962.
   A reissue of the American edition with a 'corrigenda' slip.
   (c) *Collected Poems of Hugh MacDiarmid.* Revised edition with en-
   larged glossary prepared by John C. Weston. New York: The Mac-
   millan Company (London: Collier-Macmillan), 1967.
   A revision of the *Collected Poems* published in 1962. As Hugh
   MacDiarmid has himself said (in the Prefatory Note to *A Lap of
   Honour*, 1967), the title *Collected Poems* was a misnomer: 'The MS
   I sent to the publishers of that book was much too large for their
   purpose and only a portion of it was used.' Thus, although the
   Author's Note printed in all three editions of the *Collected Poems*
   states: 'This volume does not contain all the poems I have
   written, but all I think worth including in a definitive collection',
   MacDiarmid has had to point out repeatedly that that statement 'was
   written for the large collection and unfortunately was not altered
   when only a part of that was published'. The *Collected Poems*,
   then, is 'only a big selection' of MacDiarmid's poetry, and it must
   be supplemented by the later collections, *A Lap of Honour*
   (1967), *A Clyack-Sheaf* (1969) and *More Collected Poems* (1970).
   (See MacDiarmid's letter in *The Times Literary Supplement*, 4th June
   1970.)

63 *The Ugly Birds without Wings.* Edinburgh: Allan Donaldson, 1962.
   There was also a large-paper edition limited to 30 copies signed
   by the author.

64 *Poetry like the Hawthorn. From* In Memoriam James Joyce. Hemel
   Hempstead: Duncan Glen, 1962.
   150 numbered copies, the first 25 signed by the poet.
   First printed, with the subtitle 'On the death of W. B.
   Yeats, 28th January, 1939', in *Wales*, no. 11, Winter 1939–40.

65 *The blaward and the skelly.* Privately printed [Hemel Hempstead,
   Duncan Glen], 1962.
   10 copies only printed.
   This poem originally appeared in the *Dunfermline Press*, 30th
   September 1922, along with 'The Watergaw'.

66 *When the Rat-Race is Over: an essay in honour of the fiftieth birthday of*

John Gawsworth [*T. I. Fytton Armstrong*]. London: Twyn Barlwm Press, 1962.

> 40 copies privately printed and signed by the author and John Gawsworth.

67 *Robert Burns: Love Songs*. Selected by Hugh MacDiarmid. London: Vista Books, 1962. *The Pocket Poets*.

68 *An Apprentice Angel*. London: New Poetry Press, 1963. *A New Poetry Broadsheet*.

> This poem was printed in the *New English Weekly*, 1 (8), 9th June 1932, and reprinted in *Scots Unbound and other poems* (1932).

69 *Harry Martinson: Aniara, a review of man in time and space*. Adapted from the Swedish by Hugh MacDiarmid and Elspeth Harley Schubert. Introduction by Dr. Tord Hall. London: Hutchinson (New York: Knopf; Stockholm: Bonnier), 1963.

70 *Sydney Goodsir Smith*. Edinburgh: Colin H. Hamilton, 1963.

> Edition limited to 135 copies; 35 copies signed by the author were issued in a special binding.
>
> The text of an address at a meeting of the Edinburgh University Scottish Renaissance Society on 14th December 1962, when Sydney Goodsir Smith was presented with the Sir Thomas Urquhart Award for his services to Scots literature.
>
> Reprinted in *The Uncanny Scot* (1968).

71 *Poems to Paintings by William Johnstone 1933.* Edinburgh: K. D. Duval, 1963.

> There was also an edition of 100 copies signed by the poet. Parts of two of the poems were printed in *Lucky Poet* (1943).

72 (a) *Two poems. The terrible crystal: A vision of Scotland*. Skelmorlie: Duncan Glen, 1964.

> 55 numbered copies signed by the poet.
>
> The two poems were originally printed in *Poetry Review* and both are reprinted in *A Lap of Honour* (1967).

(b) —— New Edition. Skelmorlie: Drumalban Press, 1964.

> Approximately 50 copies.

73 *Six Vituperative Verses*. Privately printed [by Duncan Glen, The Satire Press], 1964.

> 25 copies printed 'without the permission of either Mr. MacDiarmid or Dr. C. M. Grieve'. One of the poems was later found to be not by Hugh MacDiarmid; others were absorbed into *Poet at Play* (1965).

74 *The Ministry of Water: two poems*. Glasgow: Duncan Glen, 1964.

> 125 numbered copies signed by the poet.
>
> The poems, 'Prayer for a Second Flood' and 'Larking Dallier', had been printed previously in the *Modern Scot* and the *London Mercury* respectively, and both are reprinted in *A Lap of Honour* (1967).

75 *Poet at Play, and other poems, being a selection of mainly vituperative poems.* Privately printed [by Duncan Glen], 1965.

The printer's note records that 'these poems were rescued and fifty-five copies printed without the permission of either Dr. Grieve or Mr. Hugh MacDiarmid'.

76 *The Fire of the Spirit: two poems.* Glasgow: Duncan Glen, 1965.

Edition limited to 350 numbered copies, the first 50 signed by the poet.

The poems, 'By Wauchopeside' and 'Diamond body: in a cave of the sea', had been printed previously in the *Modern Scot* (1932) and the *Welsh Review* (1939) respectively, and both are reprinted in *A Lap of Honour* (1967).

77 *The Burning Passion.* Bishopbriggs, Glasgow: Akros Press, 1965.

35 numbered copies.

This poem, previously published in *First Hymn to Lenin and other poems* (1931), had been reprinted in the first issue of Duncan Glen's periodical *Akros* (1965). It is reprinted in *A Lap of Honour* (1967).

78 *Whuchulls: a poem.* Preston: Akros Publications, 1966.

100 numbered copies.

There are a portrait frontispiece of the poet and two illustrations by Duncan Glen.

First printed in the *Modern Scot*, 'Whuchulls' was reprinted in *Akros*, 1 (3), August 1966. It is reprinted in *A Lap of Honour* (1967).

79 (a) *The Company I've Kept*, [by] Hugh MacDiarmid (Christopher Murray Grieve). London: Hutchinson, 1966.

Autobiographical, with a portrait frontispiece from a photograph by Alan Daiches.

(b) —— Berkeley, Calif.: University of California Press, 1967.

80 *On a Raised Beach: a poem.* Preston: The Harris Press, 1967.

200 numbered copies, designed and printed by students of the School of Art, Harris College, Preston, with drawings by Alan D. Powell. There is an introductory note by Duncan Glen.

First published in *Stony Limits and other poems* (1934) and reprinted in *Longer Contemporary Poems*, ed. David Wright (Penguin Books, 1966) and in *A Lap of Honour* (1967).

81 *The Eemis Stane.* Northampton, Mass.: The Gehenna Press, 1967.

500 copies; printed on one sheet of paper, with the author's portrait by Takahara after Leonard Baskin.

Reprinted from *Sangschaw* (1925).

82 (a) *A Lap of Honour.* London: MacGibbon & Kee, 1967.

A collection of poems which do not appear in the *Collected Poems* (1962, 1967), mainly 'recovered' by Duncan Glen.

(b) —— Chicago: Swallow Press, 1969.

83 *Celtic Nationalism*, [by] Owen Dudley Edwards, Gwynfor Evans and
    Ioan Rhys, Hugh MacDiarmid. London: Routledge & Kegan Paul, 1968.
    MacDiarmid deals with Scotland, p. 299–358.

84 (a) *Early Lyrics by Hugh MacDiarmid. Recently discovered among
    letters to his schoolmaster and friend George Ogilvie.* With an appreciation
    of Ogilvie by Hugh MacDiarmid. Edited with an introduction by J. K.
    Annand. Preston: Akros Publications, 1968.
    Limited edition of 350 numbered copies, the first 50 signed by poet
    and editor. Wrappers with portrait of MacDiarmid.

    (b) —— 2nd ed. Preston: Akros Publications, 1969.
    The second edition has different-coloured wrappers and a different
    portrait of MacDiarmid.

85 *The Uncanny Scot: a selection of prose by Hugh MacDiarmid.* Edited with
    an introduction by Kenneth Buthlay. London: MacGibbon & Kee, 1968.
    40 copies of the first edition were specially bound in buckram, each
    numbered and signed by the author.

86 *An Afternoon with Hugh MacDiarmid.* Interview at Brownsbank on
    25th October 1968. Hugh MacDiarmid – Duncan Glen, with Valda
    Grieve and Arthur Thompson. Privately printed [by Duncan Glen and
    the photographers – James Bamber, Geoff Green and Arthur Thomp-
    son], 1969.
    55 numbered copies signed by the poet, Duncan Glen and the
    photographers.

87 *A Clyack-Sheaf.* London: MacGibbon & Kee, 1969.
    A further collection of poems not included in the *Collected Poems*
    (1962, 1967).

88 (a) *Selected Essays of Hugh MacDiarmid.* Edited with an introduction
    by Duncan Glen. London: Jonathan Cape, 1969.
    There is a portrait frontispiece from a drawing by Rosalie M. J.
    Loveday.

    (b) —— Berkeley, Calif.: University of California Press, 1970.

89 (a) *More Collected Poems.* London: MacGibbon & Kee, 1970.
    'The poems in this volume were not included in *Collected Poems* and
    are collected here for the first time.'

    (b) —— Chicago: Swallow Press, 1970.

90 *The MacDiarmids: a conversation* – Hugh MacDiarmid and Duncan
    Glen, with Valda Grieve and Arthur Thompson. Recorded at Browns-
    bank, Candymill, on 25th October 1968. Preston: Akros Publications,
    1970.
    There was also a limited edition of 50 signed and numbered copies.
        Reprinted from *Akros*, 5 (13, 14), April 1970, which was a special
    Hugh MacDiarmid issue in two parts. Similar to no. 86 above.

91 *Selected Poems.* Selected and edited by David Craig and John Manson.
    Harmondsworth: Penguin Books, 1970. *The Penguin Poets.*

B PERIODICALS

1   *The Scottish Chapbook: a monthly magazine of Scottish arts and letters.* [Edited by C. M. Grieve.] Montrose. Vol. 1, no. 1, August 1922 – vol. 2, no. 3, November–December 1923.

2   *The Scottish Nation.* [Edited by C. M. Grieve.] Weekly. Montrose. Vol. 1, no. 1, 8th May 1923 – vol. 2, no. 8, 25th December 1923.

3   *The Northern Review.* [Edited by C. M. Grieve.] Monthly. Edinburgh. Vol. 1, no. 1, May 1924 – no. 4, September 1924.

4   *The Voice of Scotland: a quarterly magazine of Scottish arts and affairs.* Edited by Hugh MacDiarmid. Dunfermline: Vol. 1, no. 1, June–August 1938 – vol. 2, no. 1, June–August 1939. Glasgow: Vol. 2, no. 2, December 1945 – vol. 5, no. 3, June 1949. Edinburgh: Vol. 5, no. 4, January 1955 – vol. 9, no. 2, August 1958.

5   *Poetry Scotland.* No. 4. Editor, Maurice Lindsay. Guest editor, Hugh MacDiarmid. Edinburgh: Serif Books, 1949.

6   *Scottish Art and Letters.* Fifth Miscellany. P.E.N. Congress Number, Edinburgh Festival, 1950. Literary editor, Hugh MacDiarmid. Glasgow: Maclellan, 1950.